Four Centuries of Opera

MANUSCRIPTS AND PRINTED EDITIONS
IN THE PIERPONT MORGAN LIBRARY

J. RIGBIE TURNER

with Robert Kendall and James Parsons
Introduction by Patrick J. Smith

THE PIERPONT MORGAN LIBRARY
in association with
DOVER PUBLICATIONS, INC.
New York

*The publication of this volume has been made possible by a grant from
The Carl and Lily Pforzheimer Foundation, Inc.*

Published in Canada by General Publishing Company, Ltd., 30 Lesmill Road, Don Mills, Toronto, Ontario.
Published in the United Kingdom by Constable and Company, Ltd., 10 Orange Street, London WC2H 7EG.

Four Centuries of Opera is a new work, first published in 1983 by The Pierpont Morgan Library in association with Dover Publications, Inc.

International Standard Book Number: 0-486-24602-7

Book design by Carol Belanger Grafton

Manufactured in the United States of America
Dover Publications, Inc., 180 Varick Street, New York, N.Y. 10014

Contents

Preface

This volume illustrates the history of opera through slightly more than 50 examples, from the earliest known opera to one first performed in the last five years. Some were chosen for their importance, some for their rarity, some for the special light they shed on a period or genre, and some simply because they sparked the interest of the writers of the catalogue. Many of the operas are known around the world, but a few are obscure even to opera historians. *Le nozze di Figaro, Die Meistersinger von Nürnberg, Pelléas et Mélisande,* and *Wozzeck* can, with little effort, be seen on stage or heard on a number of recordings. Cavalli's *Il Titone,* Alessandro Scarlatti's *Tutto il mal von vien per nuocere,* Méhul's *Valentine de Milan,* and David's *Lalla-Roukh* are undoubtedly terra incognita even to the most devoted operagoer.

The manuscripts and books described here span some 380 years, from Rinuccini's libretto for Peri's *La Dafne* (1598)—by consensus called the first opera—for which little music but much commentary survives, to John Eaton's *Danton and Robespierre* (1978), for which the Morgan Library has the composer's own working manuscript, a typescript of the libretto annotated by the composer, and a communication from Mr. Eaton on the writing of the opera. For the nearly four centuries in between, most of the important genres are represented, often by notable examples.

The music for all but three of Monteverdi's operas is lost; included here is a rare early edition of Rinuccini's libretto for *L'Arianna* (1608), Monteverdi's second opera. Francesco Cavalli, the most performed composer of opera in the quarter-century after Monteverdi, is represented by three librettos in their first editions. Lully's *Thésée* (1675) and *Roland* (1685) are examples of the French *tragédie lyrique* that flourished under the artistically enlightened reign of Louis XIV. Rameau's *Les Indes galantes* (1735), Rousseau's *Le devin du village* (1753), and Gluck's *Orphée et Euridice* are all works that signaled revolts against either French or Italian operatic traditions—as did Gay's *Beggar's Opera* (1728), which is hardly an opera at all, but which is included because of the unique place it holds in the story of opera in England. A descendant of Gay's play with music was the German *Singspiel,* represented here by Mozart's *Der Schauspieldirektor* (1786); that composer's *Le nozze di Figaro* of the same year is counted among the great comic operas.

The last flowering of the Italian *bel canto* tradition is shown in works of its three most famous composers: Bellini, by an *opera seria, Il pirata* (1827), and a *melodramma, La sonnambula* (1831); Donizetti by *Buondelmonte* (1834), an opera hastily refashioned when censors forbade it in its first version, *Maria Stuarda;* and Rossini, with cadenzas written in 1858 to ornament *Tancredi* (1813), his first international success. French op-

era of the 1830's is shown in two contrasting examples: Meyerbeer's *Les Huguenots* (1836), a work that epitomizes French grand opera, and Berlioz's neglected *Benvenuto Cellini* (1838), that vivid evocation of an artist's life and a passionate defense of artistic freedom. The two Verdi manuscripts span 43 years: from 1844, an aria especially written for Nicola Ivanoff to sing in *Ernani;* from 1887, sketches for *Otello.* During the intervening years are found, among other works, two staples of the French opera repertory: Offenbach's *Les contes d'Hoffmann* (1881) and Massenet's *Manon* (1884); *La Gioconda* (1876), the only Ponchielli opera still regularly performed; Wagner's comic masterpiece *Die Meistersinger von Nürnberg* (1868); and two works in a lighter vein, Lecocq's *Le petit duc* (1878) and Gilbert & Sullivan's *The Pirates of Penzance* (1879).

The twentieth century opens with one of its most important works, Debussy's *Pelléas et Mélisande* (1902), an opera whose esthetic still stirs controversy long after its historic première. Converse's *The Pipe of Desire* (1906) would, in 1910, become the first opera by an American composer to be performed at the Metropolitan Opera House; Puccini's *La fanciulla del West* was given its triumphant world première in the same house later that year. Ravel's enchanting *L'enfant et les sortilèges* (1925) continues to weave its bewitching spell on audiences as well as on the eponymous child; Berg's *Wozzeck,* from the same year, remains a powerful and disturbing work of enduring importance. Strauss's *Die ägyptische Helena* (1928) is rarely heard today, but we are allowed a fortunate glimpse at the composer's working method in sketchbooks for the opera. Einem's *Dantons Tod* (1947) and Dallapiccola's *Il prigioniero* (1950) were both written in the long and tragic shadow of World War II. *Amahl and the Night Visitors,* Menotti's 1951 Christmas opera for children, is probably the most frequently performed opera in the world, by one of the most successful composers of the century. Schoenberg's *Moses und Aron* (1957), composed in the early 1930's, is counted among the few twentieth-century operas of lasting significance.

The entries are arranged chronologically by date of first performance, which in some cases differs considerably from the date of the manuscript or printed score or libretto. The entry for Rossini's *Tancredi,* for example, will be found under 1813—the date of the première—although the manuscript itself contains ornaments written in 1858; the printed full score of Glinka's *A Life for the Tsar* appeared only in 1881—45 years after the première in 1836, the date under which the opera is discussed; and Schoenberg's *Moses und Aron* comes under 1957, the year of its first stage performance, although the draft of Act I dates from 1930.

This volume is a record, in part, of an exhibition held at The

Pierpont Morgan Library in New York from 1 September through 6 November 1983. Because 1983 marks two notable centenaries in the world of opera—the death of Richard Wagner on 13 February 1883 and the opening of the Metropolitan Opera House in New York on 22 October 1883—and since the collection of music manuscripts housed in the Morgan Library is the finest in this country, we thought it appropriate that the Library place on display its most important opera manuscripts and printed scores and librettos, and publish this volume.

Neither the book nor the exhibition should be construed as documenting the entire history of opera. No single institution could mount so comprehensive a show without borrowing extensively from private and public collections around the world, and the writing of a correspondingly exhaustive catalogue would be far beyond our scope here. Rather, we selected for this work 53 operas from the roughly 100 included in the exhibition.

We are grateful to James Parsons and Robert Kendall for their contributions to this catalogue. Mr. Parsons wrote the entries for the Peri-Rinuccini *La Dafne* (1598) and *Euridice* (1600), the Monteverdi-Rinuccini *L'Arianna* (1608), the three librettos for Cavalli (1640, 1645, and 1664), Lully's *Thésée* (1675), Scarlatti's *Tutto il mal non vien per nuocere* (1681), Lully's *Roland* (1685), Campra's *Tancrède* (1702), Rameau's *Les Indes galantes* (1735), Rousseau's *Le devin du village* (1753), Verdi's *Ernani* (1844), and Strauss's *Die ägyptische Helena* (1928). Mr. Kendall wrote the entries for Mercadante's *La schiava saracena* (1848), Ponchielli's *La Gioconda* (1876), Puccini's *Le villi* (1884), Verdi's *Otello* (1887), and Puccini's *La fanciulla del West* (1910). All of the other entries, and the two Checklists, were prepared by Rigbie Turner. He is our Curator of Music Manuscripts, and has devoted many months to the preparation of this work, and we are especially thankful to him. Our gratitude is extended as well to Patrick J. Smith, who kindly consented to write the Introduction, bringing to that task his wide knowledge of operatic literature.

It is a pleasure to acknowledge the many persons who helped the writers of this catalogue: their prompt and informed replies to our enquiries made our work easier. First, a collective thanks to the staff of the Music Division of The New York Public Library; without the resources of that vast and rich collection the preparation of this catalogue would have been a far more daunting task than it was. Individually, we acknowledge Antonio de Almeida, James R. Anthony, Leo F. Balk, A. Peter Brown, Martin Chusid, Michael Collins, Lenore Coral, John Eaton, Rudolf Elvers, Alice Garrigoux, Louise Goldberg, Philip Gossett, Peter Jeffery, Hugh Macdonald, Catherine Massip, Albi Rosenthal, Lois Rosow, Denis Stevens, R. Larry Todd, and Alan Tyson. From the Morgan Library, special thanks go to Herbert Cahoon, Ruth Kraemer, Jane V. Shoaf, and to Charles V. Passela and C. Mitchell Carl, who made the photographs for the catalogue. We are also grateful to Hayward Cirker and Stanley Appelbaum of Dover Publications, and to Carol Belanger Grafton, for their invaluable help in producing, editing, and designing this volume.

All the manuscripts, and printed scores and librettos described in this catalogue are housed in the Morgan Library. Several items are from two collections on deposit; we should like to thank Robert O. Lehman, Frederick R. Koch, and the Frederick R. Koch Foundation for allowing us to include manuscripts from their respective collections.

The exhibition has been supported by grants from the National Endowment for the Arts, the American Can Company Foundation, the Henry and Lucy Moses Fund, Incorporated, and the DeWitt Wallace Fund.

CHARLES RYSKAMP
Director
The Pierpont Morgan Library

Introduction

Any book or exhibition about opera is a daunting task, for opera encompasses a profusion of worlds. Indeed, it is the very complexity of the makeup of what is termed opera that ensures its continued popularity, since those who love this most elaborate of art forms are in continual search for an ideal of its realization. That ideal is ever elusive, for it must include the auditory (both instrumental and vocal) and the visual (both scenic and histrionic). At various stages in its history opera has reflected the dominance of one or another of its various facets: masque, poetry, melisma, the scenic, machines, vocal embellishments, voice, orchestra, sonority, the idea and the totality of its disparity. Opera has, at many points in history, been at the center of artistic achievement, both musical and visual, and at the center of popular culture. It has also been on the fringe, as an ancillary appendage. Yet the common bromide often heard that opera today is an outdated and semiextinct species is certainly false, less because the viable new works are central to musical and intellectual consciousness than because the museum nature of the form—and the richness of its history—has been combined with new works and with new modes of opera production so as continually to renew and reinvigorate the genre and to keep it within the mainstream of the performing arts.

Any book on the history of opera, however limited or fragmentary, will attest to opera's importance as a seen and heard event and as part of a cultural continuum. One of the most vital and productive areas in music since the Second World War has been that of museological inquiry into our musical past and the examination and cataloguing of the masses of information that had heretofore not been systematically studied, or even studied at all. For better or worse, this beaverlike activity has given us a far more extensive knowledge of the past and a concomitant understanding of it; this in turn has influenced the way we approach opera, both in terms of the works themselves and in terms of the performance of them.

A chronological approach will grant a picture of the art form as it existed and developed that is perhaps not entirely accurate, but one that conforms to our view of its history. For instance, it is a commonplace to state that opera grew more from the word—that is, from the poetry—than from the music. This is true enough, since the poetry was the genesis, but something different happened to poetry when it was set to music and the two were presented simultaneously in costumed form. The court masques and festivities that preceded opera as we define it, and which continued long after opera had begun, were spectacles in which poetry and even music were placed second—to the dismay of the poets and composers. The history of opera is punctuated by numerous attempts to "get back to basics" in terms of the poetry and the word, and these attempts usually invoke the Greek ideal of the chanted text. The Florentine circle out of which opera is thought to have begun, the Arcadian poets of the first reform, the Gluck reform of the eighteenth century, and the operas of Wagner are all examples of these attempts. But the process can be traced right down to the present day in the word-dominant settings of such disparate composers as Carl Orff (*Antigonae*) or Erik Satie (*Socrate*).

The importance of the word from the beginning is clearly shown by the earliest items here. They are mostly librettos, available today because they were printed either for sale or for the elite. Music was rarely printed and the manuscripts, to be used for a single production, were considered expendable. We are lucky that some Monteverdi operas have survived in manuscript, but most are lost. Manuscripts of many Cavalli operas are preserved in Venice; regrettably, the music he may have composed for Busenello's great epic libretto *La prosperità infelice di Giulio Cesare dittatore* (1646) has disappeared.

Librettos were generally of two contrasting types, of which this volume has good examples. One was the practical guide to the words, usually sold in the theatre, that was printed on inferior paper, often with numerous misprints (owing both to changes and last-minute printing). The Faustini libretto for Cavalli's *Il Titone* (1645) is of this type. The other type was intended as a more permanent record and represented an elaboration of the bare bones of the first. Minato's libretto for Cavalli's *Scipione affricano* (1664) contains an engraving and listings of the various machines and ballets that were to be presented along with the words and music, and is a much better job of printing. The amount of information contained in librettos has recently been used to amplify our knowledge of the performance of music: the size of the orchestra or the changes for a variety of productions. In addition, the often witty prefaces written by the poets (and by the composers) tell us a great deal about conditions of opera at various times and locales.

This codification of knowledge was likewise evidenced in collections of librettos, beginning in the seventeenth century and brought to culmination in the collections of *opera seria* librettos of Apostolo Zeno and Pietro Metastasio in the eighteenth. After that, the primacy of the libretto gave way to that of the music, with the publication of scores and parts. Yet the continuing importance of the words is shown in this catalogue by the autograph manuscript for Wagner's *Die Meistersinger*. Wagner's texts were not only used for private readings (as were Metastasio's) but were printed and distributed before the opera was performed. And, because his operas were staged with relative infrequency, these texts were often read by a public independent of the musical envelope.

An earlier instance of an attempt to codify a composer's works can be seen in the publication of the operas of Jean-Baptiste Lully (born Giovanni Battista Lulli), court composer and favorite of Louis XIV. Ballard's editions of Lully's operas began before the composer's death and continued after it; examples can be seen here in the scores of *Thésée* and *Roland*. Lully's operas were considered to be the musical representation of French culture in the age of the Sun King, and were printed in appropriately sumptuous editions. Ballard held a royal monopoly on music publishing in France, but printed by letterpress, a technique rapidly becoming obsolete for music by the end of the seventeenth century. When other firms issued Lully's operas in the early 1700's they printed from engraved plates, a process exempt from the monopoly.

The enshrinement of a "classic" can also be noted in a later, very famous example: Rousseau's *Le devin du village*, a light entertainment first presented before Louis XV at Fontainebleau in October 1752. Although this Italian-influenced work stirred up an acrimonious debate, the fact that it was in a sense protected by the king meant that it instantly became part of the culture of France and thus could be accorded a printed status denied to other lighter French works.

This kind of official imprimatur can be seen, much later, in the lavish complete score of the more famous of Mikhail Glinka's two operas, *A Life for the Tsar*. Although it was first performed in 1836 and was an instant success, its stature as a seminal Russian opera grew slowly during the nineteenth century (it was accused of being too Italianate). But by the time of this handsome edition (1881) its reputation justified the publication. These two operas are examples of works that have never become part of the core repertory, either in terms of performance (the Rousseau faded in the early nineteenth century; the Glinka has rarely been produced outside Russia) or in terms of strictly musical excellence, but that are of considerable importance in the history of opera.

Two important facets of opera can be noted in this book. One is that the story, whether from classical mythology, epic poem, or history, is extensively repeated in new musical guise. The story of Orpheus and Eurydice is, of course, intimately linked to music itself, since Orpheus's playing was supposed to animate even the stones. It is fitting that two famous operas still played today—those of Monteverdi and Gluck—were written about this subject, as was one of the earliest librettos extant.

But the Orpheus legend is only one of many which saw dozens of different treatments down through the years from 1600 to 1800. Operagoers were expected to know their literary heritage and to be familiar with the tales of Armida and Semiramis and Xerxes and Pompey. Metastasio's fame as a librettist, however, led to his texts being considered sacrosanct, to be set by many different composers—although they were not so sacrosanct that arias were not added, eliminated, or juxtaposed.

There was thus an immense variety within the form, which spread outward from the standardized stories that were used and reused. The idea that one could see the same opera in two productions presented exactly alike may have had currency in the court theatre of France. But in Italy all sorts of changes could and did occur, not only through the aforementioned substitution of arias, but even through newly written texts (supplied by local librettists) and music (by local composers), as well as different machines, ballets, and scenic effects. The example of Haydn's recomposition of an aria in an opera by Traetta, shown

in the volume, is only one of many emendations that were regularly made. Even in the nineteenth century such changes were common, as Verdi's insertion of an aria written for the tenor Nicola Ivanoff in *Ernani* attests. This situation has an odd, contemporary resonance for though we today pride ourselves on fidelity to the original score, in performance the claim is to an extent hollow. An opera like *Parsifal* is quite differently presented at Bayreuth, the Metropolitan Opera, and in the film of Hans-Jürgen Syberberg, although the music is the same in each case.

But there is a further area of change in opera—that between one country and another. If Italian was the common operatic language, Italian operas were nonetheless translated into German or French when they traveled to those countries, and they took on local colors. Thus Gluck's *Orfeo*, first performed in Vienna in 1762, became "Frenchified" a dozen years later when, among other changes, the castrato role gave way to a tenor and additional ballet music was added. The example of Gluck's German setting of his *Iphigénie en Tauride* demonstrates the lengths to which the composer was willing to go to reconstitute his opera for a German-speaking audience.

Another cause for change, one that became endemic in nineteenth-century Italy, was the question of censorship. The various Italian states each had a differing view of what could and could not be presented on stage, and this view moreover was subject to willful change depending upon the ruler or the censor in control. Verdi's operas are classic examples of the censor's delicate artistry, but this volume includes one from Donizetti. His opera *Buondelmonte* was fashioned from his *Maria Stuarda* when—for whatever reason—King Ferdinando II objected to the original.

Opera, of course, has always included more than simply the high-toned *tragédie lyrique* of France, or the *opera seria* and later Grand Opera genres. It has always included lighter works, usually of a comic nature, which grew out of entertainments for the lower classes but which, long before Mozart canonized the development, could concern themselves with serious subjects. Thus any book on the range of opera should present not only the lighter works, but also those that fall partially outside the arena of opera, if only because they are musico-dramatic, have their own validity, and are today quite often seen in the same theatre the night after *Aïda*. Gay's *The Beggar's Opera*, with its frank use of popular tunes, and Rousseau's *Le devin du village* influenced the more elevated forms, and such nineteenth-century examples as Lecocq's *Le petit duc* and Sullivan's *The Pirates of Penzance* demonstrate the extent to which opera influenced operetta. In Sullivan's case, it may be added: and the extent to which operetta mercilessly parodied opera.

One of the chief features of the nineteenth century was its growing awareness of the past, and this is directly reflected in opera. If vast areas of the past were still undiscovered, some of the peaks of achievement were being played and studied, and thus influenced contemporary composition. The inclusion of Berlioz's copy of Gluck's *Iphigénie en Tauride* is a striking example. Here, Berlioz copied out the score in its entirety, out of love for it, and he incidentally put in directions for traditional cuts that are of historical importance in telling us how the opera was performed in Berlioz's day. The fruits of his inordinate (to us) admiration for Gluck's works can be clearly heard in his epic opera *Les troyens*.

If in the early years of opera the scores were considered less important than the librettos and even manuscripts were not treated with care, the change in status of the composer vis-à-vis the librettist ensured a greater likelihood not only that the score would be published but also that manuscripts and sketches would survive. They were of primary value when musicology as a formal discipline came to prominence and are important today as students of textual criticism seek to understand the workings of the composer's mind and the way in which opera was performed.

Take the question of cadenzas in *bel canto* opera, which were musically quite different from cadenzas in *opera seria*. They were, however, only sketchily rendered in scores since the singer was expected to interpolate them extempore (and therefore they would vary from night to night and singer to singer). What exactly was sung? This volume includes an autograph manuscript, written out by Rossini for a Madame Grégoire in 1858, of ornaments for *Tancredi*. Here, from the pen of someone who was trying to eliminate the excesses of vocal display, is what Rossini felt would be appropriate and which was, even 45 years after the première, an authentic response.

Take the question of forgotten operas of major composers. Mendelssohn was never known as an opera composer and many music lovers are unaware that he even wrote an opera. He in fact completed two, the second of which, *Die Heimkehr aus der Fremde*, is included here in an autograph manuscript.

Take the question of historical sources. Berlioz no less than any other composer wanted to make money and one way to do so was through the sale of excerpts from popular operas. His *Benvenuto Cellini* may have been a failure but several of its pieces, if played, could still become famous and sell to an interested public. The set of highlights from the opera shown here, however, differs from other such groupings in that it includes a piece part of which was later cut. Berlioz corrected two notes in this copy; since the autograph of the deleted section is lost any musicologically complete edition of the score, which would include variants, must be similarly corrected.

Variants are a treasure trove for the scholar/hunter. In the manuscript score of *The Pirates of Penzance* W. S. Gilbert's words for the Major General's patter song read: "I am the very pattern of a modern major general." At some point the preferable, alliterative word "model" was substituted.

Composer's sketches are obviously of prime importance not only as indications of the way a specific composer worked with his material but also how he developed over his career. The sketches included here—and they cover nearly 200 years of compositional activity—range in appearance from the tiny, fastidiously neat pencil handwriting of Richard Strauss in his sketchbook for *Die ägyptische Helena* to the violent scrawls of Saverio Mercadante in his draft for *La schiava saracena*. It takes an extremely knowledgeable and diligent editor to make sense of the hodgepodge of notes that Offenbach left in his *Contes d'Hoffmann* sketchbook, a collection that bears out the traditional picture of Offenbach at work: always in a whirlwind, scribbling down ideas as they came to him, knowing that only a few would survive to the final work, because they would either be early discarded, cut in rehearsal, or cut after opening night (and quite often used again in something else). It is a good thing

for scholarship that Ponchielli's most famous opera, *La Gioconda*, has not achieved the status of Verdi's *Otello*, for that Venetian gallimaufry went through a variety of changes—indicated by the mass of sketches and drafts—that are guaranteed to give a conscientious editor a severe headache if he should attempt to prepare a musicologically exact score.

There are also extramusical curiosities. Menotti's *Amahl and the Night Visitors* was the first, and arguably the most famous, opera specifically written for television. John Eaton's doodlings in his short score of *Danton and Robespierre* give a glimpse of the composer at play, between trying to write quarter-tone harmonies—although the doodles may be the result of such ratiocination! Massenet's scores are delights since at the end of each day he regularly provided them with footnotes detailing the weather, his health, and which of his operas were on the boards.

Puccini's drafts for two of his operas—the early *Le villi* and the much later *La fanciulla del West*—are quite interesting in that, in the later score, there is clear evidence of a richer harmonic texture. Although the Italians considered *Le villi* to be influenced by Wagner, by the time Puccini wrote *Fanciulla* (ca. 1908–09) he had come under the stronger influence of a number of later composers—and most notably of his contemporary Debussy—who were working with an expanded orchestral palette and a more complex harmonic language. The evidence of the short-score draft can be heard in the final form in the opera.

Debussy's own opera, the magical *Pelléas et Mélisande* (1902), is represented by a manuscript that once belonged to the New England Conservatory of Music. The autograph of the short score, the result of work begun nearly a decade earlier, is of singular value in documenting the final stages of Debussy's continuing revisions of the opera. It is also fascinating to look over the Conservatory's library card pasted in the score and see to whom *Pelléas* was issued. The earliest name is Charles Martin Loeffler (1924); one of the latest, Luigi Dallapiccola (1967). Loeffler was an avid reader of the French Symbolists—including, of course, Maurice Maeterlinck—and his music is colored throughout with the spirit of Impressionism. Gustav Holst and Arthur Honegger also examined the score, as did the Debussy scholars Léon Vallas and Edward Lockspeiser. And in 1930, the year he began his historic series of Beethoven recordings, Artur Schnabel—a name not immediately associated with Debussy and the French—also signed out the score.

All of these sketches are, of course, mines for the specialist. But they are also of interest to the casual operagoer since, at least to the trained eye, they can accurately reflect the compositional stages characteristic of each composer. At a time when music threatens to become overfamiliar through a multiplicity and ubiquity of performance there is the ever-present danger that *La bohème* or *Aïda* or *Tristan und Isolde* will become as faceless as Muzak. The core of individuality of each separate work will become obscured. The reality of compositional sketches, even to the nonspecialist, reinforces the uniqueness of each work, and may give us a temporary insight into the creative act, which is alike for genius and journeyman.

PATRICK J. SMITH

ALPHABETICAL LIST OF
Composers and Librettists

Note: Only those names are listed here that appear in the main headings of the 53 items illustrated, and the page numbers refer to those headings.

[*Jacopo Peri, 1561–1633.*]
OTTAVIO RINUCCINI, 1562–1621.

La Dafne d'Ottavio Rinuccini rappresentata alla sereniss. gran duchessa di Toscana dal Signor Iacopo Corsi. Florence: Giorgio Marescotti, 1600. [24] p. 21.5 cm. Probable first edition of the libretto.
First performance: Florence, Carnival 1598 (new calendar).
Mary Flagler Cary Music Collection.

The inception of opera in the closing years of sixteenth-century Italy was at once a joining of the old and new: on the one hand a backward glance at the courtly entertainments and philosophical speculations of the Renaissance, on the other a tentative and experimental first step towards the emergence, in music, of the Baroque. Writing about his libretto for what is today considered the first opera, the poet and courtier Ottavio Rinuccini left little doubt as to his debt to the past or the novelty which he sought:

> It has been the opinion of many . . . that the ancient Greeks and Romans, in representing their tragedies on stage, sang them throughout. But until now this noble manner of recitation has been neither revived nor (to my knowledge) even attempted by anyone, and I used to believe that this was due to the imperfections of modern music, by far inferior to the ancient. But the opinion thus formed was wholly driven from my mind by . . . Jacopo Peri, who . . . set to music with so much grace the fable of *Dafne* (which I had written solely to make a simple test of what the music of our age could do) that it gave pleasure beyond belief to the few who heard it.

With the possible exception of Gabriello Chiabrera, librettist for Giulio Caccini's resplendent *Il rapimento di Cefalo* of 1600, few figures were to play a more prominent role in influencing the literary direction of the first decade of opera than Rinuccini. Described by the Florentine court chronicler Bastiano de' Rossi as "a very fine connoisseur" of music, Rinuccini was, as we learn elsewhere, both a "good poet and musician in one." His "simple trial" of *Dafne*, first heard during Carnival in 1598, was followed two years later by *Euridice*, set separately to music by Peri (see p. 4) and Caccini, and in 1608 by *Arianna* for Claudio Monteverdi (see p. 7).

Impelled by the resurgence of humanist philosophy, Rinuccini desired a revivification of the tragedy of antiquity. This desire was widely shared by Italian literary circles of the late sixteenth century, although few at first agreed on how such a goal might actually be achieved. It was Rinuccini's opinion that the drama of the ancients had been sung, yet among many of his contemporaries the idea was slow to win acceptance. The path was cleared by the classicist Girolamo Mei, an editor of Greek texts as well as a respected authority on Tuscan poetry. Mei, working in Rome, began in 1568 a systematic study of the writings on ancient music, which he expounded in *De modis musicis antiquorum*. In Book IV, completed in 1573, Mei announced for the first time the contention, based on Aristotle's *Poetics*, that the tragedies of old had been entirely sung.

Mei's theory soon reached Florence, where it took root within the city's numerous academic fraternities. For the early years of opera, one of the most important of these would be the Accademia degli Alterati, founded in 1569 for the "alteration" or "improvement of [its] members through the cultivation of elegant speech, good conduct, and a knowledge of all the arts and sciences." Among its number were several musicians as well as the young Rinuccini; two other members, influential for their efforts toward the development of the union of drama and music, were Count Giovanni de' Bardi and Jacopo Corsi, each of whom sponsored his own Camerata. Bardi's was devoted to discussions of learned topics and occasional impromptu music-making, while Corsi's was a sort of semiprofessional musical and dramatic workshop given over to experimental theatrical productions.

Once it was agreed that the dramas of the Greeks had been sung, there remained the problem of determining how, in music, to revive their "noble manner of recitation." Rinuccini, along with many intellectuals of his day, believed that "the imperfections of modern music"—the learned polyphony of the Renaissance—rendered it "far inferior to the ancient." In a letter of 1634, important for what it reveals about the inception of opera, Pietro de' Bardi, Giovanni's son, wrote that his father's Camerata had as one of its chief goals the improvement of modern music in order to "raise it in some degree from the wretched state to which it has been reduced." One of the most influential members of Bardi's group was Vincenzo Galilei, father of the astronomer, who, as Pietro tells us, added to "practical music" by his study of Greek and Latin music. Basing his findings largely on the work of Girolamo Mei, it was Galilei, Pietro continues, who advanced the course of music and was "the first to let us hear singing in *stile rappresentativo*." An attempt to imitate the ancient Greek theatre, Galilei's "representative style" was characterized by the use of rapidly repeated notes mirroring a quickly declaimed text, sung over a largely improvised accompaniment of either lute, theorbo, or harpsichord. It was but one of the many new stylistic features that signaled the beginning of the Baroque in music. According to Pietro, its "novelty, although it aroused considerable envy among the professional musicians, was pleasing to true lovers of the art," and it was not long before the innovation was recognized for its potential in recapturing the "noble manner" of the ancients. With pride of place, Pietro, in describing an evening's entertainment hosted by Jacopo Corsi, recounts that "the first poem sung on the stage in *stile rappresentativo* was the story of *Dafne*, by Signor Ottavio Rinuccini [and] set to music by Peri." After its performance, Pietro states, "I was left speechless with amazement."

In returning to the authority of the ancients, Rinuccini offered a bold and new program, a union of words and music in emulation of the drama of old. For opera, as it was subsequently to develop, his pastoral depiction of Apollo and Daphne provides a fitting starting place with its story of the "pangs and frustrations of love, the all-pervading subject in the history of opera." In tracing the fortunes of opera in the almost four centuries that will follow, we shall note a variety of responses and solutions to the wide array of problems the genre has posed. And yet with *Dafne* the stage had been set: opera was born.

Unfortunately for both posterity and the history of music, neither Rinuccini nor Peri sought to publish the musical portion of their "operatic experiment." Aside from six numbers, preserved in manuscripts in Florence and Brussels, all music for *Dafne* is lost.

LA DAFNE
D'OTTAVIO
RINVCCINI
Rappresentata alla Sereniss. GRAN DVCHESSA
DI TOSCANA
Dal Signor Iacopo Corsi.

IN FIRENZE
APPRESSO GIORGIO MARESCOTTI.
MDC.
Con Licenza de' Superiori.

[PERI] / RINUCCINI: *La Dafne*

Le musiche di Iacopo Peri nobil fiorentino sopra L'Euridice del Sig. Ottavio Rinuccini rappresentate nello sponsalizio della cristianissima Maria Medici regina di Francia e di Navarra. Florence: Giorgio Marescotti, 1600 [new calendar, 1601]. [6] [2] 3–52 p. 32 cm. First edition.
First performance: Florence, 6 October 1600.
Mary Flagler Cary Music Collection.

Encouraged by the "pleasure and astonishment" that greeted the "simple trial" of *Dafne* in 1598 (see the preceding entry), Peri and Rinuccini continued their efforts in the new genre of opera two years later with *Euridice*, a *favola per musica* (or "tale [written] for music"). First performed in a small room of the Pitti Palace before a select audience of nobility, the work was but one of the many splendid entertainments mounted in Florence in October 1600 to celebrate the marriage by proxy of Maria de' Medici and King Henry IV of France. Among those attending the first hearing of the work was the composer Marco da Gagliano; his remarks seem particularly well chosen in describing the first opera for which music has survived.

> I shall not grow tired of lauding it; indeed there is no one who does not bestow infinite praise upon it, no lover of music who does not have constantly before him the songs of Orfeo. Let me say truthfully that no one can completely understand the gentleness and the force of his [Peri's] airs if he has not heard him sing them himself. He gives to them such grace and so impresses on the listener the affection of the words, that he is compelled to weep and rejoice, as the composer wills. How much the representation of this *favola* pleased would be superfluous to relate, since there is the testimony of so many princes and lords, the cream of the nobility of Italy, one might say, who convened at those magnificent wedding festivities.

In structure and in general layout Rinuccini's libretto for *Euridice* closely resembles his *Dafne*. In both, rhymed dialogue in freely alternating lines of seven and eight syllables is interspersed with more regular strophic verses; similarly, each work is divided into five scenes, and concludes with a formal chorus in strophes of four or six lines. *Euridice* is longer (790 lines) than *Dafne* (448 lines), contains greater variety, and, by all accounts, was more successful dramatically. The story of *Euridice*, like that of *Dafne*, is simply constructed. In the opening prologue La Tragedia sings that she has abandoned her traditional role as the spectre of pity and terror in exchange for a more "pleasing mien for the royal nuptials," and so "I tune my song to happier strings to give sweet pleasure to the noble heart." In the first scene, nymphs and shepherds rejoice at the impending wedding of Orpheus and Eurydice. Eurydice enters, expressing her happiness, and suggests that she and those present retreat "to the pleasing shade of that flowering wood, and there to the sound of the limpid stream let us sing happy songs and dance." Orpheus appears in Scene 2 and delivers a monologue in praise of nature, telling the flora and fauna around him that they will henceforth

hear from him no songs of sadness: "No longer will my noble lyre / Move you to tears with its plaintive song: / With ineffable mercy, into great delight / Courtly Love has today changed my plaint."

Arcetro, Orpheus's friend, joins him and the two reflect on the comfort and joy brought by love. Interrupting their conversation, the rustic Thyrsis begins to play his panpipes and dance in anticipation of the coming wedding. Thyrsis has scarcely finished his song when Daphne breaks in to recount the tragic news of the death of Eurydice. The grief-stricken Orpheus sings of his sorrow, and then hurries off in search of his beloved, followed by Arcetro, who goes to comfort him. The nymphs and shepherds return from the woods, bewailing the loss of their mistress. In the third scene, Arcetro describes how Orpheus threw himself down on the spot where Eurydice died, whereupon a goddess (later revealed to be Venus) suddenly descended in a golden chariot and carried him away. In Scene 4, Venus leads Orpheus to the gates of hell where he sings a lament for the dead Eurydice. The intensity of his passion forces open the gates; following a protracted argument, Pluto, moved by Orpheus's entreaties, agrees to return Eurydice to him—without, however, the traditional warning that he not look back. (Rinuccini states in his dedication to the libretto that since the opera was to be performed at a wedding he was compelled to alter the ending to one befitting "a time of such great rejoicing.") In the concluding fifth scene the shepherd Amyntas announces the joyous news to the other shepherds and nymphs; Orpheus and Eurydice arrive and the opera ends with an elaborate chorus of rejoicing and celebration.

Comparing this libretto with the one for *Dafne*, Rinuccini remarked that "greater favor and fortune have been bestowed upon the *Euridice*," for it was "set to music by . . . Peri with wonderful art." As he had in *Dafne*, Peri employed in *Euridice* the monodic *stile rappresentativo* (see the preceding entry). In his foreword to the printed edition of the music he informed the reader of his aims in composing the work:

> I knew . . . that in our speech some words are so intoned that harmony can be based upon them and that in the course of speaking it passes through many others that are not so intoned until it returns to another that will bear a progression to a fresh consonance. And having in mind those inflections and accents that serve us in our grief, in our joy, and in similar states, I caused the bass to move in time to these, either more or less, following the passions, and I held it firm through the false [that is, nonhar-

PROLOGO
LA TRAGEDIA.

O che d'alti sospir vaga, e di pian ti Spars'or di doglia hor di minaccie il volto Fei negl'ampi te atri al popol folto Scolorir di pietà volti, e sembian-ti. Ritornello.

2
Non sangue sparso d'innocenti vene
Non ciglia spente di Tiranno insano
Spettacolo infelice al guardo humano
Canto su meste, e lacrimose scene,

3
Lungi via lungi pur da regij tetti
Simulacri funesti, ombre d'affanni
Ecco i mesti coturni, e i foschi panni
Cangio, e desto ne i cor più dolci affetti

4
Hor s'auuerrà, che le cangiate forme
Non senza alto stupor la terra ammiri
Tal ch'ogni alma gentil ch'Apollo inspiri
Del mio nouo cammin calpesti l'orme

5
Vostre Regina fia cotanto alloro
Qual forse anco nó colse Atene, ò Roma
Fregio non vil su lonorata chioma
Fronda Febea fra due corone d'oro

6
Tal per voi torno, e con sereno aspetto
Ne Reali Imenei m'adorno anch'io
E sù corde più liete il canto mio
Tempro al nobile cor dolce diletto

7
Mentre Senna Real prepara intanto
Alto diadema, onde il bel crin si fregi
E i manti, e seggi dè gl'antichi Regi
Del Tracio Orfeo date l'orecchie al cáto.

Pastore del Coro.

INFE Ch'i bei crin d'oro Sciogliete lie te allo scherzar de venti E

PERI: *L'Euridice*

monic tones] and true proportions until, running through various notes, the voice of the speaker came to a word that, being intoned in familiar speech, opened the way to a fresh harmony.

Peri's explanation is actually little more than a description of one of the new characteristics of the emerging Baroque style, the *basso continuo*. In performance the bare two-part texture is filled out at sight by instrumentalists who, playing chords or occasionally more elaborate passage work, realize the harmonies indicated in the score by numbers—hence the term "figured bass"—written either below or above the bass line. Peri's use of both the *stile rappresentativo* and *basso continuo* is illustrated in the opening page of the prologue, sung by La Tragedia, which is reproduced here. The poetry is in rhyming four-line stanzas which Peri has set in strophic recitative; the music is supplied for the first stanza and is repeated unaltered for the remaining six. Peri's setting begins with a somewhat static repetition of the same pitch—the "speaking in harmony" referred to above. In the second and third measures, where the text is more charged with emotion, climaxing on the word "pianti" (tears), the melody and harmony move more rapidly, mirroring the inflection and accent of the text.

The influence of a musical drama such as *Euridice* on future works was significant, for from this time on poetry and music entered a new partnership. Among the many who recognized the importance of the achievement was Marco da Gagliano, from whom we quoted above; he remarked that Peri's "artful manner of reciting in song" was admired by "all Italy." To this we may add the comments of Giovanni Battista Doni, who named the poet Rinuccini as one of the "true architects of this Theatrical Music," and the musician Peri as one of "the first shapers [*formatori*] of this style." Surely the most lasting testimony to the achievements of Peri and Rinuccini's *Euridice* was that of Claudio Monteverdi and his librettist Alessandro Striggio, who in their *L'Orfeo* (1607, Monteverdi's first opera) adapted and emulated, in true Renaissance fashion, many of the essential musical and dramatic features found in *Euridice*.

Autograph material of Rinuccini is extremely rare; the Morgan Library owns an autograph document signed by Rinuccini, dated 1610. The Library also has the rare first edition of Gabriello Chiabrera's libretto for Caccini's *Il rapimento di Cefalo*, first performed in Florence three days after *Euridice*.

1608

[Claudio Monteverdi, 1567–1643.]
OTTAVIO RINUCCINI, 1562–1621.

L'Arianna tragedia del Sig. Ottavio Rinuccini . . . . Florence: Giunti, 1608. [2] [7]–52 p. 20.5 cm. An early edition of the libretto.
First performance: Mantua, 28 May 1608.
Mary Flagler Cary Music Collection.

On 28 May 1608, in a recently constructed theatre outside the walls of Mantua with a capacity estimated by contemporary observers as between 4000 and 6000, Claudio Monteverdi's second opera, *Arianna*, was performed for the first time. It was the main event in celebration of the homecoming of the newly wed Francesco Gonzaga, hereditary prince of the city, and his bride, Margaret of Savoy. The work was a triumph and those who heard it were unanimous in their praise. The composer Marco da Gagliano, writing in the preface to his *Dafne* (1608), declared that *Arianna* "renewed the excellence of the ancient music, in that [it] . . . visibly moved the whole theatre to tears." Much the same was recorded by Acquilino Coppini, a Milanese friend of Monteverdi's youth, when he wrote that "whoever heard it afterwards" shed "thousands and thousands of compassionate tears."

More than a little of the credit for the success of the work must surely reside with its librettist; as we read in Giovanni Battista Doni's *Trattato della musica scenica* (written 1633–35), "Monteverdi . . . received much aid from Rinuccini in *L'Arianna*, even though this poet was not trained in music (making up for this with the fine judgment and astute ear apparent in the nature and structure of his lyric poetry) . . . ." This was the third of Rinuccini's operatic texts (his fourth and last, *Narciso*, was considered by Monteverdi but ultimately rejected because of the large number of sopranos and tenors required, and its tragic ending). *Arianna* clearly ranks as the poet's most accomplished libretto, for it is marked by a richness of expressive devices, affective parallelisms, incisive rhythmic gestures, and, most importantly, by a cultivation of human emotion rarely encountered in either *Dafne* or *Euridice*. Rinuccini himself considered *Arianna* to be among the grandest of his works, and in fact came to Mantua in February 1608 to confer with Monteverdi concerning the singers and all the distribution of the musicians.

Given the quality of Rinuccini's text it is indeed unfortunate that Monteverdi's music for the opera has not survived. One fragment, however, has come down to us, the famous "Lamento d'Arianna," which, in the words of the composer, was "the most essential part of the work." Others in Monteverdi's day held the piece in high esteem for, as Doni asserted, "the lament . . . is perhaps the most beautiful composition which has been done in our time." Severo Bonini, a composer and writer on music, wrote as late as the 1640's that "there was not a house which, possessing harpsichords or theorbos, did not also have the lament of Arianna."

With Rinuccini's libretto, and the vivid description provided by Federico Follino in his *Compendio delle sontuose feste . . .* (Mantua: Aurelio and Lodovico Osanna, 1608, in which, incidentally, Rinuccini's libretto was apparently first published), we are able to piece together a fairly accurate account of the first performance of *Arianna*. The stage was set with a rocky sea reef; to "very sweet instrumental music," a cloud "full of the most brilliant light" slowly descended bearing Apollo, and then vanished "in a moment" as he stepped to earth. The prologue is sung by Apollo, who reveals his new guise: armed not with bows and arrows, he comes instead with a kithara (an instrument something like a lyre), eager to delight the heart and vanquish weighty cares with the sweet strains of tender love songs. Venus and Cupid appear in Scene 1 and relate the journey made to Crete by Theseus, prince of Athens, as one of seven youths and seven maidens to be sacrificed to the Minotaur, a creature half-man, half-bull, in tribute to King Minos of Crete. Once there, Theseus meets Ariadne, daughter of Minos, and the two fall in love. She gives him a sword with which to slay the Minotaur, and a thread to trail behind him on his way through the creature's labyrinth in order that he may find his way out again.

Triumphant, Thesus escapes from Crete with Ariadne, and they sail to the island of Naxos where, in Scene 2, Theseus's feelings for Ariadne begin to change. She retires and Theseus reveals his shameful sentiments at the thought of betraying the woman who is the very "cause of my glory and my life." In Scene 3, advised by his counsellor, Consigliero, that he is not bound by vows made in the heat of passion and incautious love, Theseus sets sail, leaving Ariadne. With her attendant, Dorilla, Ariadne expresses in Scene 4 her growing fear concerning the whereabouts of Theseus; the reports of a chorus of fishermen do nothing to allay her suspicions. In Scene 5 a messenger arrives with the dreaded news: Ariadne has indeed been abandoned by Theseus. In the next scene Ariadne sings the famous lament, "Lasciatemi morire": "Ah, let me die! Who shall comfort me in so cruel a fate, in such great martyrdom? Let me die!" Yet all is not lost, for to the sounds of trumpets, drums, and horns, Dorilla exclaims: "to the shore . . . see Theseus, who returns." But it is not Theseus, nor would Ariadne trust him again if it were, for to her the past is now dead.

In Scene 7 we learn from another messenger what has happened. It is Bacchus who has crossed the sea; fulfilling the remedy planned by Venus and Cupid, he falls instantly in love with Ariadne. All past sorrows are forgotten in the ballet of the concluding scene during which Cupid—appropriately for a celebration in honor of Francesco and his bride, Margaret of Savoy—admonishes both gods and mortals to "admire the lofty glory of love." Ariadne sings that "happy above all human desire is the heart which has for comfort a god"; Venus, "rising from the sea," and Jove, in "the heavens," add their blessing. Bacchus, inviting his bride "to the eternal sky," promises that "the bright stars will make of your beautiful hair a garland of gold, glorious reward of a soul which despises, for the sake of heavenly desire, mortal beauty."

Monteverdi seems to have cherished a special affection for *Arianna*, and in particular Ariadne's lament. In 1620 he eagerly participated in Duke Ferdinand Gonzaga's proposal for a revival of the opera—protesting, however, to Alessandro Striggio (librettist for his first opera, *L'Orfeo*, 1607) that "if I had had more time, I would have revised it more thoroughly and even perhaps greatly improved it." (The performance did not take place.) He reworked the lament into a four-part cycle of five-voice madrigals which were printed in 1614 in the Sixth Book of madrigals. A monodic version was published in 1623, of which only a single copy is known (Ghent, Rijksuniversiteit, Centrale Bibliotheek). Monteverdi once again returned to the material of the lament in his *Selva morale e spirituale*, published in 1641, set this time to a sacred text with the title "Pianto della Madonna." In 1640 Monteverdi, now long since moved to Venice, undoubtedly retouched the score of the entire opera for its revival at the opening of the Teatro San Moïse.

As noted above, Rinuccini's text for *Arianna* in all likelihood first appeared in Follino's *Compendio*. Three other printings, all of which date from 1608, are also recorded: Mantua, "gli heredi di Francesco Osanna"; the Florence, Giunti edition shown here; and Ciotti in Venice. The question of precedence has not been definitively settled. Solerti, in *Le origini del melodramma* (1903), states that the *Compendio* printing is the first; Sonneck, in the *Catalogue of Opera Librettos Printed before 1800* (1914), lists the "heirs of Francesco Osanna" edition as the first; and the Florence printing is given precedence in the *Primo tentativo di catologo unico dei librettti italiani a stampa fino all'anno 1800*, published by the Biblioteca Nazionale Braidense, Milan (ten volumes, typed and duplicated, undated). But apparently neither Sonneck nor the Braidense cataloguer knew of the *Compendio* edition, so Solerti's claim—which, it seems, no one has challenged—could well be accurate.

One other detail of bibliographic interest found in extant copies of *Arianna* might be noted here. The gap in the pagination between title page and page [7], the beginning of the text, "points to a practice not noticed hitherto," observes Albi Rosenthal: "that the quire of the libretto containing the synopsis may have been sold separately at performances."

There are no known autograph manuscripts of Monteverdi's. The manuscript of *L'incoronazione di Poppea* in the Biblioteca Nazionale Marciana, Venice, parts of which were thought to be holograph, is now identified as being mostly in the hand of Maria Cavalli, wife of the composer Francesco Cavalli (see the next entry).

L'ARIANNA
TRAGEDIA
DEL SIG OTTAVIO
RINVCCINI.
GENTIL'HVOMO DELLA CAMERA
DEL RE CRISTIANISSIMO.

Rappresentata in musica nelle reali nozze del Sereniβimo
Principe di Mantoua, e della Sereniβima
Infanta di Sauoia.

IN FIRENZE,
Nella Stamperia de' GIVNTI. MDCIIX.
Con licenzia de' Superiori.

[MONTEVERDI] / RINUCCINI: *L'Arianna*

1640 [Francesco Cavalli, 1602–1676.]
GIOVANNI FRANCESCO BUSENELLO, 1598–1659.

Gli amori d'Apollo e di Dafne . . . . Venice: Andrea Giuliani, 1656. engr. plate [4] 64 p. 15.5 cm. First edition of the libretto.
First performance: Venice, Carnival 1640.

1645 [Francesco Cavalli, 1602–1676.]
GIOVANNI FAUSTINI, ca. 1619–1651.

Il Titone. Drama per musica. Venice: Francesco Valvasense, 1645. [3] 4–66 p. 14 cm. First edition of the libretto.
First performance: Venice, Carnival 1645.

1664 [Francesco Cavalli, 1602–1676.]
NICOLÒ MINATO, ca. 1630–1698.

Scipione affricano. Drama per musica . . . . Venice: Steffano Curti e Franc. Nicolini, 1664. engr. plate [12] 74 [2] p. 13.5 cm.
First edition of the libretto.
First performance: Venice, 9 February 1664.
Purchased as the gifts of Mr. James J. Fuld.

The opening of the first public opera house in Venice in 1637, the Teatro S Cassiano, must certainly rank as one of the most significant events in the social history of opera. Whereas the genre had previously existed for the "delight of princes," as the composer Marco da Gagliano had written, the advent of a public theatre devoted to the budding art form of drama in music, supported by a combination of broad public appeal and the patronage of the upper classes, was to be of lasting consequence. The popularity of opera in Venice was nothing short of amazing; by the end of the century almost 400 productions had been given (in as many as nine different houses).

For Venice the arrival of opera was propitiously timed. Politically in decline after more than a century of territorial, maritime, and trading losses, the city was in need of an all-embracing diversion for her citizens which opera readily provided. And others in Europe found the Venetian panacea equally alluring, for yearly, during Carnival season, foreign visitors flocked in huge numbers to that city in its pursuit. An Englishman, Robert Bargrave, concluded a seven-year grand tour of Europe with a stay in Venice in 1655. Recording his impressions of the city, he noted that

> the Varieties of Carneval enterteinments are as unconfin'd, as are mens Fancies, Every minute and every place affording new. But above all, surpassing whatsoever theyr Inventions can else stretch to, are theyr Opera's (or Playes) represented in rare Musick from the beginning to end, by select Eunuchs and women, sought out through all Italy on purpose . . . . Nay I must needs confess that all the pleasant things I have yet heard or seen, are inexpressibly short of the delight I had in seeing this Venetian Opera; and as Venice in many things surpasses all places else where I have been, so are these operas the most excellent of all its glorious Vanities.

One of the most accomplished and prolific composers of these "glorious Vanities" was Francesco Cavalli. Known in his lifetime as "the Amphion of Music," he has been praised in our own day as "the greatest opera composer of the generation which succeeded Monteverdi." Twenty-seven operas attributed to Cavalli survive, out of 33 for which librettos are known. His works, which span the tentative beginnings of public opera in Venice and the establishment of the city as one of the major operatic centers of Europe, are of central importance to the history and understanding of the development of *seicento* opera.

Gli amori d'Apollo e di Dafne, the second of Cavalli's operas for which music survives, was composed to a libretto by Francesco Busenello (author also of the libretto for Monteverdi's *L'incoronazione di Poppea*, Venice, 1642), and first performed at S Cassiano during Carnival 1640. The libretto, Busenello's first, exhibits close ties to the pastoral play in its mythological subject matter and contemplative poetry, a point borne out in the preface, in which the librettist pays homage to Battista Guarini's *Il pastor fido*, as well as citing it as a precedent for the number of amorous entanglements found in his work. The poem, loosely constructed in three acts with further divisions into separate scenes, shows additional relationships to the pastoral tradition in its use of ballet numbers—the prologue includes a *ballo dei fantasmi*, Act I, Scene 4 a *ballo di ninfi e pastori*—stage machinery, and extended, set declamatory speeches.

Il Titone, the music for which is lost, was written for S Cassiano in 1645 to a libretto by Giovanni Faustini. Author of eleven librettos during the years 1642 to 1651, most of which Cavalli set to music, Faustini was one of the very few writers in Venice who proudly confessed to being a professional librettist. In the preface to his *Oristeo* (1651) he offered as his artistic credo:

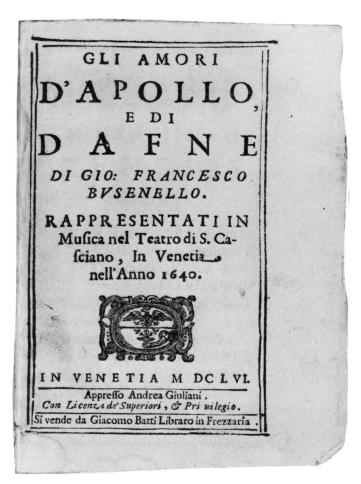

[CAVALLI] / BUSENELLO: *Gli amori d'Apollo e di Dafne*

[CAVALLI] / FAUSTINI: *Il Titone*

[CAVALLI] / MINATO: *Scipione affricano*

I am not one of those writers who writes for mere diversion [Busenello, a lawyer by profession, published his five librettos in 1656 in a volume entitled *Delle hore ociose*—"From Idle Hours"]. I strain my pen, I confess, to see if it can raise me above the ordinary and common achievements of dull and plebeian talents. This honored madness that began to assault me when I had scarcely emerged from swaddling clothes and has not yet abated, forces me to the assiduous creation of various compositions.

From the preface to another contemporary libretto, written perhaps by Marco Faustini, Giovanni's brother, we learn:

Giovanni Faustini, at an age too young for proper enjoyment, applied his genius to music-dramas, in which he excelled above all at invention. Therefore during the course of only nine years (for he died suddenly in 1651, aged only 31) the theatres of this city presented, to great applause, La Virtù de' strali d'Amore, Egisto, Ormindo, Titone, Doriclea, Ersilda, Euripo, Oristeo, Ronsinda, Calisto, Eritrea, and after his death, Eupatra, then Elena rapita da Teseo, clothed with the verse of a sublime Virtuoso; all set to music either by the singular virtue of Francesco Cavalli, a most honored organist in the most Serene Republic; or Pietro Andrea Ziani . . . . They met not only the joy and satisfaction of this city, which hears so many similar productions, but also those in many other major cities of Italy, where they are heard increasingly often with every amount of applause; indeed his many inventions have often met with more than one musical setting.

Nicolò Minato, librettist of *Scipione affricano*, was one of the most prodigious librettists in the history of opera, with over 200 works to his credit. He began his career in Venice and concluded it in Vienna as court poet for Emperor Leopold I. Author of twelve librettos for Venetian theatres between 1650 and 1665, Minato, in contrast to the aims of Faustini, declared that he wrote librettos for no other end than his own caprice—"compogno per mero capriccio"—and claimed elsewhere that he had written dramas for music during the time he would otherwise have spent sleeping. Such sentiments were no doubt spawned by the growing fickleness of a fee-paying public who increasingly demanded novelty at all costs. Indeed Benedetto Ferrari, librettist of the first opera performed in a public theatre in Venice, after several seasons of experience with the public lamented: "Though a veteran of scenic compositions I am afflicted by the sophistication of the century; its fickleness torments me." Ferrari was not alone in this complaint, for another writer, as early as 1642, had characterized the Venetian public as those "who are only content with miracles and would scorn the very harmony of heaven if they were to hear it more than once." The librettist Aurelio Aureli expressed his disillusionment even more strongly, writing in 1665:

The Venetian audiences have got to such a point that they no longer know how to enjoy what they see; nor do authors know how to invent something to satisfy the bizarre tastes of this city . . . . Man cannot always work as he chooses, but he is constrained to obey the wishes of others.

Minato, one of the librettists most adept at catering to the whims of Venetian audiences, hit upon the formula of classical historical subjects—adapted, however, to public tastes ("all'uso corrente"). Not only historical situations, but often also entire characters and their motivations were made subordinate to the amatory involvements of the principals. The *argomenti* (summaries) of Minato's librettos therefore consist of two sections. The first part, entitled "Di quello, che si hà dall'historia" ("that which comes from history")—Plutarch for *Scipione affricano*—is immediately followed by "Di quello che si finge" ("that which is fictitious"). Minato's librettos call as well for an increased use of machines for rapid changes of scenes, occasions for disguise and deception, and the use of action scenes depicting sacrifices, battles, deaths, and prisons.

The plight of Minato and his fellow Venetian librettists has been shared by many. The composers and librettists of seventeenth-century Venice would certainly have been sympathetic to Samuel Johnson's eloquent verse:

> Hard is his lot, that here by Fortune plac'd,
> Must watch the wild Vicissitudes of Taste;
> With ev'ry Meteor of Caprice must play,
> And chase the new-blown Bubbles of our Day.
> Ah! let not Censure term our Fate our Choice,
> The Stage but echoes back the publick Voice.
> The Drama's Laws the Drama's Patrons give,
> For we that live to please, must please to live.

Manuscripts of nearly all of Cavalli's operas are found in the Biblioteca Nazionale Marciana, Venice; seven of them are largely in Cavalli's hand. The remainder, most of which include autograph corrections, are in copyists' hands, mainly that of his wife, Maria, his chief copyist until her death in 1652. The Marciana manuscripts form part of the Contarini Collection, willed to the library in 1839, which includes over 100 manuscript scores of the period 1639–1685, a major source of seventeenth-century Venetian opera.

JEAN-BAPTISTE LULLY, 1632–1687.

Thesée, tragedie mise en musique . . . . Paris: Christophe Ballard, 1688. [8] 372 [2] p. 37.5 cm. First edition of the full score. First performance: Saint-Germain-en-Laye, 12 January 1675. Mary Flagler Cary Music Collection.

French opera of the seventeenth century has aptly been described as "a product directed toward a specific audience of one, the king"—*le Roi Soleil.* In an age of absolutism the apocryphal remark attributed to Louis XIV, "L'état, c'est moi," reflected not only a political reality but also a social hierarchy that touched all aspects of intellectual and artistic life. Aided by his administrator, Jean-Baptiste Colbert, he exercised his passion for order within these domains by establishing five academies, one each for literature, dance, science, and architecture, and an Académie de Musique, founded in 1669. Their primary function was to insure the centralization of taste which reflected at once the greater glory of France and of Louis himself. To achieve this goal the king sought the assistance of capable and ambitious men of the bourgeoisie, and in music found a worthy advocate in Jean-Baptiste Lully, a man whose efficiency and absolutism paralleled his own. And so, on 13 March 1672, Louis placed Lully in charge of the academy of music, noting that

> in order to assure greater success, we believe it appropriate to give control to an individual whose experience and capacity we know well . . . . These reasons moving us, and being well acquainted with the intelligence and great attainments which have been acquired by our dear . . . Jean-Baptiste Lully in music . . ., we charge on him the honor of the post of *surintendant et compositeur de la musique.*

Lully created a union of drama, music, and spectacle that satisfied in every way the king's desire to further the aims of state and monarchy. Lully and his librettist, Philippe Quinault, designated their operas *tragédies lyriques,* and from 1673 to the end of his life the composer completed thirteen works in this genre of which Quinault was librettist of eleven. With stories drawn usually from Greek mythology, and less often from Italian and Spanish chivalric romance, the *tragédies lyriques* of Lully and Quinault were divided into five acts preceded by a prologue. The prologues, most often only partially related to what followed, were especially written to allow for thinly veiled allegorical allusions to the qualities of Louis, the military victories of France, or, when the country was not at war, the virtues of peace; the remaining five acts constituted the central drama of the opera. Lully's goal in the *tragédie lyrique* was a synthesis of drama, poetry, music, dance, and elaborate stage machinery—in short, an *"agréable meslange."* (See also the discussion of Lully's *Roland,* p. 18.)

The published full score of *Thesée,* Lully's third *tragédie lyrique,* was first issued a year after the composer's death by the monopolistic publishing firm of Christophe Ballard. The present copy has a distinguished provenance: first owned by Louis-Alexandre de Bourbon, Comte de Toulouse (a son of Louis XIV and Madame de Montespan), it then passed to the library of King Louis-Philippe, and in 1852 became part of the extensive music holdings of Sir Frederick Ouseley. The Comte de Toulouse, by the standards of his day, amassed an impressive music collection that numbered 290 copyist's manuscripts of scores and parts of the operas of Lully and his contemporaries, as well as 67 printed volumes devoted to the music of the same period. (The bulk of the collection was acquired in 1978 by the Bibliothèque Nationale and the Bibliothèque Municipale in Versailles; in addition to *Thesée,* the Morgan Library obtained a printed score of André Campra's *Tancrède;* see p. 20.)

The Comte de Toulouse copy of *Thesée* is of interest for the numerous manuscript emendations it contains—added, it seems, soon after it was acquired (the hand responsible for the additions dates from the late seventeenth or early eighteenth century). While it was not uncommon for owners or musicians in the homes of nobility to alter the early publications of Lully's operas, it is nonetheless illuminating to witness, as it were, the manner in which music of the time might have been performed. Numerous phrase markings and indications of figured bass have been added to the prologue, supplementing the printed ones, and throughout the copy, written above the vocal parts, are found abbreviations of the names of singers. The most intriguing additions perhaps are those that occur in the recitative that opens Act II.

Recitative, as in all opera in which it is employed, primarily carries the responsibility of advancing dramatic action, whereas the aria more often serves as reflection on the action. In an aria the singer may be allowed the opportunity for vocal display, but recitatives, at least when set by a composer concerned with dramatic values, demanded special attention for the clear declamation and inflection of the text. A form of heightened speech, recitative was defined by Jean-Jacques Rousseau, in the *Encyclopédie* (1765), as "a style of singing that approximates very closely to the spoken word; it is really declamation set to music, in which the singer should endeavor to imitate as much as possible the vocal inflections of the orator."

Lully, in establishing the *tragédie lyrique,* lavished considerable attention on the construction of his recitative and, as we know, was influenced in its ultimate formulation by hearing the actress Marie Champmeslé declaim the dramas of Racine. To insure that the words were clearly intelligible, Lully generally composed *récitatif simple,* one accompanied only by the basso continuo and, as described by a contemporary, intended to be performed "quickly without appearing bizarre." As for ornamentation in recitative, Lully said there should be none: "my recitative is made only for speaking." From the number of surviving contemporary scores of Lully's operas with ornaments added to the recitatives, it is evident that he was only partially successful in achieving this goal. Further documentation of this is provided by the manuscript emendations on pages 164 and 165 of the present score: a *récitatif simple*—but there is scarcely one measure that has not been embellished with one, two, or three ornaments (indicated by x's and other marks above the vocal lines).

Lully apparently prepared only skeleton scores of his operas, and left to his students the task of filling in many of the inner voices. A single autograph manuscript is known, an unidentified work in the André Meyer collection, Paris.

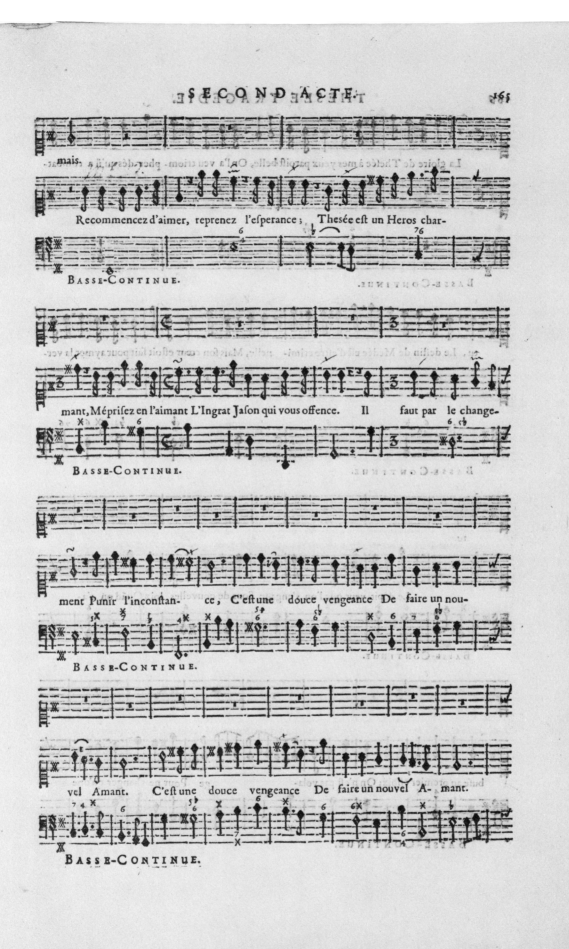

Recommencez d'aimer, reprenez l'esperance ; Thesée est un Heros char-

BASSE-CONTINUE.

mant, Méprisez en l'aimant L'Ingrat Jason qui vous offence. Il faut par le change-

BASSE-CONTINUE.

ment Punir l'inconstan- ce, C'est une douce vengeance De faire un nou-

BASSE-CONTINUE.

vel Amant. C'est une douce vengeance De faire un nouvel A- mant.

BASSE-CONTINUE.

LULLY: *Thésée*

Tutto il mal non vien per nuocere. Autograph manuscript of Olindo's aria "Luci belle, che siete d'Amore," from Act I, Scene 1. On p. 2 is a draft of an aria from Act V, Scene 1. 2 p. 20 × 25 cm.
First performance: Rome, Carnival 1681.
Mary Flagler Cary Music Collection.

Composer by his own count of 114 operas, Alessandro Scarlatti—a "prodigy of music" as he was known in his lifetime—completed his third opera, *Tutto il mal non vien per nuocere* ("Not every misfortune is harmful"), in 1681. The plot of the *commedia per musica* revolves around a succession of half-serious, half-humorous misunderstandings, disguises, deceptions, and confrontations, enlivened from time to time by quarreling and amorous entanglements of the two comic servants, all of which concludes happily in the final scene.

By the standards of the time the opera seems to have met with success, for after its initial performance at the Teatro Capranica in 1681 it was given again in Rome the same year in a private performance at the Rospigliosi Palace. From there it made its way two years later to Ancona and Siena, followed by performances in Ravenna in 1685, Florence in 1686, Naples in 1687 (this time under the title *Dal male il bene*), and finally in 1694 in Rimini.

The first aria of the opera, "Luci belle, che siete d'Amore," a version of which is preserved in the Cary manuscript, sets the tone for the serious nature of the work with Olindo's protestations of love to the indifferent Doralba. The text of the aria and a translation are given here:

> Luci belle, che siete d'Amore,
> Archi, e strali da cui non v'è scampo,
> Se uccidete con fulmini il core,
> Ravvivate i miei lumi col lampo.
>
> Molli guancie, pendici amorose,
> Ove ridon le brine et i fiori,
> Non tardate a scoprir quelle rose
> Le cui spine trafiggono i cori.

> Lovely eyes that belong to love's wonder,
> Bows and arrows which brook no escaping,
> If you kill my lost heart with your thunder,
> Oh, revive my poor eyes with your lightning.

> Softest cheeks, am'rous slopes to the lover,
> Where the frost and flow'rs laugh in the morning,
> Don't delay those pink roses to uncover
> Whose sharp thorns transfix hearts with their piercing.

That Scarlatti is known to have made at least four separate settings of the aria possibly reflects the apparent popularity of the opera. Each of the three extant manuscripts of the complete work—in the Deutsche Staatsbibliothek, Berlin; the Biblioteca dell'Abbazia, Monte Cassino (partly autograph); and the Conservatorio di Musica S Pietro a Majella, Naples—transmits a different version of the aria; the fourth is found in the leaf reproduced here. Given the operatic conventions current in Scarlatti's day, we may further speculate that the number of variants for the aria suggests a more practical consideration. In the age of the *prima donna* and *primo uomo*, composers were obliged to provide music that would show off to the greatest advantage the vocal abilities of the performer; if an aria became too closely identified with a particular singer, another would have to be written in its place.

Just which performance of the opera the present version was intended for is impossible to say, since no libretto has yet been found in which the text appears in the same wording and context as in the Cary leaf. Were it not for the fact that a draft for an aria from Act V, Scene 1 of the opera is found on the verso of the leaf, another possible explanation for the version might be that it was written for inclusion in another work or for concert performance. The present setting contains two textual differences from the 1681 and subsequent librettos: the second line of the second stanza is changed from "Ove ridono i fiori, e le brine" to "Ove ridon le brine et i fiori"; and the last line of the second stanza is altered from "Di cui sento nel core le spine" to "Le cui spine trafiggono i cori."

Autograph manuscripts of Scarlatti operas are found in libraries in London, Cambridge, Brussels, Vienna, and Naples; the Cary leaf is apparently the only operatic manuscript, and one of only two Scarlatti autographs, in this country.

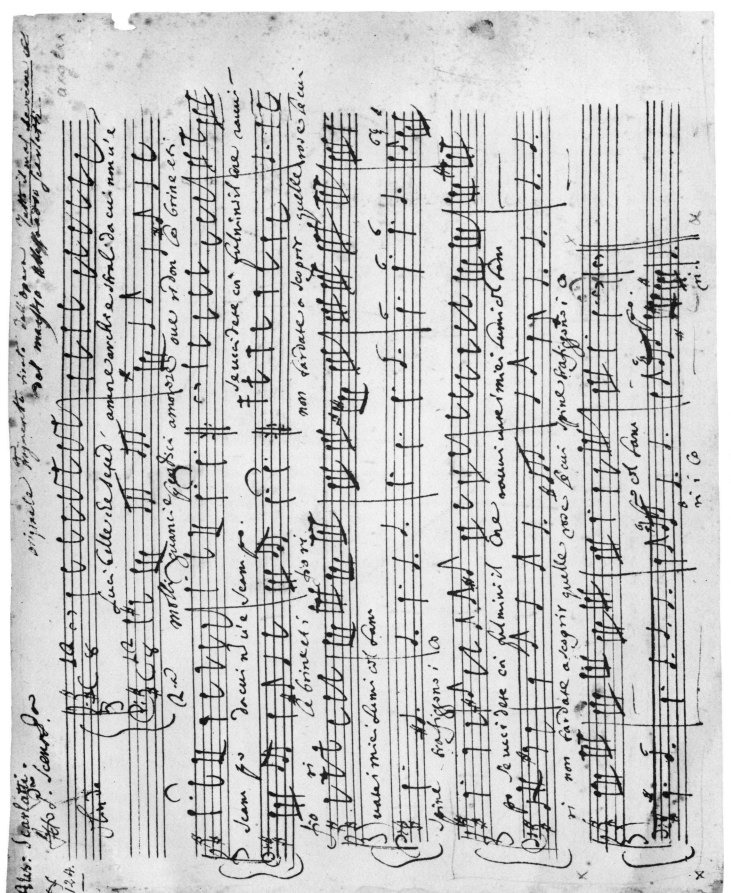

A. SCARLATTI: *Tutto il mal non vien per nuocere*

1685   JEAN-BAPTISTE LULLY, 1632–1687.

Roland, tragedie mise en musique . . . . Paris: Christophe Ballard, 1685. [vi] lvi [1] 2–344 p. 36 cm. First edition of the full score.
First performance: Versailles, 8 January 1685.
Mary Flagler Cary Music Collection.

"To set forth the delusions in which love can entangle the heart that disregards *la gloire*" is the moralizing subject of *Roland*, Lully's twelfth *tragédie lyrique*. A standard of society reflected in the mode of life of the *grand siècle*, *la gloire* (defined here as the duty to abide by exalted principle) was a virtue that *le Roi Soleil* sought to encourage, and it was at his suggestion that Lully and his librettist, Philippe Quinault, considered the topic in *Roland*. Reason, truth, and nature were values that meant much to the time, but they were tempered by *l'honneur*, *la galanterie*, and *la gloire*. To insure that these and other principles were not forgotten, Louis, as has previously been mentioned in the discussion of Lully's *Thésée* (p. 13), created an elaborate bureaucracy that set guidelines for both art and society. And opera, perhaps more than any other art form, provided the grandest of vehicles to instruct aristocracy and general public alike.

The *tragédies lyriques* of Lully and Quinault were attempts to join in a unified whole the divergent elements of music, dance, drama, and spectacle. The success of this collaboration resulted from an artistic oligarchy that has seldom been duplicated, and the genesis of their operas is perhaps as fascinating as the study of the works themselves. Quinault would first make outlines of several stories for the king's approval (those of *Persée*, *Amadis*, *Roland*, and *Armide*, it seems, originated with Louis). After the king had selected a subject that suited him, Lully and Quinault would draft a general plan. The next step has been recorded by Le Cerf de la Viéville in his *Comparaison de la musique italienne et de la musique française* (1704–06): "Quinault wrote out a plan of the action of the piece. He then gave a copy to Lully. . . . As soon as he [Quinault] had finished writing some scenes, he presented them to the Académie Française; after having profited by the judgments of the Academy, he brought the rewritten scenes to Lully . . . who examined them word for word, making further corrections and even cutting half the scene when he deemed it necessary."

Historians, drawing on both fact and legend, have dutifully recorded Lully's almost obsessive desire for musical perfection and the often harsh measures by which he sought to achieve it. Yet the autocratic *surintendant de la musique* was well aware of his debt to his librettist. Six years after Lully's death, the *Mercure galant* reported that he had called Quinault "the only poet with whom he could work and who knew as much about varying meter and rhythm in poetry as he himself knew about varying melody and cadence in music." The fruits of their collaboration earned for the composer the encomium of being "father of our beautiful French music," and in his works, according to Titon du Tillet's *Le Parnasse françois* (1732–43), "one finds . . . a just and true character, a marvelous variety, a melody and harmony that are enchanting." More fanciful descriptions were not un-common: Jacques Bonnet, in his *Histoire de la musique* (1715), asserted that Lully's music was "moving enough to melt hearts and to make the very rocks groan."

For some critics of French opera the poetry, not the music, was of greater importance. The Abbé Mably, in his *Lettre à Madame la Marquise de P[ompadour] sur l'Opéra* (1741), insisted that "although the Musician may have more talent than the Poet; although by the force of his genius he may insure the success of an Opera, his art is regarded in France as always secondary to that of Poetry." In Lully's case, however, the situation was perhaps the other way around, for Saint-Évremond, no friend of opera, wrote that while "the Musician is to follow the Poet's direction . . . in my opinion Lully is to be exempted . . . [for he] knows the passions and enters further into the Heart of man than the poets themselves."

The reliance on the *divertissement* of the ballet and spectacle in French opera was regarded by many as a decorative intrusion that contributed little to dramatic development. Saint-Évremond was certainly not alone when he wrote of the *tragédie lyrique*: "something foolish laden with music, dances, machines, scenery, is magnificently foolish, but . . . foolish all the same." One suspects perhaps that Lully was again the exception to this pronouncement, for although he occasionally employs *divertissement* for dramatic relief, he often made use of dances, choruses, and songs to heighten tragedy by contrast, as in Act IV of *Roland*. In Scenes 3 through 5 Roland has witnessed the village wedding of his beloved Angélique to Médor, an occasion that affords Lully the use of an elaborate *mise-en-scène* of choruses and dances of joyful shepherds and shepherdesses. Disrupting the happy celebration at the conclusion of Scene 5, Roland moves forward to address the faithless Angélique, saying that she has pierced his heart with "the most terrible blow." The chorus, already dramatically established, here interjects: "Ah! fuyons, fuyons tous" ("Ah! let us flee, let us all flee"), after which follows Roland's air of vengeance "Je suis trahi!" ("I am betrayed!"). The air, accompanied only by basso continuo, is a model of musical economy, a stark contrast to the forces employed in the preceding three scenes. Delivering his invective, Roland laments the folly on which he had been embarked, thereby underscoring the didactic thrust of the opera's libretto: "I am betrayed! Heaven! . . . I am betrayed by ungrateful Beauty, for whom Love caused me to betray my *gloire!*"

Despite its name, the *tragédie lyrique* usually ended happily. In Act IV Roland goes mad with love; in Act V the shades of ancient heroes appear and bid him honor his *gloire* and set free his country. Roland regains his reason and yields to their noble counsel.

TRAGEDIE.
SCENE VI.
ROLAND seul.

BASSE-CONTINUE:

BASSE-CONTINUE.

Je suis tra-

hi ! Ciel ! qui l'auroit pû croire? O Ciel !

BASSE-CONTINUE.

je suis tra- hy par l'in- grate Beauté Pour qui l'A- mour m'a

BASSE-CONTINUE.

fait trahir ma gloire. O doux es- poir dont j'e- stois enchan-

BASSE-CONTINUE.

LULLY: *Roland*

ANDRÉ CAMPRA, 1660–1744.

Tancrede, tragedie, mise en musique. . . . *Paris: Christophe Ballard, 1702. [8] i–l, 291 [1] p. 18.5 cm. First edition of the score.*
First performance: Paris, 7 November 1702.
Mary Flagler Cary Music Collection.

With the death of Lully in 1687 and the gradual lessening of Louis XIV's interest in the traditional association of music and monarchy, French opera became a troubled institution. The Sun King, distracted by setbacks at home and the large sums demanded by military entanglements abroad, found little time for pleasure or courtly ceremony. Added to this was the sobering influence of Louis's mistress, Madame de Maintenon, who saw in opera and theatre the very embodiment of evil. Pleased with her influence on Louis, she asserted in 1697 that the "taste for Pleasure is extinguished in the King's Heart: Age and Devotion have taught him to make serious reflections on the Vanity and Emptiness of everything he was formerly fond of." Thus deprived of the firm commitment of royal patronage and of Lully's formidable administrative and musical talents, the Académie de Musique had lost much of its former eminence. Indeed, one writer declared that the Opéra now "served as a depository to recruit the joyful daughters of debauched, moneyed persons of Paris or the court." Undaunted, the greater part of the French public and nobility, long accustomed to the social trappings of opera and other entertainments, retained a hearty appetite for display and diversion. Not without a measure of jaded ennui did the Duchesse d'Orléans write in 1707: "Every day people say to me, today there is going to be a new opera, or tomorrow a new play. . . . This very year there have been six new comedies and three new operas. I think the Devil has done it on purpose to tease me in my solitude."

This was the milieu in which the composer André Campra lived and worked. Remembered today as the originator of the *opéra-ballet*, Campra was first known in Paris as *maître de musique* at Notre Dame Cathedral, a position he assumed in 1694. Within three years, however, Campra had fallen victim to the lure of the stage, and in 1700 was dismissed from his post at Notre Dame, for the archbishop, along with all the clergy of the day, objected to opera on the grounds that it fostered immorality. Campra was now free to devote his full energies to music for the theatre, and he worked both as a composer and conductor at the Opéra. His new position was merrily celebrated by musicians and audiences in an amusing satirical song: "Quand notre archevesque sçaura, / L'Auteur du nouvel Opéra, / De sa Cathédrale Campra / Décampera."

Le Cerf de la Viéville, a contemporary writer of musical criticism and esthetics, ranked Campra's *tragédies lyriques* first among the post-Lully works of the genre. Rameau, the foremost opera composer of the following generation, considered Campra's third *tragédie lyrique*, *Tancrède*, a "masterpiece."

Campra was among the first French composers to combine the Lullian use of recitative as the predominant style of declamation with the rich lyricism of such Italians as Scarlatti. As a result, arias or *ariettes* took on a larger role in his operas. Two examples from *Tancrède* may be cited. Tancrède, a crusader, mistakes his disguised lover, Clorinde, for his enemy Argant, kills her, and dies of grief. In Act II, having conquered Clorinde's soldiers, Tancrède frees them, telling them to cast off their chains and enjoy a more glorious destiny ("Quittez vos fers, goûtez un sort plus glorieux"). Tancrède's short aria, laid out in firm and resolute phrases, is immediately taken up by the chorus and developed into a powerful and moving ensemble that prefigures Gluck.

The aria that opens Act IV, "Sombres forêts," is of a quite different character. It is an *air de monologue*—a type of aria that Campra usually placed at the beginning of an act or important scene, and one that marks an emotional peak in both music and words. Tancrède, shown deep in an enchanted forest, pours out his sorrow at having lost Clorinde; grieving that he will never see her again, he summons death. Arthur Pougin, who published the first extended study of Campra, wrote of this aria: "It is a brief passage, containing only two main phrases; but the musical conception is so noble and pure, the emotion released so poignant, the grief so despondent, the style so filled with loftiness and grandeur, that it is impossible to imagine anything more wonderful and accomplished in the genre."

In *Tancrède*, Campra broke with French operatic tradition by scoring the role of the heroine, Clorinde, for alto, and also in employing only bass voices for the leading male roles. According to all accounts, Campra wrote the part of Clorinde for Mademoiselle Maupin, one of the most colorful singers of her day. An unusually vivid account of her life is provided by the English music critic George Hogarth (Charles Dickens' father-in-law) in his *Memoirs of the Opera* (first published in 1838, revised in 1851):

She was born in 1673, and married at a very early age, but soon ran away with a fencing master, from whom she learned the use of the small sword. After remaining for some time at Marseilles, where she narrowly escaped the punishment of being burnt alive for setting fire to a convent, she went to Paris, appeared at the opera at the age of two-and-twenty, and was for a considerable time the reigning favourite of the day. Having on some occasion been affronted by Dumenil, a singer, she put on male attire, watched for him in the Place des Victoires, insisted on his drawing his sword and fighting her, and, on refusing, caned him and took his watch and snuff-box. . . . Thevenard, [who sang the role of Tancrède for nearly 30 years] . . ., was nearly treated in the

CAMPRA: *Tancrède*

21

same manner, and had no other way of escaping, but by publicly begging her pardon, after hiding himself in the Palais Royal for three weeks. At a ball given by Monsieur, the brother of Louis XIV, she appeared in men's clothes, and, having behaved impertinently to a lady, was called out by three friends. Instead of avoiding the combat . . . she drew her sword and killed all the three; and then, returning very coolly to the ball-room, told the story to Monsieur, who obtained her pardon. After some other adventures, she went to Brussels, where she became mistress of the Elector of Bavaria. . . . She . . . returned to the Parisian stage, which she [had] left in 1705. The conclusion of such a life is not the least extraordinary part of it. She became at last very devout; and, having recalled her husband, from whom she had long been separated, lived with him in a pious manner till her death, in 1707, at the age of thirty-four. Such is the history of the woman.

Maupin's tempestuous and eventful life inspired Théophile Gautier with material for his novel *Mademoiselle de Maupin, double amour* (Paris, 1835–36). The copy of Campra's *Tancrède* now in the Cary Collection was originally part of the outstanding music collection of the Comte de Toulouse (see p. 13). Manuscripts of Campra's operas are preserved in the Conservatoire National de Musique, Bibliothèque Nationale, and Bibliothèque-Musée de l'Opéra.

The Beggar's Opera . . . . London: printed for John Watts, 1728. [4] [1] 2–58 [2] 16 p. 19.5 cm. First edition, earliest state.
First performance: London, 29 January 1728.
Purchased on the Fellows Capital Fund, 1981.

Opera in London in the first decades of the eighteenth century meant Italian opera. In 1723 Gay wrote to Jonathan Swift: "As for the reigning Amusements of the town, tis entirely Musick. real fiddles, Bass Viols and Hautboys not poetical Harps, Lyres, and reeds. Theres nobody allow'd to say I sing but an Eunuch or an Italian woman." Joseph Addison, whose libretto for *Rosamond* (1707) was an attempt to encourage a native English opera, wrote that the only purpose of Italian opera was "to justify the senses and keep up an indolent attention in the audience." And the critic John Dennis had condemned "that soft and effeminate music that abounds in Italian opera." With *The Beggar's Opera* all that would change; two weeks after its first performance, Gay (again to Swift) writes: "Lord Cobham says that I should [have] printed it in Italian over against the English, that the Ladys might have understood what they read. The outlandish (as they call it) Opera hath been so thin of late that some have call'd that the Beggars opera, & if the run continues, I fear I shall have remonstrances drawn up against me by the Royal Academy of Musick" (which sponsored the Italian Opera).

Although *The Beggar's Opera* aims only a few specific barbs at Italian opera, the genre to which it actually belongs, and of which it is the most celebrated example, is itself fundamentally non-operatic. Ballad opera was written in the vernacular, had spoken dialogue, and used traditional or currently popular melodies in its songs. Gay's work, furthermore, was set in London's underworld of thieves, pickpockets, and prostitutes, in whose roguery was to be seen a satire on the Walpole government—"a piece of Satire," wrote Pope, "which hit all tastes and degrees of men, from those of the highest Quality to the very Rabble."

The 69 tunes that make up the music in *The Beggar's Opera* were adapted to Gay's verses by Johann Christoph Pepusch, a noted composer and teacher, and the first English musicologist. He drew on a number of sources: "Our Polly is a sad Slut," for example, is set to the music of "Oh! London is a fine town," a very popular air printed, like so many other songs in *The Beggar's Opera*, in one of the various editions of D'Urfey's *Wit and Mirth, or Pills to Purge Melancholy;* "Let us take the Road" uses music from Handel's *Rinaldo;* and an air from Purcell's *Fairy Queen,* "If love's a sweet passion, how can it torment," becomes, in the Gay-Pepusch work, "When young at the bar you first

taught me to score." An obvious advantage to adapting these tunes was that the audience probably knew most of them and was thus spared the prospect of an evening of unfamiliar music. And in place of prolix recitatives in a foreign tongue few understood, the audience must have been relieved by spoken dialogue in English. As the Beggar says in the Introduction: "I hope I may be forgiven, that I have not made my opera throughout unnatural, like those in vogue; for I have no recitatives."

The effect on London's musical life of the unprecedented success of *The Beggar's Opera* was immediate. In *The Dunciad,* Pope wrote that "it drove out of *England* for that season the *Italian Opera,* which carry'd all before it for ten years: That Idol of the Nobility and the people, which the great Critick Mr. *Dennis* by the labours and outcries of a whole life could not overthrow, was demolish'd in one winter by a single stroke of this gentleman's pen." In March Gay wrote to Swift that "there is discourse about the town that the Directors of the Royal Academy of Musick design to sollicite against it's being played on the *outlandish* [that is, Italian] Opera days . . . ." Among the many ballad operas spawned by *The Beggar's Opera,* one of the earliest was Colley Cibber's *Love in a Riddle* (1729), in which the author more than once acknowledges Gay's achievement. From the Epilogue we learn that

> Poor English mouths for twenty years
> Have been shut up for musick;
> But, thank our stars, outlandish airs
> At last have made all you sick.
> When warbling dames were all in flames
> And for precedence wrangled,
> One English play cut short the fray
> And home again they dangled.

The rude, earthy satire of Gay's work has rarely been equaled in an opera libretto; his most notable literary descendant, W. S. Gilbert, also satirized many aspects of English society, but always with an underlying respect for it, whereas Gay portrays government as venal to the core. (Gilbert & Sullivan's *The Pirates of Penzance* is discussed on p. 79.) Ballad opera was also the forerunner of the German *Singspiel,* an example of which is Mozart's *Der Schauspieldirektor* (see p. 34).

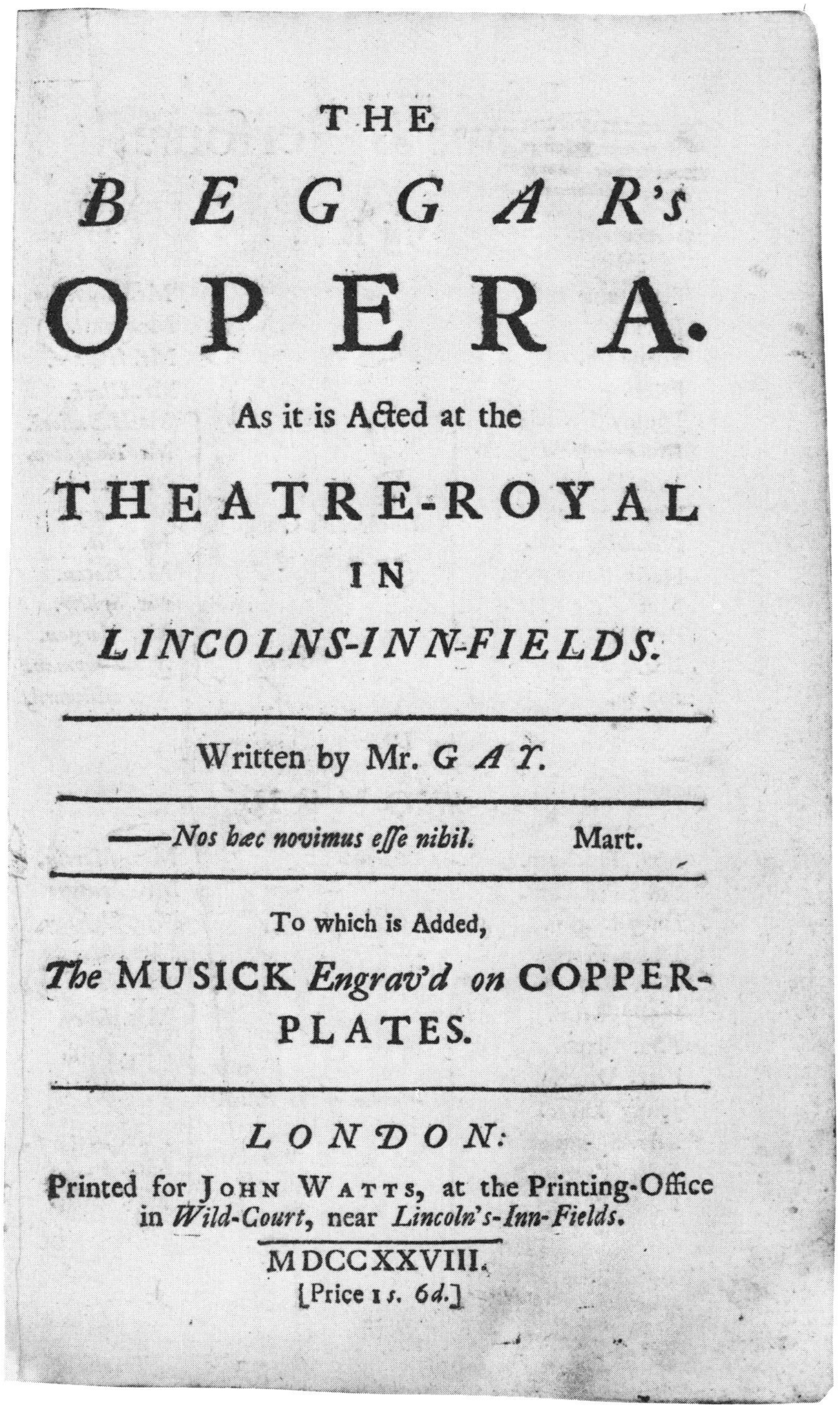

THE
BEGGAR's
OPERA.

As it is Acted at the

THEATRE-ROYAL
IN
LINCOLNS-INN-FIELDS.

Written by Mr. G *A Y*.

——*Nos hæc novimus esse nihil.*   Mart.

To which is Added,

The MUSICK *Engrav'd on* COPPER-
PLATES.

LONDON:

Printed for John Watts, at the Printing-Office
in *Wild-Court,* near *Lincoln's-Inn-Fields.*
MDCCXXVIII.
[Price 1 *s.* 6 *d.*]

Gay: *The Beggar's Opera*

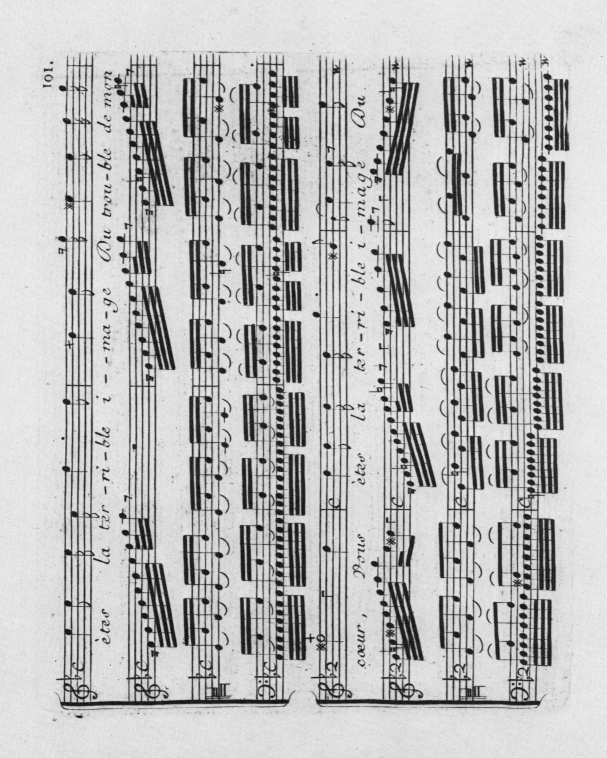

RAMEAU: *Les Indes galantes*

25

1735   JEAN-PHILIPPE RAMEAU, 1683–1764.

Les Indes galantes, ballet, réduit à quatre grands concerts: avec une nouvelle entrée complette. Paris: M. Boivin, M. Leclair, L'Auteur [n.d., ca. 1736]. [4] 226 p. 24 cm. Early edition of the opéra-ballet.
First performance: Paris, 23 August 1735.
Mary Flagler Cary Music Collection.

Weary of the tone of didacticism and moral edification epitomized by the *tragédie lyrique*, French operatic audiences by the early eighteenth century began to desire more intimate and immediately accessible theatrical diversions. Reflecting this change in taste, the November 1714 *Mercure de France* reported that Lully's "*Bellérophon* nowadays appears too tragic, *Thésée* too listless." Similar sentiments were expressed—and lamented—in the *Réflexions sur l'opéra* (1741) of Rémond de Saint-Mard: "there is no longer any need for the strong and the pathetic action demanded by the tragic. . . . People want only sensuous spectacles that are easy to follow," for "the French public is no longer inclined toward entertainment that requires concentration." The shift, actually one of degree, was motivated, one suspects, by the need for escapism. Thus Louis de Cahusac, librettist, *littérateur*, and successful man of the theatre, astutely observed the distinction when he wrote: "the opera conceived by Quinault [and Lully] is composed of one central dramatic action over the course of five acts. It is a vast concept, such as that of Raphael or Michelangelo." In its place, Cahusac continues, spectators wanted an opera comprising "piquant miniatures of pretty Watteaus" with "precision of draftsmanship, grace of brushstrokes, and brilliance of color."

The cry for the agreeable, graceful, and colorful was soon to be answered by the *opéra-ballet*. In the hands of its creator, André Campra (composer, incidentally, of six *tragédies lyriques*, of which the third, *Tancrède*, is discussed on p. 20), the *opéra-ballet*, as Pierre-Charles Roy wrote in his *Lettre sur l'opéra* (1749), "corresponds to French impatience." The change in the cultural atmosphere from the heroic posturing of the *grand siècle* is at once made clear from the opening *entrée* of Campra's *Les fêtes vénitiennes* (1710), with its title "Le triomphe de la folie sur la raison." The public had won, and Saint-Mard confessed self-consciously: "we have reached the point . . . where one desires only [opéra-]ballets. . . . Each act must be composed of a fast-moving, light, and *galante* intrigue. . . . You will find there the portrait of our mores. They are, to be sure, rather vile, but they are, nonetheless, ours."

As with many critics, Saint-Mard perhaps protests too much. The real attraction of the *opéra-ballet*, it seems, was that mythological and allegorical figures were eliminated and replaced with down-to-earth characters in recognizable, or at least plausible, settings. But the genre brought with it a new set of problems: to oblige the demand for "sensuous spectacles," dramatic interest was substantially sacrificed. Yet the poets' loss became the musicians' gain, for in reducing the drama the opportunity for increasing the elements of music and dance expanded, thereby allowing composers both greater musical freedom and room for experimentation. Dramatically, the *opéra-ballet* consists of a prologue and three or four *entrées* (acts), each with its own set of characters and independent action, but all loosely related to some collective idea expressed in the work's title. In *Les Indes galantes*, the unifying theme is some aspect of exotic love, set in a remote corner of the world—one of the magical lands suggested by the Indies: the first act is set in Turkey, the second in Peru, the third in Persia, and the fourth in a North American forest.

In *Les Indes galantes* the increased reliance on the purely musical may easily be illustrated by a brief look at its *première entrée*, "Le turc généreux." (References here are made to the complete *opéra-ballet*; the present score—"réduit à quatre grands concerts"—is condensed, and contains only selections from the work.) The setting is the garden of the generous Turk, Osman Pasha; in the background is the sea. Émilie, a French captive, pledged from birth to Valère, sings to the pasha of her abduction by cruel bandits and imprisonment by pirates "on the vast seas near all that I hate, far from the one I love." Thus separated from Valère, she relates his valorous attempts to rescue her. Presently, "the sky darkens with clouds, winds roar, and the seas rise." From the storm emerges a wind-tossed chorus of sailors who have narrowly escaped death. Scarcely believing it, Émilie spies Valère among the sailors; the lovers are reunited.

It is the "Tempeste" and "Chœur des Matelots" that draw forth Rameau's most arresting music. Graphically depicting the raging tempest, the scene is rich with abrupt changes of harmonies, enharmonic modulations, and vivid orchestral effects of violin tremolos and rapid scale passages for the flutes—all a dramatic portrayal of the sailors' terror in the grip of nature. Desfontaine's contemporary review of the work in the *Observations sur les écrits modernes* might well have been written with this section in mind: "the music is a perpetual witchery; nature has no share in it. Nothing is more craggy and scabrous; it is a road of constant jolts."

Autograph manuscripts of many of Rameau's operas are preserved in the Bibliothèque-Musée de l'Opéra and the Bibliothèque Nationale, Paris; no autograph is known for *Les Indes galantes*.

JEAN-JACQUES ROUSSEAU, 1712–1778.

Le devin du village. Intermede . . . . Paris: Mdme. Boivin, Mr. le Clerc, Melle. Castagnerie [1753]. [4] 95 p. 33.5 cm. First edition.
First performance: Fontainebleau, 18 October 1752.
Purchased by Pierpont Morgan in 1910.

It was the time of the great quarrels between the courts and the clergy. The courts had just been dissolved; the excitement was at its height; there was every danger of an approaching revolt. My pamphlet appeared, and immediately all other quarrels were forgotten. . . . The only revolt was now against me, and such was the outburst that the nation has never quite recovered from it. At court they were merely deciding between the Bastille and banishment. . . . Whoever thinks that this pamphlet probably prevented a revolution in France will think that he is dreaming. Yet it is an actual fact, which all Paris can still bear witness to, for it is less than fifteen years since that singular incident.

The year was 1753 and the protagonist none other than Jean-Jacques Rousseau, philosopher, author, and sometime composer. The great offense he thus recounted in his *Confessions* was his involvement not in some hoped-for political reform—*Du contrat social* was not published until 1762—but in the continuing fracas concerning the relative merits, particularly in opera, of French and Italian music. The pamphlet that touched off the "singular incident" was his *Lettre sur la musique française*; after its appearance, as Rousseau tells us, "no one could think of anything except the threat to French music." And small wonder, for the concluding paragraph pronounced that

there is neither measure nor melody in French music, because the language is not capable of them; . . . French singing is a continual squalling, insupportable to an unprejudiced ear; . . . its harmony is crude and devoid of expression and suggests only the padding of a pupil; . . . French "airs" are not airs; . . . French recitative is not recitative. From this I conclude that the French have no music and cannot have any; or if they ever have, it will be so much the worse for them.

Rousseau's *Lettre* was but the capstone of the so-called *querelle des bouffons*, a conflict sparked by the arrival in Paris, in August 1752, of a troupe of Italian comedians—or *bouffons*, as they came to be called—who performed a number of Italian comic *intermezzi*, of which Giovanni Battista Pergolesi's *La serva padrona* quickly became the most popular. First given in Naples in 1733, Pergolesi's work was by no means new to Paris, having been tried there as early as 1745 with little lasting effect. Yet seven years later the French capital was in an entirely different mood. Rousseau, with his battle cry, "return to nature," along with his fellow *encyclopédistes* Diderot and D'Alembert, had begun preaching that the evils of society were the outgrowth of an overlay of civilized sophistication, and few subjects, especially French opera, were to escape their critical eye. The *tragédies lyriques* of Lully and his successors, with their high-flown drama and mythological characters, were singled out for vehement and sarcastic attack. A call was made for realism and the natural, and Pergolesi's comic masterpiece was soon seen as the first step toward that goal. As Francesco Algarotti, a noted critic and operatic reformer, who would have a lasting effect on Gluck, wrote in his *Saggio sopra l'opera in musica* (1755): "no sooner was heard upon the theatre of Paris the natural and elegant style of the *Serva padrona*, rich with airs so expressive and duets so pleasing, than the far greater part of the French became not only proselytes to, but even zealous advocates in behalf of the Italian music."

None was to convert more quickly or with greater enthusiasm than Rousseau, for within a month of its performance he had set about having the Pergolesi *intermezzo* engraved. But Rousseau was not content to stop there; nothing short of his own operatic contribution would do in the struggle for the victory of Italian comic opera. And so was born his *intermède*, *Le devin du village*. In his *Confessions* Rousseau describes its inception: "when I composed my entertainment my head was full of these pieces [Italian *intermezzi*]; it was they that gave me the idea." Rousseau's work, for which he also wrote the libretto, was an immediate triumph, and in a letter of 22 October 1752 he states that "the little Opera . . . is now being shown at Court. Its success is marvelous and astonishes even me." And from Pierre de Jélyotte, perhaps the most famous tenor of the day and the first to perform the role of Colin in *Le devin*, comes the amusing report to Rousseau: "the whole Court is enchanted with your work; the King, who, as you know, doesn't like music, sings your airs all day long with the falsest voice in this kingdom."

Mention has previously been made of Rousseau's negative opinion of French recitative; for him, recitative should have been a "harmonious declamation . . . necessary in lyric drama, . . . to connect the action and preserve the unity." This description, however, would hardly seem to be a startling insight, for it closely resembles Lully's definition discussed in regard to his *Thésée* (see p. 13). Yet Rousseau also believed the function of recitative was to "set off the airs," and in this Lully's approach, in Rousseau's estimation, fell short.

In composing the recitatives for *Le devin*, Rousseau attempted to remedy this and other faults; summarizing his views in the *Confessions*, he asserted: "the part to which I had devoted the most attention, and in which I had made the greatest departure from the beaten track, was the recitative. Mine was accented in an entirely new manner and kept time with the delivery of the words." Yet despite his efforts, the tide of history was to deal

Rousseau an ironic blow, for his "greatest departure" achieved scant recognition. Although *Le devin* played on its own merits in Paris until 1829, running continuously for more than 75 years with over 400 performances, the revival of Rameau's *Castor et Pollux* and *Platée* in 1754 gave the *querelle des bouffons* its *coup de grâce*. Two weeks after the opening of *Platée* the French, weary of musical and philosophical quibbles, had moved on to other concerns, and the departure of the *bouffons* was "celebrated in the journals of the day as a national triumph."

The final performance of *Le devin* deserves mention, for it was witnessed by no less a wit and raconteur than Hector Berlioz. After declaring his "sovereign contempt" for the work, Berlioz, in his *Memoirs*, wrote:

Poor Rousseau! . . . How could he have foreseen that his precious opera, which excited such enthusiasm, would one day be extinguished for ever beneath a huge peruke, thrown at the heroine's feet by some irreverent joker? By pure chance I was present. . . . Many people, in consequence, attributed the production of the peruke to me. But I must protest my innocence.

Autograph manuscripts of *Le devin* are found in the Bibliothèque de l'Assemblée Nationale and the Bibliothèque Nationale, Paris. The Morgan Library owns autograph manuscripts of three of Rousseau's songs, as well as his own copy of the first edition of the *Lettre sur la musique française*.

LE DEVIN DU VILLAGE

INTERMÉDE

RÉPRÉSENTÉ A FONTAINEBLEAU

Devant leurs Majestés

les 18. et 24. Octobre 1752.

ET A PARIS PAR

l'Academie Royale de Musique

le 1er. Mars 1753.

PAR

J. J. ROUSSEAU.

Gravé par M.elle Vandôme, depuis la 1re. Planche jusqu'a la 50

Prix 9tt.l.

A PARIS

Chez
{
M.dme Boivin, rue St. Honoré à la Regle d'Or.
M.r le Clerc, ruë du Roule à la Croix d'Or.
M.elle Castagnerie, ruë des Prouvaires.
Et à la Porte de l'Opera.
}

de l'Imprinerie du St. Auguste. AVEC PRIVILEGE DU ROY. depuis la 1re. Pl. jusqu'a la 50.

ROUSSEAU: *Le devin du village*

Orphée et Euridice. Autograph manuscript of three passages. 2 p. 30 × 23 cm.
First performance: Paris, 2 August 1774.
Mary Flagler Cary Music Collection.

It has been said of Gluck's *Orfeo ed Euridice* that it stands at the same watershed among the composer's works as it does in the history of opera. Rejecting most of the conventions of Metastasian *opera seria*—the intrigue plots, the stock characters, the stylized scenes, the obligatory bravura arias—Gluck sought in *Orfeo* a return to the simpler, more direct modes of expression established in the esthetic principles of the Florentines who, around 1600, brought forth the first operas.

The libretto for *Orfeo* was written by Raniero de' Calzabigi, and Gluck was the first to assert that any success enjoyed by *Orfeo*, *Alceste*, and *Paride ed Elena*—his three operas to Calzabigi texts—owed more to the librettist than to himself. "Whatever talent the composer may have," he wrote to the *Mercure de France* in February 1773, "he will never create more than mediocre music, if the poet does not arouse in him that enthusiasm without which all artistic productions are weak and spiritless." *Orfeo*, first performed in Vienna in 1762, did not, in fact, win immediate popularity; its success grew only after Gluck's second reform opera, *Alceste* (1767).

By the early 1770's Gluck had turned his attention to Paris, where he hoped to effect reforms on the French *tragédie lyrique* similar to those he had on the Italian *opera seria*. The first attempt was *Iphigénie en Aulide*; the première was on 19 April 1774, but subsequent performances were interrupted by the death, on 10 May, of Louis XV. While we do not know when work began on the second opera for Paris, *Orphée et Euridice*, the most concentrated effort probably took place during the period of public mourning. But Gluck's collaboration with his translator, Pierre-Louis Moline, must have begun well before the *Aulide* première, since the engraved full score of *Orphée* was published around the time of its first performance.

In planning his second French reform opera Gluck undoubtedly chose to adapt an older work, rather than compose a new one, because of the daunting tasks that he would face in preparing both the *Aulide* and *Orphée* premières. *Orfeo* was a short opera, even by Italian standards, and for France it might have filled the evening as an *opéra comique*, but hardly as a *tragédie lyrique*. An expedient way of lengthening the work was to provide more ballet music, an addition fully in the French tradition and wholly consonant with Parisian tastes. And the dances were sure to come off with good effect since at that time the Académie Royale, where *Orphée* was first given, had the most illustrious ballet troupe in Europe. Gluck added the well-known "Air de Furies" (Act II, Scene 1), most of the ballet in Act II, Scene 2,

and three movements of the concluding ballet—all newly composed or adapted from earlier works.

A set of copyist's orchestral parts in the Bibliothèque de l'Opéra, prepared either for the December 1776 or the 1778 revival of *Orphée*, contains five additional ballet movements, one of which is preserved in the Gluck autograph shown here. It is assumed that the other four are by him as well, although their autographs have not survived. The other two entries in the Morgan manuscript are an orchestral "Maestoso" from the Act III, Scene 3 ballet, and an otherwise unidentified two-measure modulation for strings with "Atto Pmo" at the beginning, and "Cœur [sic] Orféo [sic]" at the end, that does not appear in the first edition of *Orphée* (1774).

Both *Orphée et Euridice* and *Iphigénie en Aulide* are dedicated to Marie Antoinette, wife of Louis XVI. Sometime before the première of *Orphée*, Gluck wrote to the Queen acknowledging her approval of the dedication: "I have thought that I might try setting to French words the new type of music which I adopted in my three last Italian operas. . . . The genre I am trying to introduce seems to me to restore art to its original dignity. The music will no longer be confined to the cold, conventional beauties, to which composers have been obliged to adhere." Marie Antoinette, who had for a time been a pupil of Gluck's in Vienna, promised him an annual pension of 6000 livres for writing new operas and for tutoring the French singers. Shortly thereafter the Austrian empress, Maria Theresa (Marie Antoinette's mother), appointed him imperial court composer at an annual salary of 2000 florins. Gluck's fame and financial security were assured: In September 1776 it was reported in Bachaumont's *Mémoires secrets* that no composer before had achieved such financial success, and that up to that date *Aulide* and *Orphée* had jointly earned no less than 334,000 livres.

Orphée continued to be played with great popularity throughout the time of the Revolution, but not without textual adjustments. Early in that period a line in the final chorus was changed from "Sa chaîne agréable est préférable à la liberté" to "Sa chaîne agréable est le doux charme de la volupté"—nothing, obviously, being preferable to liberty.

Other autograph fragments of the opera are found in the Bibliothèque de l'Opéra and the Bibliothèque Nationale, Paris; the Deutsche Staatsbibliothek, Berlin; the Saltïkov-Shchedrin Library, Leningrad; and the Memorial Library of Music, Stanford University. Two copyist's manuscripts of the full score are in the Bibliothèque de l'Opéra.

GLUCK: *Orphée et Euridice*

CHRISTOPH WILLIBALD GLUCK, 1714–1787.

Iphigenie auf Tauris. Autograph manuscript of the voice parts, from the middle of Act I, Scene 3 to the end of Act IV, Scene 3.
8 p. 30.5 × 23 cm.
First performance: Vienna, 23 October 1781.
Mary Flagler Cary Music Collection.

On 10 February 1780 Gluck wrote to Grand Duke Carl August of Saxe-Weimar: "I have now become very old and have lavished on the French nation most of my spiritual powers, notwithstanding which I still feel an inner urge in me to accomplish something for my nation, and I am filled with a burning desire to be able to hum something German to Your Serene Highness . . . ." Gluck was 65 years old and had composed 43 operas, including the Italian reform operas *Orfeo ed Euridice* (1762), *Alceste* (1767), and *Paride ed Elena* (1770), all first performed at Vienna's Burgtheater. Among the operas "lavished on the French nation" were *Iphigénie en Aulide* (1774), *Armide* (1777), and, considered by many to be his greatest work, *Iphigénie en Tauride* (1779). That "something German" he hoped to accomplish became, in the event, his only opera with a German text, *Iphigenie auf Tauris*. It would be as great a success as the French version had been and, except for his *De Profundis*, was his last major undertaking. After a series of strokes he died, in Vienna, on 15 November 1787.

The translator of the French Iphigenia—possibly chosen by Gluck himself—was the young Viennese poet Johann Baptist von Alxinger. Working from the first French edition of the full score (1779), he translated Nicolas-François Guillard's libretto into German. Gluck then set the new text to the "French" music, making occasional changes in the words, but more often recasting the melodies and rhythms of the voice parts; the result was this manuscript. It was once owned by the noted Viennese collector Alois Fuchs, who acquired it from Joseph Püringer; he is said to have known Gluck in the last years of the composer's life and to have frequently visited Gluck's widow. In 1843 Fuchs, who called the manuscript "the crown of my entire collection," sold it to Dr. Felix Bamberg in Paris; it was subsequently part of the Musikbibliothek Peters in Leipzig. Another three pages, containing the voice parts for Act IV, Scene 4 to the end of the opera, are in the Deutsche Staatsbibliothek, Berlin; that part of the manuscript preceding the Morgan leaves is lost.

The German Iphigenia is much more than a singing translation of *Iphigénie en Tauride*; it is virtually a recomposition of the opera, for hardly a measure of the singers' parts remained unaltered. Other substantial changes made for the Vienna production included lowering Thoas' part for the German bass Ludwig Fischer and recasting the baritone Orestes as a tenor—a change more of timbre than tessitura, since the part has not been transposed. The first Viennese Orestes was Joseph Valentin Adamberger; nine months later he and Fischer would sing, respectively, the roles of Belmonte and Osmin in the première of Mozart's *Die Entführung aus dem Serail*. Mozart, in fact, was present at most of the rehearsals of *Iphigenie auf Tauris*, which, with Gluck's *Alceste* (in Italian), was in rehearsal at the Burgtheater. On 6 October 1781 Mozart wrote to his father: "Nothing would be gained if the whole opera [*Entführung*] were finished, for it would have to lie there until Gluck's two operas were ready—and there is still an enormous amount in them which the singers have to study." Mozart also had praise for Alxinger's contribution: "The translator of 'Iphigenia' into German is an excellent poet," he wrote his father on 16 September, "and I would gladly have given him my Munich opera [*Idomeneo*] to translate."

In 1795 a new translation was introduced in Berlin, and during the next century and a half a number of others appeared; Alxinger's text was all but forgotten. A new edition—the first to make use of the Gluck manuscript—was published in 1958 but that score, too, was found wanting, being in effect a conflation of the German and French versions. It was not until 1966 that the first scholarly edition of *Iphigenie auf Tauris* appeared, finally incorporating the Gluck-Alxinger text. Those who now venture to improve upon Gluck's work would do well to heed Alxinger's advice in the Preface to the first edition of the libretto (1781): "Whoever thinks this German Iphigenia careless or unpolished is invited to translate another Gluck opera better, or even as well. In that way, the Translator will very gladly see himself criticized."

Copyist's manuscripts of *Iphigenie auf Tauris* are found in the Österreichische Nationalbibliothek and the Gesellschaft der Musikfreunde, Vienna; the Moravské Museum, Brno; and the Württembergische Landesbibliothek, Stuttgart. For a copy of *Iphigénie en Tauride* in Berlioz's hand, see p. 46.

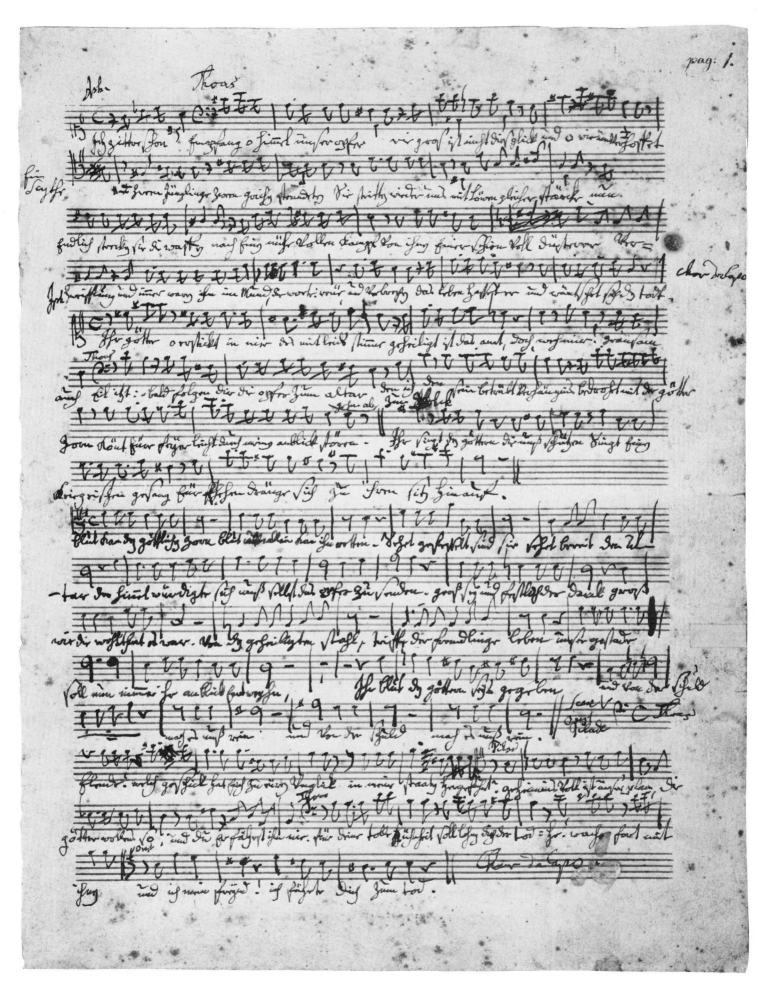

GLUCK: *Iphigenie auf Tauris*

WOLFGANG AMADEUS MOZART, 1756–1791.

*Der Schauspieldirektor. Autograph manuscript of the full score. 84 p. 23 × 32 cm. Dated on the first page of the "Terzett":
"Vienna li 18 gennajo 1786."
First performance: Schönbrunn, 7 February 1786.
Mary Flagler Cary Music Collection.*

On 7 February 1786, Emperor Joseph II of Austria presented an evening of entertainment at Schönbrunn, his summer residence near Vienna. The occasion was a reception in honor of Duke Albert of Sachsen-Teschen, the governor-general of the Austrian Netherlands, and his wife, the Archduchess Marie Christine, Joseph's sister. The emperor had commissioned two works to be performed that evening: an Italian *opera buffa* by Antonio Salieri and a German *Singspiel* by Mozart. The choice of works in those particular genres was no doubt suggested in part by the architectural design of the remarkable hall selected for the festivities. The Orangerie at Schönbrunn, built in 1755, was a hothouse. It was an enormous room, possibly the largest of its kind in Europe: nearly 600 feet long and 32 feet wide, filled with an assortment of exotic plants and fruit trees. The emperor had the hall designed with a stage at either end, one for plays, one for operas—an arrangement probably unique in Europe. The Orangerie was, not incidentally, the only hall at Schönbrunn that would have been warm enough for such midwinter entertainment.

Salieri's contribution to the evening was *Prima la musica e poi le parole*, an *opera buffa* with a libretto by Giovanni Battista Casti—a work nearly forgotten today (although Richard Strauss's last opera, *Capriccio*, is loosely based on the same story). It is, like Mozart's composition, a comic treatment of the difficulties faced by a theatre manager. The playwright in *Prima la musica* was intended as a caricature of Lorenzo da Ponte, Mozart's librettist for *Le nozze di Figaro* (see p. 37) and Casti's rival. (Da Ponte called the work "a thorough muddle, without wit, formal construction, or characterization," and claimed that the caricatured librettist resembled Casti more than himself.)

Mozart's librettist was Gottlieb Stephanie, a producer and prolific playwright who has been called the most notorious intriguer in the theatrical world of his day. He is remembered mainly as the librettist for Mozart's *Die Entführung aus dem Serail*. His one-act comedy *Der Schauspieldirektor*, the basic idea for which was suggested by the emperor himself, concerns an actor, Puf, and his manager, Frank the impresario, and their attempts to assemble a company of actors for a production in Salzburg. The singers, Herr Vogelsang, Madame Herz, and Mademoiselle Silberklang, enter; the sopranos vie for the honor of *prima donna*, while Herr Vogelsang tries to arbitrate the dispute: "No artist must berate a rival, it brings to art an evil name." The Finale is a vaudeville quartet for the three singers and Puf; their moral is that artists must work together for a nobler cause.

Mozart composed the music, comprising an overture, two arias, a trio, and a finale, between 18 January and 3 February 1786—that is, in a little over two weeks. January 27th was his thirtieth birthday. The Trio was composed first, the Overture last; the day after the first performance an account appeared in the *Wiener Zeitung* which treated the whole affair as a royal social function (which of course it was), describing in detail the arrival and departure of the guests, the botanical riches and splendid lighting of the Orangerie, and so on—but mentioning neither Mozart's nor Salieri's name. Although it is very likely that both composers were present, and probably conducted their works, the operas were apparently quite incidental to the evening's activities. As so often happened at the time, the importance, even identity, of the composers was overshadowed by the pomp and circumstance of the occasion. The first critical mention of the work comes from the diary of Count Carl von Zinzendorf, a member and indefatigable chronicler of the court circle in Vienna. He too described the splendid Orangerie, called *Der Schauspieldirektor* thoroughly mediocre, and also failed to mention either composer by name.

Christopher Raeburn argues convincingly that the decidedly cool reception accorded the little opera may very well have reflected derogatory reactions not to composer or librettist, but rather to the farcical tone of the production itself. He suggests that the performers, rather than engaging in a subtle satire of contemporary theatrical practices (which was probably Stephanie's intention), presented instead a kind of burlesque, emphasizing broad humor and farce. "To an audience which was more concerned with the social aspect of the occasion," Raeburn writes, "the temperate reception was not altogether surprising." As for Stephanie's libretto, it "is no worse a vehicle than other eighteenth-century trifles. The cause of the initial failure appears to have been more with the nature of the production."

The first public performance of *Der Schauspieldirektor*, along with *Prima la musica*, was on 11 February at the Kärntnertor Theatre in Vienna. Unlike the Schönbrunn production, it was enthusiastically received and was repeated on the 18th and the 25th. These were the only performances during Mozart's lifetime. Since his death the work has been given in numerous versions in half a dozen languages; some have incorporated additional music by Mozart, some have appended excerpts by Cimarosa, Dittersdorf, and others, and all have probably adapted the libretto to include more topical and contemporary subjects. Among those who composed additional music was Mozart's younger son, Franz Xaver Wolfgang. On Constanze Mozart's birthday it was customary for the family to put on a

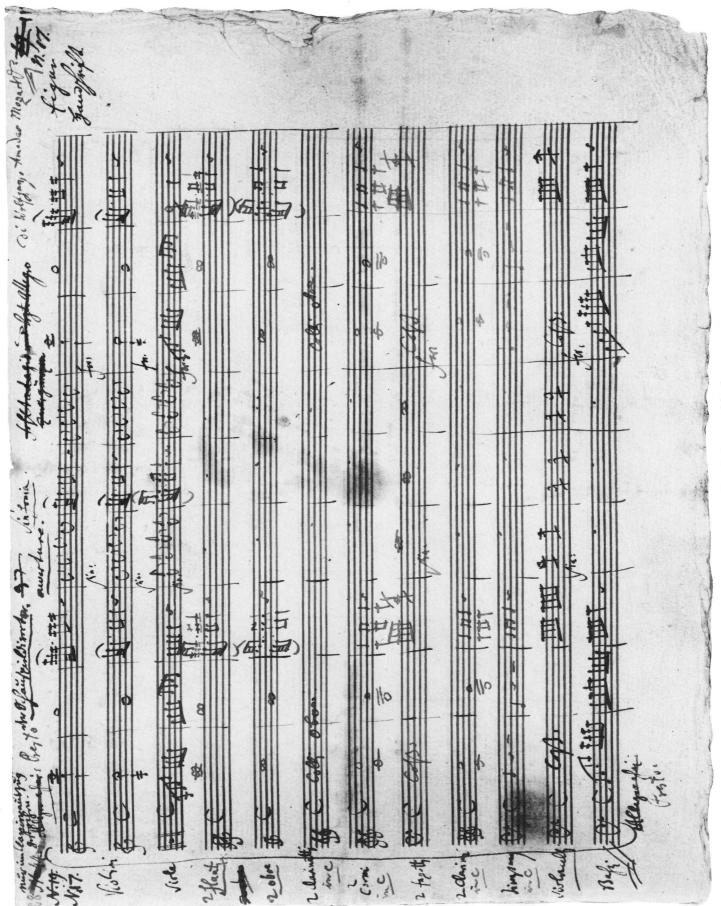

MOZART: *Der Schauspieldirektor*

private performance of one of Mozart's operas as their principal amusement for the evening; for the celebration in Vienna in 1808 Franz Xaver wrote an *aria buffa* to be interpolated into *Der Schauspieldirektor*. Constanze gave the manuscript of the aria to Vincent Novello in 1829; he in turn presented it to the British Museum in 1843, where it is today.

The early provenance of the manuscript of *Der Schauspieldirektor* followed the same path as many other works in the composer's legacy. After Mozart's death in 1791 his widow, Constanze, retained ownership of his musical estate. In May 1798 the Leipzig publishing firm of Breitkopf & Härtel, for its proposed *Œuvres complettes de W. A. Mozart*, asked Constanze if any unpublished works of her late husband were still in her possession. She enlisted the help of the Abbé Maximilian Stadler, an Austrian composer and a friend of Mozart, in preparing an inventory of manuscripts. The registry itself is in the hand of Georg Nikolaus von Nissen, the legation secretary of the Danish embassy in Vienna and a close friend of Constanze; they were married in 1809. On the first page of the manuscript Nissen has written the title, "Der Schauspieldirector," and his authentication, "eigen[e] Handschrift," which is found on dozens of Mozart autographs.

Toward the end of 1799 a second contender for Mozart's manuscripts entered the picture: Johann André, the 24-year-old son of Anton André, the late founder of the publishing firm in Offenbach. After several offers and counteroffers between Constanze and the two publishers, she agreed to sell the entire legacy, some 280 manuscripts, to André. The works were sent to André in fifteen packets; the number "19" on the first page of the manuscript indicated that *Der Schauspieldirektor* was the nineteenth item in one of the packets.

André died in 1842 and in 1854 his remaining manuscripts—he had disposed of several over the years—were divided among his six surviving sons and his son-in-law, J. B. Streicher. The number of manuscripts each heir received was not the same, but the seven lots were supposed to be of approximately equal value. In 1841 André had published a thematic catalogue of all of his Mozart manuscripts, with a separate price list, offering to sell them, individually or as a group, to the highest bidder. *Der Schauspieldirektor* appears as number 43 in this catalogue; the number was written at the bottom center of the first page of the manuscript, but has since been erased.

Der Schauspieldirektor went to André's eldest son, Carl August, head of the Frankfurt branch of the publishing house. In 1865 it belonged to Carl Meinert, a well-known collector in Frankfurt, later to Siegfried Ochs in Berlin, and then joined Louis Koch's distinguished collection of music manuscripts in Switzerland.

Four pages of drafts and one of sketches are known. A draft of the beginning of the first aria is found on one leaf in the Music Division of The New York Public Library. A second leaf, which is a continuation of this draft, is in the Augsburg Stadtarchiv. A third leaf, with one page of sketches identified as relating to the "Terzett," is in the Alfred Doppler Nachlass in Graz.

This is the only complete autograph of a Mozart opera in this country. Except for the manuscripts of *Don Giovanni* and parts of *Mitridate*, which are in the Bibliothèque Nationale, the autographs of Mozart's other stage works are in German libraries, are lost, or are presumably among those manuscripts, recently resurfaced in Poland, that were removed from the former Preussische Staatsbibliothek in Berlin during World War II. The information above was taken from the Introduction to the facsimile of *Der Schauspieldirektor* published by the Morgan Library in 1976.

Le nozze di Figaro. Autograph manuscript of Cherubino's aria "Non so più cosa son," arranged for voice, violin, and piano. 4 p. 22 × 31 cm.
First performance of the opera: Vienna, 1 May 1786.
Dannie and Hettie Heineman Collection.

In a letter of 11 November 1785, Leopold Mozart wrote to his daughter: "At last I have received a letter of twelve lines from your brother, dated November 2nd. He begs to be forgiven [for not writing], as he is up to his eyes in work at his opera 'Le Nozze di Figaro' . . . . I know the piece; it is a very tiresome play, and the translation from the French will certainly have to be altered very freely if it is to be effective as an opera. God grant that the text may be a success. I have no doubt about the music." Leopold was perhaps too severe on the play, and, in the event, need not have worried about the libretto: both Beaumarchais's *La folle journée, ou Le mariage de Figaro* and da Ponte's *Le nozze di Figaro* are counted among the exemplars of their respective genres—as, needless to say, is Mozart's opera.

Eric Blom has traced the literary ancestry of Beaumarchais's characters in *Figaro* to the *commedia dell'arte*, where his Chérubin (da Ponte's Cherubino) was usually called Leandro, "a boyish and ingenuous lover who constantly (or rather inconstantly) fluttered around the ladies with the alternate shyness and boldness of adolescent devotion. . . . [He] is a butterfly of the Almaviva species at the point of emerging from the chrysalis stage." (Cherubino is Count Almaviva's page; Kierkegaard characterized him as a Don Giovanni *in potentia*.) According to Beaumarchais, the basis of Chérubin's character "is an undefined and restless desire. He is entering on adolescence all unheeding and with no understanding of what is happening to him." (It was Beaumarchais, incidentally, who insisted that the part be played "by a young and very pretty woman; we have no very young men in our theatre who are at the same time sufficiently mature to appreciate the fine points of the part.")

It is in this emotionally turbulent state that we first encounter Cherubino. *Figaro* is about love and desire in their many guises (and, especially in the last act, disguises), and it is Cherubino, in "Non so più," who first uses the word "amore"—the first of over 50 occurrences in the libretto of "amore," "amare," "amante," "amoroso," "amatore," and "amabile." There are more than 60 uses of the French equivalents in Beaumarchais. Brigid Brophy has called *Figaro* the most purely erotic opera ever written, and sees Cherubino as the embodiment of Eros, presiding symbolically over the opera's amorous intrigues, much like Puck in *A Midsummer Night's Dream*. Mozart's musical depiction of the febrile yearning of adolescence is almost palpable, and Brophy even construes "Non so più" as a graphic apostrophe to the boy's erotic turmoil. (Analogously, Octavian's youthful passion in Strauss's *Der Rosenkavalier* is vividly portrayed by the orchestra, even before the curtain rises. Both Cherubino and Octavian are

sung by a woman dressed as a man who, in the course of the opera, is called upon to dress as a woman—a double transformation that reinforces the skein of masks and reversed identities that plays an important role in *Figaro*; the humor there, however, is touched by irony, a device largely absent from the more sentimental affects of *Rosenkavalier*.)

In a libretto printed for a 1788 performance of *Figaro* in Florence, "Non so più" was replaced by a short aria for Susanna beginning "Senza speme ognor s'aggira." Alfred Einstein thought that the music for it might have been composed by Bartolomeo Cherubini (Luigi's father), who conducted the performance. Jack Westrup has made the ingenious suggestion that "Senza speme" was in fact composed by Mozart, and used the opening theme of his G minor symphony (K. 550), composed in 1788. (Indeed, "Non so più" can comfortably, if incongruously, be sung to the same melody.) A libretto for a Monza performance in 1787 shows an odder change: the Count enters as usual, just as Susanna has hidden Cherubino behind the chair, and sings "Voi che sapete," Cherubino's own Act II arietta, with the text altered to reflect the Count's more seasoned ways. Mozart originally planned a third number for Cherubino, at the end of Act III, Scene 6; it seems to have been a last-minute deletion, since the text of the arietta, beginning "Se così brami," is printed in the libretto for the first performance.

Nothing is known about the occasion for which the Heineman setting of "Non so più" was made; the safest guess is that Mozart simply found himself with soprano, violinist, and pianist at hand, and quickly produced the *pièce d'occasion*. But it is unique among Mozart's works, being the only complete arrangement of an operatic number he is known to have made. (There are fragmentary voice and piano reductions of two arias from *Die Entführung aus dem Serail*, and a few voice and bass-line autographs from which singers could learn their parts.) Alan Tyson's watermark and rastrology study of this manuscript strongly suggests that the arrangement was made between November 1785 and March 1786—that is, before work on the opera was completed. The paper type used in "Non so più" is found in all or part of five works composed during those five months, as well as four leaves from the Act II finale of *Figaro*. The autograph full score of Acts I and II of the opera are in the Deutsche Staatsbibliothek, Berlin; Acts III and IV were removed during World War II, and have only recently resurfaced in Poland. An autograph draft of "Non so più" is found in the Stefan Zweig Collection, on permanent loan to the British Library.

MOZART: *Le nozze di Figaro*

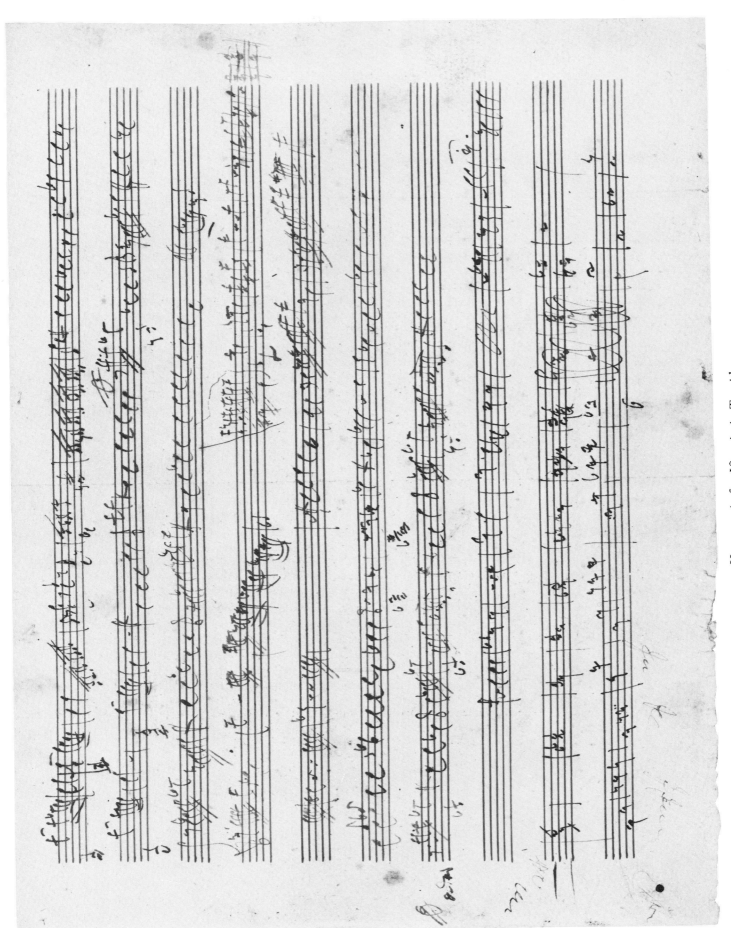

HAYDN: aria for *Ifigenia in Tauride*

"Ah tu non senti amico / Qual destra omicida"; sketches for the recitative and aria for insertion in Tommaso Traetta's Ifigenia in Tauride. 2 leaves. 22.5 × 30 cm.
First performance: Eszterháza, probably 4 July 1786.
Purchased by Pierpont Morgan about 1907.

In 1761, a year that would mark a major turning point in Haydn's life, he entered the service of the Esterházys, one of the wealthiest and most influential families of the Hungarian nobility. Haydn was to work under the Esterházy patronage for nearly 30 years, mostly at Eszterháza, the splendid late-Baroque palace in Hungary, partly at the Esterházy residences in Eisenstadt and Vienna. Haydn's musical duties at court changed over the years. Up to about 1775 he was largely occupied with composing and directing instrumental music for various functions. But from 1776 on, as Dénes Bartha has written, "a large part of his energy was absorbed in selecting, preparing, coaching, and performing an Italian opera repertory that ranked, as we now know, second only to those of the great centers of Italian operatic life—Venice and Naples—and equalled or surpassed the important Viennese repertoire."

During the fifteen years between 1776 and 1790, when, with the death of Prince Nikolaus Esterházy, Haydn's patronage ended, there had been at least 87 different operas performed: six were Haydn's own, and the remainder were by many of the foremost contemporary opera composers, such as Cimarosa, Anfossi, Paisiello, Salieri, and Grétry. Perhaps the most active year was 1786, with 125 performances of seventeen operas—all rehearsed and directed by Haydn. Among the eight works new to the Esterházy repertory that year was Tommaso Traetta's *Ifigenia in Tauride*, performed first on 4 July, with four repetitions. (It had first been given in Vienna in 1763.) Haydn regularly revised—often drastically—the operas he presented, and occasionally added arias of his own. Between 1776 and 1790 he wrote sixteen such insertion or replacement arias; for Traetta's *Ifigenia* he rewrote Orestes' opening scena, and more musical documents survive for this revision than for any other. They comprise Traetta's recitative and aria "Ah tu non senti amico / Qual destra

omicida" in a copyist's manuscript annotated by Haydn (now in the National Széchényi Library, Budapest); Haydn's sketches for the replacement (using the same text), shown here; and his autograph full score of the scena (also in Budapest).

Why did Haydn replace Traetta's dramatically powerful music—one of his most arresting passages—with one of his own making? Peter Brown suggests that "perhaps the primary catalyst . . . was that *Ifigenia in Tauride* had been set with some success by two of the most progressive operatic composers active during the second half of the century: Traetta and Gluck." A German version of Gluck's *Iphigénie en Tauride* was given in Vienna in 1781 (see p. 32) and an Italian one in 1783; Haydn may well have seen the latter production. "Such a situation," writes Brown, "must have presented a challenge to a composer especially proud of his operas who at the same time realized that his own works were tailored to the tastes and theatrical requirements at Eszterháza. What better way could Haydn assert his originality than by composing this *scena* which was a dramatic *tour de force*? Its position at the beginning of Coltellini's libretto would immediately transfer the attention of the audience from Traetta to the resident composer-conductor."

Haydn sketches are relatively rare—only about 58 have survived—and when Pierpont Morgan acquired his he was no doubt unaware of its significance, and possibly even of its existence. About 1907 he bought an extra-illustrated edition of Thackeray's *The Four Georges* (London, 1861). On p. 138, in the chapter on George III, Thackeray writes that "the queen would play on the spinnet—she played pretty well, Haydn said." This fleeting reference was illustrated by the Haydn sketch, which was bound into the volume along with the Ott/Bartolozzi portrait of the composer.

Tancredi. Autograph manuscript of "Quelques ornements sur L'air de Tancredi pour l'usage de Madme. Gregoire par son ami G. Rossini. Passy ce 15 Août 1858." 3 p. 27 × 34.5 cm.
First performance: Venice, 6 February 1813.
Mary Flagler Cary Music Collection.

Tancredi, a serious opera, was Rossini's first international success. With the première of *L'italiana in Algeri* in Venice three and a half months later, Rossini was to demonstrate his mastery of the comic opera genre as well, and his standing as the leading Italian opera composer of his time was assured. One aria from *Tancredi*, "Di tanti palpiti," soon swept across Europe, winning a popularity and familiarity (at least in Italy) usually achieved only by folksongs. (A measure of its international fame can be found in Canto XVI of Byron's *Don Juan*: ". . . the long evenings of duets and trios! / The admirations and speculations; / The 'Mamma Mia's!' and the 'Amor Mio's!' / The 'Tanti palpiti's' on such occasions: / The 'Lasciamo's,' and the quaverings 'Addio's.' ") The aria was not sung at the first performance; the Tancredi, Adelaide Malanotte-Montresor, apparently did not care for it, so Rossini wrote for her a more elaborate cavatina, "Dolci d'amor parole." Far from being an exception, such substitution was common practice among all Italian opera composers in the *primo ottocento*, roughly the first half of the nineteenth century.

The demands of singers, stage managers, impresarios, and censors, whether motivated by capricious whim or official fiat, frequently took precedence over the composer's intentions. If a singer was unhappy with an aria she could—as Malanotte did—demand (and get) a replacement. If another singer, with different vocal abilities, later essayed the role, she might return to the original aria—or demand (and get) her own piece, sometimes written by another composer. Such substitutions were not limited to arias: when Maria Malibran sang Bellini's *I Capuleti e i Montecchi*, she regularly replaced his tomb scene with the one from Nicola Vaccai's *Giulietta e Romeo*. Censors could forbid a word, verse, scene, or, in the case of Donizetti's *Maria Stuarda* (see p. 54), an entire libretto. Roman audiences did not like unhappy endings; when Rossini revived his *Otello* for Rome in 1820, he introduced a last-minute reconciliation between Otello and Desdemona. If his operas were produced in France, he supplied them with ballets.

When a successful opera began its tour of the Italian opera houses—Milan, Bologna, Florence, Rome, Naples, and so on—the composer often went along, supervising rehearsals, conducting the first performance, and frequently being called on to write new music. And many later revivals, although the composer rarely oversaw them, called for textual and musical changes. According to Philip Gossett, "there are half as many new pieces associated with revivals of *Tancredi* as there are in the original version." The first major change was made for the second production, in Ferrara, several months after the Venice première. The Venetian *Tancredi* had a happy ending; for Ferrara Rossini substituted a tragic finale, one more closely paralleling Voltaire's *Tancrède*, on which the opera is based. By 1814, the year of the first production in Genoa, Gossett writes that "the music from all versions of *Tancredi* is treated as a reservoir from which a musical director, singer, or impresario can draw elements best suited to local conditions." The printed libretto is a primary source for tracing some of these changes, since it was reset and printed anew for each production and revival. Unlike French practice, it contains not the original, polished text to be read for its literary accomplishment, but the specific version that would be sung at that evening's performance. Gossett has identified 43 different librettos of *Tancredi* printed between 1813 and 1834.

The modern editor who attempts to establish a critical version of a Rossini opera is thus faced with literally dozens of sources, both textual and musical, each of which can claim its legitimate place in the *Urtext*. Most operagoers assume that their libretto contains the single, authentic text for the evening's performance, and that the music they will hear is all (or most) of what the composer wrote for the work. For an opera by Wagner or Richard Strauss those assumptions are usually warranted; for one by Rossini, they almost never are. While there exist editions of, say, *Die Meistersinger* or *Der Rosenkavalier* that faithfully transmit the composer's final thoughts on his opera, attempts to establish a corresponding degree of authenticity for a Rossini opera are still in their infancy. Difficult as it may be to believe, the edition of *Il barbiere di Siviglia* published by Ricordi in 1968 was the first critical edition of a nineteenth-century Italian opera—which is to say, the only edition of any opera by Rossini, Donizetti, Bellini, or Verdi to get all the notes right, not to mention the text, orchestration, articulation, and so on.

While common sense (and wishful thinking) might lead one to assume that there must somewhere exist Rossini's final, complete, and authentic autograph manuscript of an opera—the Platonic idea of, say, *Tancredi*—such is not the case, and the search for it will be elusive. First, there is no final version; Rossini, and others, continually added to, deleted from, rearranged, and revised his operas. Second, a "complete" performing version—that is, one that included all the musical and textual variants introduced into each separate production or revival of the opera, whether or not supervised by Rossini—would be of Wagnerian proportions and Kafkaesque absurdity. The problem of authenticity is somewhat easier to address: Gossett defines an authentic version of a Rossini opera as one with which he was directly connected as composer, director, or arranger. By extension, an authentic number in an opera would be one he wrote or the performance of which he sanctioned.

But even having established something approaching an authentic edition, there remains the question of ornamentation. Ornamentation could be defined as singing (or playing) notes not written, but suggested—even demanded—by the performance practice and musical conventions of the day. This tradition of improvisation was a long-standing one among singers of Italian opera, who were expected, by both audience and composer, to embellish their parts with ornaments and cadenzas. The extraordinary skills and equally remarkable excesses of these singers are recorded at great length by contemporary chroniclers. "Performer licence amounted to a disease," writes Julian Budden, "and Rossini decided to treat it homeopathically" by "devising for his singers ornaments more ingenious than any they could invent for themselves." Rather than allow singers complete freedom to improvise their embellishments, Rossini began, about 1814, to write his own elaborated vocal lines, which then became the authentic version—or rather *an* authentic version, since he always reserved the right to alter anything he had written.

The Mme. "Grégoire" for whom Rossini composed "quelques ornements" has not been identified, but she may have been married to one of the Gregoir family of Belgian musicians and critics who were active in the mid-nineteenth century. To the original version of "Oh patria! dolce, ingrata patria"—the scena that directly introduces Tancredi's "Tu che accendi / Di tanti palpiti"—Rossini has added many expressive indications: crescendi and decrescendi, directions such as "animato," "dolce," "Lento," accents, phrase marks, and so on. The rhythmic regularity of the original is shown to be only an approximation that needs the composer's license or the performer's invention to bring it to life. Further examples of Rossini's added ornamentation are found in another manuscript in the Cary Collection. For Giuditta Pasta, one of the most famous Tancredis of her day, Rossini, in the 1820's, embellished the beginning of the Tancredi-Amenaide duet from Act II, "Lasciami, non t'ascolto."

The introductory motive in the Act II aria "Torni alfine ridente, e bella" is taken from Rossini's song "Se il vuol la molinara"—his earliest known work—the manuscript of which is in the Cary Collection. The opening of the tragic finale for *Tancredi*, mentioned above, is a short chorus beginning "Muore il prode," the tune of which clearly appealed to Rossini, for he used it in two later works. One is a chamber duet for soprano, tenor, and piano, "Amore mi assisti"; Rossini's manuscript of this work is also in the Cary Collection. The full-score autograph manuscript of *Tancredi* is in the La Scala archives in Milan.

ROSSINI: *Tancredi*

Valentine de Milan. Autograph manuscript of an ensemble from Act III. 32 p. 34.5 × 26 cm.
First performance: Paris, 28 November 1822.
Mary Flagler Cary Music Collection.

Méhul occupied an important position among the French composers of his time; he has been called the greatest French symphonist between Gossec and Berlioz, and several of his operas were successful at the Opéra-Comique and the Théâtre Favart. In 1793 he became one of the first staff members of the Institut National de Musique, the immediate predecessor of the Conservatoire. Among his many patriotic songs, the "Chant du départ" was widely sung, at times rivaling the "Marseillaise" in popularity.

His orchestral writing was especially innovative, and much of his most original music is to be found in three surviving symphonies and his opera overtures. Of his operas, *Joseph* (1807), which has been singled out as the first unashamedly Biblical opera, is considered the major work. Weber, in whose music Méhul's influence can be detected, thought highly of *Joseph*, characterizing it as a musical fresco (an apt phrase for a work less opera than sacred oratorio); Wagner, too, admired it, and conducted it in Riga in 1838. Berlioz, who considered *Euphrosine et Coradin* Méhul's operatic masterpiece, praised the simplicity, economy, and restraint of the orchestration in *Joseph* and *Valentine de Milan*, but found it lacking in coloring and strength. In a moving letter of 31 August 1824 to his father, Berlioz wrote: "I wish to make a name for myself, to leave behind on earth some trace of my existence; and such is the strength of that feeling—which in itself is nothing but noble—that I would rather be Gluck or Méhul dead than that which I am in the prime of life."

Valentine de Milan was the brother of Charles VI and the wife of Louis, Duc d'Orléans. The opera was left incomplete at Méhul's death; his nephew, the composer Daussoigne-Méhul, completed the score, and the librettist, Jean-Nicolas Bouilly, was influential in persuading the Opéra-Comique to produce it. (Bouilly wrote the libretto for Gaveaux's *Léonore*, later adapted

for Beethoven's *Fidelio*). Bouilly's text was harshly criticized at the time, being deemed, among other things, too somber and melodramatic for the Opéra-Comique. An odd spectacle took place immediately after the opera's première; intended as homage to Méhul's memory, it assumed unintentionally comic overtones. All the writers and musicians associated with the Opéra-Comique had been asked to appear (in costume, according to one account) in the balconies of the theatre. As the opera ended, the cast, singing verses specially composed by Bouilly for the occasion, brought on stage a bust of Méhul; the writers and musicians rose in tribute to the composer. A contemporary chronicler of the Parisian theatre wrote that a more fitting homage would have been to have produced the opera in Méhul's lifetime. "The success of the work is assured," he went on, "and should not be confused with the manner in which the great man was memorialized. If the work does not remain in the repertory, the reason may be sought in the low quality of the libretto . . .; the score contains much of Méhul's best work, and individual numbers of the first order." Castil-Blaze, Berlioz's predecessor as music critic for the *Journal des Débats*, also faulted Bouilly; he judged Act III to be the best in words and music.

The manuscript, which once formed part of the full score of the opera, was given by Daussoigne-Méhul to Felix Mendelssohn on 12 June 1846 in Liège, where Mendelssohn's *Lauda Sion* had first been performed the day before. The sequence "Lauda Sion" was written by St. Thomas Aquinas about 1264 for Corpus Christi, a feast introduced to Catholic liturgy in 1246 in Liège; the city was celebrating the 600th anniversary of that occasion.

The Bibliothèque Nationale houses complete or partial autograph manuscripts of about a dozen Méhul operas.

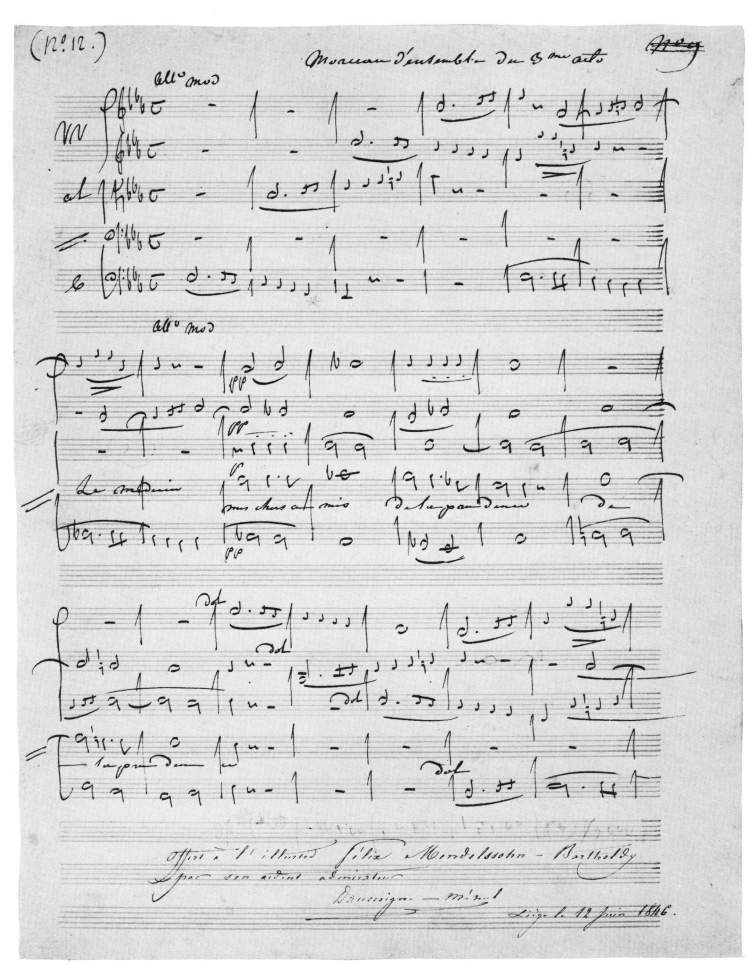

MÉHUL: *Valentine de Milan*

HECTOR BERLIOZ, 1803–1869.
[Christoph Willibald Gluck]

"Iphigénie en Tauride. Tragédie en quatre actes par Mr Guillard. Mise en musique et dédiée à la Reine par M^r le Chevalier Gluck."
Autograph manuscript copy of the full score, dated April 1824. 209 p. 29.5 × 21.5 cm.
The gift of Robert Owen Lehman.

When the seventeen-year-old Berlioz arrived in Paris, in late October or early November 1821, it was as a student at the École de Médecine. But his passion for music had taken hold years earlier and it was inevitable that, as an antidote to "that human charnel house" of the dissecting room, he would attend operas and concerts at every opportunity. On 26 November he saw one of his first operas, Gluck's *Iphigénie en Tauride*. "I vowed as I left the Opéra," he later wrote in his *Memoirs*, "that in spite of father, mother, uncles, aunts, grandparents, friends, I would be a musician." One passage from the opera made a particularly strong impression. In a letter of 13 December 1821 to his sister—the first letter of Berlioz to his family to have survived—he wrote:

> I can't describe to you even approximately the feeling of horror one feels when Orestes, overwhelmed, falls down and says, "Calm returns to my heart." Half asleep, he sees the shade of his mother whom he has killed; she is hovering about with other shades holding infernal torches above his head. And the orchestra! It's all in the orchestra. If you could only hear how the situations are depicted in it, especially when Orestes is calm: there is a long hold in the violins suggestive of tranquility—very *piano*; but below, the basses murmur like the remorse which, despite his calm, throbs in the heart of the matricide.

Berlioz was by no means the first person to comment on that scene. In an anonymous article that appeared in the 15 June 1779 issue of the *Mercure de France*, less than a month after the première of *Iphigénie*, the author cites two passages "where M. Gluck is at once painter and poet." He first discusses the opening scene, which depicts a raging storm, and then the third scene of Act II. Orestes, son of Clytemnestra (whom he has killed) and sister of Iphigenia, has been shipwrecked on Tauris with his friend Pylades. In this scene the friends are separated. "After his first fits of rage," the article continues, Orestes falls prostrate on a stone bench and sings these words:

> Calm returns to my heart,
> My sorrows have wearied the wrath of heaven,
> I near the end of my misery.
> Just gods! Avenging heaven!
> Let breathe the matricide Orestes!

But listen to the instruments: they tell you that there is dejection, not repose; they tell you that Orestes has lost not the feeling of his sorrows, but only the power to vent them. . . . His song is accompanied by violas that depict a voice hollow and menacing with remorse, while the violins express a deep agitation, mingled with sighs and sobs. In the same way, waves after a storm are seen to move and rock long before they subside and become smooth.

This scene is possibly the most famous in all of Gluck's operas; few commentators since have failed to single it out as, in Patrick J. Smith's words, "the symbolic moment when music finally displaced the word as primary. From that time on, music would not necessarily serve to clarify or enhance the meaning of the word . . ., but would act as commentary on it."

Berlioz himself must now be counted among those exegetes, for on the title page of this copy of *Iphigénie* he has written: "Look at Act II, Scene 3, where Orestes, overcome, says: 'Calm returns to my heart.' The roaring of the violas, the murmuring of the double basses, the screaming of the violins. Why this contradiction, one asks Gluck? '*He lies,*' the great man answers, '*he has killed his mother.*' " (Inexplicably, however, Berlioz has misnotated the viola part, a misreading that robs it of the very syncopations that so effectively belie Orestes' words.)

Berlioz has added one other editorial comment to this copy, in the first scene of Act II, six measures before the end; a footnote to the double-bass line reads: "Whoever, on hearing this E natural in the double basses, and being in possession of the requisite frame of mind, does not tremble in all his limbs, obviously lacks all feeling for dramatic music."

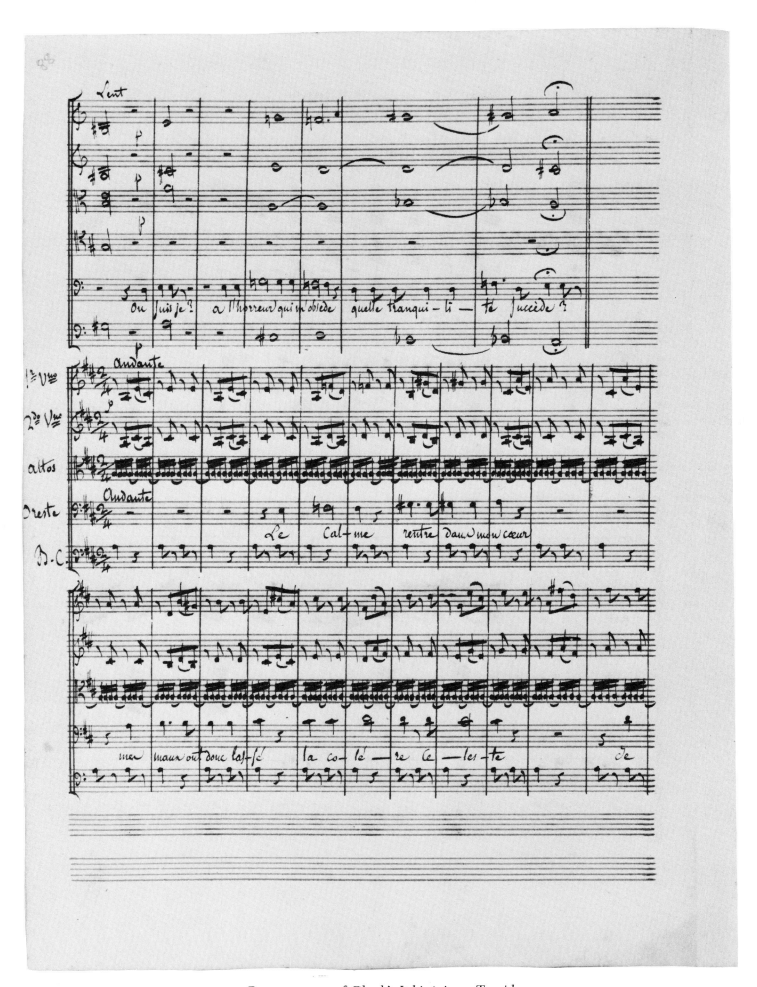

BERLIOZ: copy of Gluck's *Iphigénie en Tauride*

Il pirata. Autograph manuscript of part of the Trio from Act II. 8 p. 24 × 30 cm.
First performance: Milan, 27 October 1827.
Mary Flagler Cary Music Collection.

Few composer-librettist collaborations in operatic history have been as fruitful as that between Bellini and Felice Romani. Beginning with *Il pirata* and ending with *Beatrice di Tenda* (1833), Bellini and Romani produced a series of operas that, except for *Zaira*, were all enormously successful. (The success was not always immediate, however: *Norma*, considered by many to be their finest work, was, Bellini reported after its première, a "Fiasco! Fiasco! Solemn fiasco!") Bellini's last opera, *I puritani*, to a libretto by Carlo Pepoli, was also a great triumph.

Shortly after Bellini's death, in September 1835, Romani wrote a *Necrologia*, describing his early favorable impressions of Bellini's music, but decrying the "ignorance of the theatrical poets and the still greater innocence of the composers of music." Sensing that "a new *dramma* was wanted . . ., I first tested the young Bellini, writing for him *Il pirata*, which seemed to me a subject likely, so to speak, to touch the most responsive chords in his heart. Nor was I mistaken. We understood one another from that day forward."

Il pirata, Bellini's first international success, takes place in thirteenth-century Sicily. ("The country regions of my fatherland are so dear to me," Bellini once wrote, "that the first two subjects I have so far set to music [*Bianca e Fernando* and *Pirata*] take place on Sicilian soil.") To save her father's life, Imogene has married Ernesto, Duke of Caldora, although she was in love with Gualtiero. Gualtiero has become a pirate in hopes of taking revenge on Ernesto and winning back Imogene. (The pirate is a familiar figure in Italian opera—Verdi's *Corsaro* is the best-known example—as is the exile, such as Tancredi and Ernani.) The opera opens as Gualtiero is shipwrecked near Caldora. When Gualtiero and Imogene meet he urges her to leave with him, but she begs him to go before Ernesto learns of his presence. In this Trio, Ernesto encounters Imogene and Gualtiero; the pirate challenges the Duke to combat, and they leave. In the ensuing duel, Ernesto is killed, after which his followers swear vengeance and condemn Gualtiero to death. Imogene goes mad. (The madwoman, nearly always a thwarted lover, is another familiar character in Italian opera: Lucia, Anna Bolena, Linda di Chamounix, Elvira [in *I puritani*]; the male counterpart—for example Nabucco—is rarer.)

Bellini was apparently obliged to shorten this Trio, and part of it is missing from the full-score autograph in Naples. A critic, writing of the première, asked, with reproach: "Why have we been given only a flash of a trio [*un lampo di terzetto*]?"—suggesting that the cut was made as early as the first performance. Part of the excised portion of the Trio is in the manuscript shown here; these pages are not, however, those missing from the Naples autograph, for the watermark in the Cary manuscript does not appear in the Naples score nor in the autograph fragments in Catania, Palermo, and Siena. Copyist's manuscripts of the opera in Naples, Milan, and Venice, being based on the Naples holograph, do not include this music, but the uncut Trio is found in the first printed edition, and its text is found in the earliest printed libretto. Two days after the première Bellini wrote to Vincenzo Ferlito, his uncle, describing the performance in some detail: in Act II, he notes, there is "a trio for all the leading singers, and it creates a furor . . . ." This is one of Bellini's earliest surviving letters; the (incomplete) autograph is owned by the Morgan Library.

Gioachino Rossini, passing through Milan in August 1829 after the première in Paris of what would be his last opera, *Guillaume Tell*, saw *Il pirata* and met Bellini for the first time. Writing to Ferlito, Bellini comments: "Rossini has been telling all Milan that he found in the whole opera a finish and an organization worthy of a mature man rather than of a young one, and that it is full of feeling and, in his view, carried to such a degree of philosophic reasoning that the music lacks some degree of brilliance. That was his feeling," Bellini continues, "but I shall go on composing in the same way, on the basis of common sense, as I have tried it out that way in my wild enthusiasm."

Romani's librettos and Bellini's music occupy transitional stages in their respective spheres: the texts look back to Metastasian classicism, and forward to the full-blown romanticism of Cammarano and Piave; the music, deeply influenced by Bellini's elder contemporary Rossini, was itself to influence Donizetti, Pacini, and Verdi, and elements of its style can be traced in later German and French opera as well.

BELLINI: *Il pirata*

FELIX MENDELSSOHN BARTHOLDY, 1809–1847.

[Die Heimkehr] Aus der Fremde, ein Liederspiel gedichtet von C. Klingemann, componirt von Felix Mendelssohn Bartholdy zur Feyer des 26 December 1829. Autograph manuscript of the piano-vocal score. 56 p. 31.5 × 22.5 cm.
First performance: Berlin, 26 December 1829.
First public performance: Leipzig, 10 April 1851.
Dannie and Hettie Heineman Collection.

Although we do not ordinarily associate Mendelssohn with the world of opera, he maintained a lifelong interest in the genre, considering and rejecting numerous librettos and subjects for them. He wrote a number of *Singspiele*, mostly intended for private performance, and incidental music for several plays, that for *A Midsummer Night's Dream* being the best known. His only full-scale opera, *Die Hochzeit des Camacho* (based on an episode from *Don Quixote*), was a failure, and was withdrawn after its first performance in 1827.

Mendelssohn made an extended visit to England in 1829. In late July and early August, he toured Scotland with Carl Klingemann, secretary at the Hanoverian embassy in London, where he sketched the first musical ideas for the *Hebriden* overture. (A manuscript of this work is on deposit in the Morgan Library.) On 29 October, anticipating his return to Berlin, he wrote to his friend Eduard Devrient: "I shall probably bring home with me an operetta that I have written for the silver wedding anniversary of my parents, and that Klingemann [who wrote the libretto] and I planned on our Scottish tour. It is nothing but a little Idyll, takes place in summertime, and in the country, and, of course, the principal part in it is written for you."

Mendelssohn arrived in Berlin in early December, orchestrated the work, and began rehearsing the singers. The slender plot of *Die Heimkehr* concerns Hermann—who, like Mendelssohn, has just returned home from travels abroad—and his courting of Lisbeth, a childhood sweetheart. He is repeatedly thwarted by Kauz, also a traveler recently come to town, who appears in a number of disguises; Hermann eventually unmasks him, and the lovers are reunited. At the first performance, which took place in the house of Mendelssohn's parents on the eve of their fiftieth wedding anniversary, Lisbeth was sung by Mendelssohn's younger sister, Rebekka; Kauz by Devrient; the Overseer (Lisbeth's father) by Wilhelm Hensel, Mendelssohn's brother-in-law; and Hermann by Eduard Mantius. Devrient, a successful actor, singer, and playwright, had the previous March sung the part of Christ in Mendelssohn's historic performance of Bach's *St. Matthew Passion*. For Hensel, a painter, Mendelssohn wrote a part requiring him to sing on only one note; Devrient reports that the performance went off "without fault, with the exception of Hensel's part in the trio, he, as usual, not being able to catch the note, although it was blown and whispered to him from every side." Mantius, a singer "much sought after in Berlin," according to Devrient, became a leading tenor at the Berlin Opera in the 1830's and '40's. (Berlioz, who heard him there in 1843, described the voice as "a little lacking in flexibility and of limited range.")

The fifth number in this manuscript, Hermann's aria "Wenn die Abendglocken läuten," is not in Mendelssohn's hand. It tells of the vigilant watch kept by a soldier far from home, and borrows melodic material from *Die Hebriden*—another allusion to the composer's own prolonged absence. Mendelssohn apparently attached some importance to this aria, for he wrote out two separate copies of it shortly after the first performance. One, dated 31 December 1829, is inscribed to Eduard Mantius (in the Music Division of The New York Public Library). A few weeks later Mendelssohn sent a copy to Betty Pistor, a close family friend who may have been at the celebrations; the manuscript, decorated with drawings by Wilhelm Hensel, is dated 14 January 1830 (in the Rudorff collection).

MENDELSSOHN: *Die Heimkehr aus der Fremde*

La sonnambula. Sketches and drafts for Act I. 6 p. 28 × 40.5 cm.
First performance: Milan, 6 March 1831.
Mary Flagler Cary Music Collection.

By mid-1830, fresh from the success of his sixth opera, *I Capuleti e i Montecchi*, Bellini and his librettist, Felice Romani, had settled on a subject for the seventh. It would be based on *Hernani*, Victor Hugo's play that had first been given in Paris earlier that year. Composer and librettist worked on the project, probably in November and December; but on 3 January 1831 Bellini wrote to a friend: "You know that I am no longer composing *Ernani* because the subject would have to undergo some modifications at the hands of the police, and that therefore Romani has abandoned it so as not to compromise himself, and is now writing *La sonnambula, ossia I due fidanzati svizzeri,* and just yesterday I began the introduction; you will see that it falls to my lot to compose this opera too in a short space of time . . . ."

La sonnambula was completed within less than two months, and the extraordinary speed of composition can be attributed to at least two factors. First, some music from the aborted *Ernani* found its way into *Sonnambula* (as well as into *Norma* and *I puritani*); Bellini, like Rossini, frequently drew on previously used tunes to fit new words. Second—and this is closely allied to that practice—Bellini regularly drafted melodies in sketchbooks, and so always had a considerable reserve of them to draw on when work began on a new opera. In a letter of 12 May 1828, Bellini offers us a rare glimpse of this procedure: "I have begun my daily exercises [*studi giornalieri*] and it seems they don't go badly, for I have composed some beautiful phrases which will be developed according to the piece in which they are played." And in another letter he speaks of having resumed his *studi* "to prepare me for the opera which (I don't know when or where) I will be obliged to write." Given the similar metrical scheme for so many of the verses supplied to him—the so-called *ottonario*, or eight-foot verse—it is not surprising that he could sketch melodies with no specific text at hand; having received the libretto, he could set about finding the suitable *ottonario* to go with them.

Not infrequently a mismatch resulted, and a tune set to one text in the sketch will eventually accompany another in the final version. On one page of these *Sonnambula* sketches, for example, the text of Lisa's aria "Tutto è gioja, e tutto è festa" is set to a melody which, in the completed opera, accompanies Amina's cabaletta "Sovra il sen la man mi posa." The page shown here contains the beginning of the Elvino-Amina duet "Son geloso del zefiro errante" ("I am jealous of the wandering gentle breeze"); it has some uncommonly elaborate vocal writing and, according to Friedrich Lippmann, contains, except for the first Adalgisa-Norma duet, the longest *a due* coloratura in Bellini's operas.

The role of Amina, the somnambulist, was written for Giuditta Pasta, one of the legendary sopranos of the early nineteenth century; she also created the title roles in Bellini's *Norma* (1831), and *Beatrice di Tenda* (1833). Later notable sopranos who sang the part include Maria Malibran (1833, her English stage debut), her sister-in-law Eugénie García (1834), Malibran's sister Pauline Viardot-García (1848, her London debut), Jenny Lind (both Chopin and Queen Victoria praised her Amina), Adelina Patti (her European debut, at Covent Garden, 1861—she was eighteen years old—and her Paris and Vienna debuts, 1862 and 1863), Minnie Hauk (who, in 1866, made her operatic debut as Amina, in Brooklyn, at the age of fourteen), and Emma Albani (her world debut, Messina, 1870; London debut, 1872; and American debut, 1874). In 1851 *La sonnambula* was the first opera to be performed in San Francisco. And on 29 July 1850, it was the first opera to be performed in Chicago; on the second night, after Act I, the Chicago Theatre caught fire and burned to the ground.

Giuseppe Verdi, writing in 1898, said of Bellini that "even in the least well known of his operas, in *La straniera*, in *Il pirata*, there are long, long, long melodies such as no one before him produced." Probably the most famous of such melodies is that of "Casta diva" from *Norma*. But Verdi could well have had in mind Amina's penultimate aria from *La sonnambula*, "Ah! non credea mirarti sì presto estinto, o fiore" ("Ah! I did not think to see you dead so soon, o flower"); it is that phrase of Romani's which is incised on Bellini's tomb in the Duomo in Catania.

The autograph manuscript of *La sonnambula* is in the Ricordi archives, Milan.

BELLINI: *La sonnambula*

Buondelmonte. Part of the additional music composed by Donizetti in altering Maria Stuarda into Buondelmonte, the form in which the opera was first given. 31 p. 26.5 × 38 cm.
First (and only) performance: Naples, 18 October 1834.
First performance as Maria Stuarda: Milan, 30 December 1835.
Mary Flagler Cary Music Collection.

Thomas Carlyle called Schiller's *Maria Stuart* "a tragedy of sombre and mournful feelings; with an air of melancholy and obstruction pervading it; a looking backward on objects of remorse, around on imprisonment, and forward to the grave." It contains, in short, many of the ingredients of *bel canto* opera. Published in 1800 and considered by some critics to be Schiller's finest drama, *Maria Stuart* includes the confrontation of strong personalities, here of royal rank; ardent passions attendant on thwarted love; intrigues involving both matters of state and affairs of the heart—all these form the common stock from which countless nineteenth-century Italian operas drew.

On 12 April 1834 Donizetti signed a contract with the Teatro San Carlo in Naples for a new opera. He tried, without success, to secure as his librettist Felice Romani (who had previously provided texts for his *Anna Bolena, L'elisir d'amore,* and *Lucrezia Borgia*), but was forced, possibly in some desperation, to turn to a seventeen-year-old law student, Giuseppe Bardari, whose text for *Maria Stuarda* was his first, and only, libretto. Bardari based his libretto on Andrea Maffei's verse translation of Schiller's tragedy. (Among Maffei's later librettos was that for Verdi's *I masnadieri,* based on Schiller's play *Die Räuber.*)

On 19 July Bardari's libretto was submitted to the Neapolitan censors, who, on 4 September, summoned the librettist and demanded extensive changes. On that same day Monsignor Giuseppe Caprioli, private secretary to Ferdinando II, King of the Two Sicilies, had sent a directive to the Minister of Police: "I take the liberty of reminding you of what I indicated to you verbally last Monday concerning the two theatrical pieces: Lucrezia Borgia and Maria Stuart: I must then inform you that it is His Majesty's wish that upon gala court evenings in the Royal theatres the presentation of operas and ballets of tragic argument should always be prohibited." (Romani's *Lucrezia Borgia* libretto had been submitted to the censors in late May; it is possible that because both texts were likely to offend the conservative censors, the fact that they were under consideration at the same time increased the chances that neither would be accepted. *Lucrezia* was not given in Naples until 1848, *Stuarda* until 1865.) The reasons for the king's proscription can only be conjectured: possibly it was the (historically spurious) confrontation between the two queens; possibly the execution of a crowned head; or perhaps it was that both Ferdinando and Queen Maria Cristina were descendants of Mary Stuart and felt that she had been misrepresented.

Donizetti was now faced with a dilemma: he must either let others recast the work, eliminating the offending passages, or himself adapt the existing music to a less inflammatory subject. He chose the latter course. Bardari was either unavailable or unwilling to rewrite the libretto; the eleventh-hour revision was therefore assumed by Pietro Salatino, the author of Donizetti's *Sancia di Castiglia.* The first dress rehearsal for *Buondelmonte,* the *rifacimento* (or refashioning) of *Maria Stuarda,* took place on 7 October 1834; in a letter of the same date to Jacopo Ferretti (yet another librettist, most familiar as the author of Rossini's *Cenerentola*), Donizetti gives a lively and ironic account of what happened that deserves to be quoted at length:

> *Stuarda* has been forbidden, heaven knows why! but better not ask, as it is the King himself who has ordered it. . . . I suggested another subject, *Maria Stuarda* not being permitted, but *Giovanna Grey* [Lady Jane Grey] met the same fate: the opera died a second time before it could be resurrected. "What can we do? Maestro, help!" the management shouted. And then, noble bugger that I am, I answered: "It will take money. You were going to give me 1400 ducats for the opera; add 600 to that and I will be able to help." That was settled in a few words. Thus, *Buondelmonte* came to light, and Maestro Donizetti tears up parts of his work and then revises and re-revises. . . . A new duet and new choruses have been pasted together; spurious recitatives have already been copied. Today the first rehearsal of this concoction was held. If I get out of this safe and sound, never again, never again will I meddle like this! . . . You will get some idea if I tell you that the big prayer in *Stuarda* has been turned into a fine, full conspiracy in *Buondelmonte.* The leading female character went to her death? Now it is the tenor Pedrazzi who dies. . . . There used to be six characters in all? Now there are ten or more. You can imagine what the opera has become! The same scenery, appropriate or not, will be used.

Donizetti's *rifacimento* consisted, it seems, mostly in adapting the existing *Maria Stuarda* music to Salatino's text, and supplying new recitatives; the Cary manuscript contains several of these recitatives, all fully accompanied, and largely unpublished. The manuscript consists of the following items:

1: "Dopo l'Introduzione Atto 1"; 3 pages of recitative with strings, for Elisabetta, Irene, Tedaldo, and Mosca.

2: "Sullo Spartito di Stuarda"; 2 pages of recitative with strings, for Buondelmonte and Tedaldo.

3: "Dopo il Duetto di Buon: con Tedaldo"; 5 pages of recitative laid out for full orchestra, but with only a few chords, mainly for strings; for Buondelmonte and Irene.

DONIZETTI: *Buondelmonte*

4: "Dopo il Coro prima del Finale Att. I"; 1 page of recitative with strings, for Elisabetta, Buondelmonte, Tedaldo, Irene, and chorus.

5: "Dopo il Terzetto"; 1 page of recitative with strings, for Irene, Buondelmonte, and Eleonora.

6: "Dopo il Terzetto, Atto 2d."; 16 pages, a large scena in recitative accompanied by full orchestra, for Lamberto, Mosca, Oderigo, Uberto, and chorus.

7: "Après la Conjuration"; 1 page of recitative with strings, for Lamberto, Uberto, Bianca, and Tedaldo.

8: [No heading]; the continuation of a recitative, subsequently abandoned by Donizetti, for Tedaldo, Bianca, and Giovanna.

The autograph full score of *Maria Stuarda* is in the Stiftelsen Musikkulturens Främjande, Stockholm. The partly autograph orchestral score of *Buondelmonte* is in the Conservatorio di Musica S Pietro a Majella, Naples; those sections in Donizetti's hand are clearly part of the original *Maria Stuarda* score, since they contain the names of several *Stuarda* characters crossed out and replaced by their *Buondelmonte* counterparts. *Maria Stuarda* is one of nine Donizetti operas set in the British Isles, the best known of them being *Anna Bolena*, *Lucia di Lammermoor*, and *Roberto Devereux*. At least fourteen other operas have been based on Mary Stuart, the most recent being Thea Musgrave's *Mary, Queen of Scots* (1977).

The Morgan Library also owns the manuscript of an insert aria for *Lucrezia Borgia*, composed for the tenor Nicola Ivanoff (for Verdi's *Ernani* aria for Ivanoff, see p. 64), and two drafts of the Act II, Scene 2 duet between Anna and Giovanna from *Anna Bolena*.

Les Huguenots. Autograph manuscript of Valentine's aria "Parmi les pleurs," arranged for voice and piano, dated 13 May 1836. 2 leaves. 16 × 25 cm.
First performance: Paris, 29 February 1836.
Fellows Fund, the gift of Mr. Frederick Koch.

With *Robert le diable* (1831), Meyerbeer was launched on a career matched by few composers before or since. *Robert* was followed by a half-dozen extraordinary, if widely spaced, successes, each only serving to increase his fame (and his fortune; he became one of the richest men in Europe): *Les Huguenots* (1836), *Ein Feldlager in Schlesien* (1844), *Le prophète* (1849), *L'étoile du nord* (a reworking of *Feldlager*, 1854), *Le pardon de Ploërmel* (1859), and *L'africaine* (posthumous, 1865). Four of these—*Robert*, *Huguenots*, *Prophète*, and *Africaine*—now virtually epitomize the genre of French grand opera. Heinrich Heine, who wrote laudatory essays on Meyerbeer (later revising them as biting criticism), once remarked that Meyerbeer's mother was only the second woman in history to see her son accepted as divine.

In October 1832, Meyerbeer signed a contract with the Paris Opéra for a new work, *La St. Barthélemy*, as *Les Huguenots* was originally called: the climactic final act of the opera—often cut in early performances—depicts scenes from the St. Bartholomew's Day Massacre in August 1572, the Catholics' attempted extirpation of the Protestant Huguenots. His correspondence over the next few years with his wife, Minna, documents the anxieties and frustrations associated with the composition and rehearsals of the opera. The anxiety is in part explained by the fact that he was faced with the improbable task of equaling or surpassing the unprecedented triumph of *Robert le diable*. Frustrating delays were occasioned by a number of events. On 26 November 1834, he wrote to his wife: "I read in a *Figaro* article that one of my most brilliant and unforeseen musical effects, which was to lend great luster to the end of Act IV, will be found complete in Halévy's new opera." (*La Juive*, Halévy's greatest success, was first performed three months later.) "I was obliged to cut entirely your favorite piece, 'laissez moi partir,' as well as the whole finale of the act." The fourth act suffered additional rearrangements at the hands of the censors: on 24 December 1835 he wrote to Minna that "the character of Catherine de' Medici, the ending [of the opera], and the monks' scene have been forbidden; the first two points are possible with considerable alterations, which will impose new work on me; the last, unless I rewrite the second half of Act IV, is not possible."

The première, one of the most memorable in opera history, merely reaffirmed Meyerbeer's standing as the leading European opera composer. The first-night reviews were ecstatic: "It is hardly possible to describe the impression this opera made. No other work, either by Meyerbeer or any other contemporary opera composer, has been received with such thunderous applause." And even: "The opera is one of the most wonderful creations of the human spirit." One writer punned that "at the première, the *Huguenots* found no protestants in the hall."

The months following the première were spent preparing the *morceaux détachés* and the piano-vocal score. On the same day that Meyerbeer copied out Valentine's aria shown here—which may have been cut at the first performance—he wrote to Minna describing the arduous work involved in the piano-vocal reductions, and then suggesting, as his letters do more than once, a conspiracy among his rivals to undermine the opera's popularity. "Unfortunately, the *Huguenots* performances have been interrupted owing to Falcon's ostensible cold, and I've just learned that she will not sing next Monday . . . . [Cornélie Falcon sang the first Valentine.] Rossini on one side, Halévy on the other, do what they can to detract as much as possible from the opera's great success, and unfortunately their influence is powerful. Since Falcon is very loyal to both, maybe they will try to persuade her (under pretext of her indisposition) not to sing at all before her departure [on vacation]. That would be a mortal blow to the *Huguenots*." A week later he wrote that "a number of persons at the Opéra maintain . . . that Falcon's hoarseness is feigned, at the instigation of R[ossini] or H[alévy], to thwart the work's success." (Falcon's problems may well have been genuine: overwork so damaged her voice that she retired permanently from opera in 1840, at the age of 26.)

Among the early champions of *Les Huguenots* was a composer who would later become one of the most virulent critics of French grand opera: Richard Wagner. He, and many critics since, singled out Act IV for special praise. In his later years he could no longer openly admit his admiration, but apparently retained something of his old enthusiasm. During the Bayreuth years he saw the opera "and was positively wrought up by the fourth act. I implore you not to let a soul know it—otherwise the Wagnerites will flay me alive!"

The autograph manuscript of *Les Huguenots* was removed from Berlin during World War II along with the autographs of three other Meyerbeer operas, and is presumably among the manuscripts that have recently resurfaced in Poland.

MEYERBEER: *Les Huguenots*

ЖИЗНЬ ЗА ЦАРЯ

БОЛЬШАЯ ОПЕРА

ВЪ ЧЕТЫРЕХЪ ДѢЙСТВІЯХЪ СЪ ЭПИЛОГОМЪ

слова

БАРОНА РОЗЕНА

МУЗЫКА

М.И. ГЛИНКИ

ПОЛНАЯ
ПАРТИТУРА
СЪ ПРИЛОЖЕНІЕМЪ
Цѣна 30 руб.

Собственность издателя
С.ПЕТЕРБУРГЪ у Ѳ.СТЕЛЛОВСКАГО
въ большой Морской № 27

GLINKA: *Zhizn' za tsarya*

MIKHAIL IVANOVICH GLINKA, 1804–1857.

Zhizn' za tsarya [A Life for the Tsar]. *St. Petersburg: F. Stellovsky, 1881. [8] [i–iii] iv–xxvii, 3–716 p. 32 cm. First edition of the full score.*
First performance: St. Petersburg, 9 December 1836.
Mary Flagler Cary Music Collection.

Gerald Abraham, in tracing the antecedents of A *Life for the Tsar*, the earlier of Glinka's two operas, sums up as follows the wholly non-Russian characteristics of Russian opera in Glinka's time:

> Russian opera for more than half a century was composed by through-and-through Italians, by superficially Russianised Italians, by Italian-trained Russians, and by Russian amateurs who took this Italo-Russian music as their model. . . . Apart from its historical interest, their collective output (as far as one can judge from the specimens obtainable) is an insipid pot-pourri of the musical platitudes of the day, faintly flavoured with native condiments.

Glinka was largely self-taught and took as his models, as Abraham and others have demonstrated, the Western music he heard in his early years. He arrived in St. Petersburg in 1817, the year Rossini's *Tancredi* was first given there, and the year that marked the beginning of Rossini's ascendancy in Russia. (In 1828 no fewer than eleven Rossini operas were in the St. Petersburg repertory.) Boieldieu, Cherubini, Méhul, Weber—Glinka heard them all and assimilated some of the more superficial characteristics of their music. The works that he wrote under this Western influence show that he learned by imitation; few exhibit an individual voice or more than a rudimentary mastery of the traditional principles of musical composition. In 1830, partly on doctor's orders but largely because he was determined to do so anyhow, Glinka, traveling with the tenor Nicola Ivanoff, left for Italy, where he would spend the next three years. They settled in Milan, the center of Italian operatic life. In their first season they saw the premières of Donizetti's *Anna Bolena*, at which Glinka "wallowed in rapture, the more so since at that time I was still not indifferent to virtuosity, as I am now," and Bellini's *La sonnambula*, at which he "shed tears of emotion and ecstasy." (For a discussion of *Sonnambula*, see p. 52.) Glinka and Ivanoff parted company in 1832, and the tenor made his Italian debut the same year in *Anna Bolena*. The Morgan Library owns the manuscripts of two insert arias composed for Ivanoff: one by Donizetti, for *Lucrezia Borgia*; one by Verdi, for *Ernani* (see p. 64).

Around the end of 1832 Feofil Tolstoi, a dilettante composer and singer, visited Glinka in Milan. In the reminiscences of his friend, written some 40 years later, Tolstoi recalled that Glinka "had set out in detail a plan which he had conceived for a grand five-act opera. . . . The proposed subject was completely na-tional with a strongly patriotic colouring, and was rather gloomy. . . . He was already playing . . . the melody 'When my mother was killed' [later to become the Orphan's song in Act III of A *Life for the Tsar*], and lovingly pointed out the counterpoint in 'My Vanya is singing to himself all about a fledgling,' " the words of Susanin's first vocal entry in the act.

In August 1833 Glinka left Italy, traveling first to Vienna, where he wrote the theme of the *krakoviak* (a Polish dance) that appears in Act II of A *Life for the Tsar*, and then went on to Berlin, where for five months he studied harmony and counterpoint with the noted pedagogue Siegfried Dehn. This was the only systematic course in composition that Glinka ever undertook. "There is no doubt that I am more indebted to Dehn than to all my other teachers," Glinka wrote later. "After his teaching I began to work clearheadedly, not gropingly." During this period of rigorous instruction Glinka's thoughts were never far from the opera he had contemplated in Milan. From Berlin he wrote to a friend in Russia: "The main thing is the choice of subject. In any case I want everything to be national: above all, the subject—and the music likewise—so much so that my dear compatriots will feel they are at home, and so that abroad I shall not be considered a braggart or a crow who seeks to deck himself in borrowed phrases. . . . Who knows whether I shall be able to fulfill the promise I have made myself?"

Glinka returned to Russia in the spring of 1834, and soon thereafter "came upon the idea for a Russian opera. I had no words, but [Zhukovsky's] *Mar'ina Grove* was running through my head and I played several bits on the piano, some parts of which I later used in A *Life for the Tsar*." Vasily Zhukovsky, a poet and the most important precursor of Pushkin, introduced to Russia through his superb translations many German and English writers, including Goethe, Schiller, and Byron. When Glinka mentioned to Zhukovsky his plan for a Russian opera, the poet approved enthusiastically, and suggested the subject of Ivan Susanin, the Russian peasant who in 1612 or 1613, at the cost of his own life, had saved that of the first Romanov tsar by diverting a group of Poles who were hunting him. Zhukovsky was but one of four persons who would eventually contribute to the libretto; most of the work fell to Baron Gregory Rosen, a writer of German extraction who was at that time secretary to the Tsarevich. But Glinka's imagination "soon ran ahead of the industrious German; as if by an act of magic the plan of the whole opera was suddenly formed. . . . Many themes and even details of their workings flashed into my head at once. I began to work, but completely haphazardly—to wit, I began with the overture, with which others finish." Glinka had, in fact, completed most of the first two acts before Rosen was finally called upon to rewrite the libretto, fitting his text to music already composed. "Zhukovsky and others used to say jokingly that Rosen had lines already written and distributed among his pockets, and that all I had to do was to say what meter I needed, and how many lines, and he would take out as many of each sort as were required—each variety from a different pocket."

Rehearsals began in the spring of 1836, under the direction of Catterino Cavos, a Russianized Italian who, in 1815, had himself composed an opera *Ivan Susanin*. Shortly before the première the Tsar, Nikolai I, attended a rehearsal, and soon afterward granted Glinka permission to dedicate the opera to him— requesting, at the same time, that the title be changed to *A Life for the Tsar*. (The historical tsar of the opera was the founder of Nikolai's own dynasty. After the 1917 Revolution the title reverted to *Ivan Susanin*; the libretto has since been completely rewritten.) The opera was received with great popular acclaim, and for many years it opened the opera seasons in both St. Petersburg and Moscow.

The question of precedence—who did what first—is a notoriously troublesome one to address, in the arts no less so than in other fields. No sooner has something been designated "the first" than someone is sure to find an earlier instance of it. Tradition has long maintained that *A Life for the Tsar* was the first Russian opera. It was neither the first opera composed by a Russian, nor the first to be based on a Russian subject. But the consensus is that it was the first important composition by a Russian—hence the first Russian opera of significance—and by virtue of that precedence has had considerable influence. Borodin, Musorgsky, Rimsky-Korsakov, and Tchaikovsky all stood in Glinka's debt, and if his first opera is hardly the masterpiece against which their works in the genre should be measured, it nonetheless broke ground in a nearly virgin field; its progeny, if not direct descendants, all inherited something from Glinka's pioneering example.

Benvenuto Cellini. Opéra Semi Seria en deux Actes. . . . Paris: Maurice Schlesinger [1839]. [82] p. 33 cm. The first-edition piano-vocal score of nine morceaux détachés, with autograph annotations and corrections.
First performance: Paris, 10 September 1838.
Mary Flagler Cary Music Collection.

Shortly after Berlioz won the Prix de Rome in 1830, he traveled to Italy for the obligatory internship at the Villa Medici. While he was largely indifferent to Italian art, and claimed that their music, "beginning with Rossini, is odious to me, except in the comic genre," during the fifteen months he spent there he was to receive impressions that would stay with him for life and that would reappear in various transmutations in many of his later compositions. "By the time Berlioz returned to Paris in the fall of 1832," writes Jacques Barzun, "he had sketched or conceived or been drawn to the subject of every one of his major works." The most obviously Italian of them were, one would suggest, *Harold en Italie* and *Benvenuto Cellini.*

Soon after completing the first of his five surviving operas, *Les francs-juges,* in 1826, Berlioz began to dismantle it; today only the overture and six fragments remain. He incorporated passages from the opera into later works, starting with *Benvenuto Cellini,* composed between 1834 and 1837—although we will never be certain what parts of *Cellini* or *Les troyens,* for example, originated in the earlier opera. The 1830's were for Berlioz years of solid successes in the concert halls and intense frustrations elsewhere, chief among them being the desire to win recognition at the Opéra; *Benvenuto Cellini* was his first—and, it turned out, only—opera to appear in that house during his lifetime. Blame for the failure of the opera has long been placed on the libretto, drawn by Léon de Wailly and Auguste Barbier from Cellini's *Vita,* a book, writes Hugh Macdonald, "whose abundant incident and ardent idealization of the artist hero appealed strongly to [Berlioz] . . . and provided, too, the irresistible local colour of Renaissance Italy." (Berlioz himself admitted that the libretto "lacked the essential ingredients of what is known as a well-constructed drama," but liked it nonetheless.) What more likely doomed the work was Berlioz's highly individual music, which must have been met with puzzlement, if not open hostility, by an Opéra clientele accustomed to the more comfortable idioms of Rossini, Auber, and Meyerbeer. At the première, Berlioz wrote in his *Memoirs,* "the overture was extravagantly applauded; the rest was hissed with exemplary precision and energy." (The overture, incidentally, is not the familiar "Roman Carnival," a work, based on material from the opera, composed in 1844.) *Cellini* was repeated three times; two days before the final performance on 11 January 1839, Berlioz wrote to a friend: "As for the chorus, they exhibit an indolence and apathy to drive a saint to despair. I've given up trying to animate that troop of corpses. The orchestra's not bad. . . . In short, this unhappy *Benvenuto* is unlucky: it is really *malvenuto.*" (A critic, reporting the opera's lack of success the previous November, had called it *Malvenuto Cellini.*)

Frustrated in his attempts to further his career in France, and having heard of the growing number of performances of his works in other countries, Berlioz undertook the first of the many tours that would occupy much of his time over the next 20 years. From December 1842 to May 1843 his travels took him to Brussels and a dozen cities in Germany. The *morceaux détachés* from *Cellini* were published in February 1839; our copy was probably sent on to a German translator, perhaps in 1842, in preparation for Berlioz's tour the following year. Four of the numbers—2, 4, 8, and 9—are marked in Berlioz's hand "à traduire." The Cavatine, no. 2, was sung in German in Dresden, Hamburg, Berlin, and Darmstadt on the tour (and also in Vienna on a tour in 1845; a year later it was published there in German for the first time). The two Dresden concerts included the *Symphonie fantastique,* movements from the *Requiem* and *Grande symphonie funèbre et triomphale,* and a few vocal pieces; the performances, Berlioz reports, were magnificent.

> [But] the Cavatine from *Benvenuto,* which I had taken it into my head to add to the programme, gave me more trouble than the whole of the rest of the concert. It could not be offered to the prima donna, Madame Devrient, the tessitura of the piece lying too high for her and the florid passages requiring a lighter, more flexible voice. Mlle Wüst, the second soprano . . ., declared the German translation bad, the andante too high and too long, the allegro too low and too short; she wanted cuts and alterations, she was suffering from a cold, etcetera, etcetera—you know the whole comedy by heart: the *cantatrice* who can't and won't.

Hugh Macdonald, who is editing *Benvenuto Cellini* for the *New Berlioz Edition,* has kindly provided the following information about our copy of the *morceaux*—one of nine known to him.

> The main point of musical interest in this copy is the correction on p. 1 of the *Duo,* no. 6, since the autograph of this page is lost and since this part of the duet was cut and never revived. Thus the edition is the only source and all uncorrected copies are therefore wrong for the two notes. The simplified cadenzas on pp. 5 and 8 of no. 2 [the Cavatine] are interesting since the simplifications are different from those found in the autograph full score and those in the later Litolff vocal score. . . . All the annotations and corrections are in Berlioz's hand.

When Franz Liszt revived *Benvenuto Cellini* for a production in Weimar in 1852, Berlioz drastically revised the opera; the autograph manuscript of the Weimar version, which Berlioz accepted as the definitive text of *Cellini,* is in the Bibliothèque Nationale, fonds du Conservatoire—the single largest repository of Berlioz manuscripts. The library of the Paris Opéra houses a set of non-autograph orchestral parts and a "violon-conducteur" score partly in Berlioz's hand, from which most of the 1838 version can be reconstructed.

BERLIOZ: *Benvenuto Cellini*

GIUSEPPE VERDI, 1813–1901.

Ernani. Autograph manuscript of the full score of the "Aria con cori per l'Ernani" written for Nicola Ivanoff. 48 p. 33 × 24 cm.
First performance of the opera: Venice, 9 March 1844.
First performance of this scena: Parma, 26 December 1844.
Mary Flagler Cary Music Collection.

When Verdi's first opera, *Oberto, Conte di San Bonifacio*, was produced at Milan's La Scala on 17 November 1839 its composer was at the ripe age of 26; compared to the youthful careers of his predecessors Rossini, Donizetti, and Bellini, it was a relatively late start. Rossini had composed his first opera before he was seventeen and by 37 had retired to a comfortable life in Paris as bon vivant. Donizetti, who wrote his first opera at nineteen, would be dead within nine years of the première of *Oberto*, while Bellini was never to know of Verdi's achievements, dying in 1838 at the age of 33. And yet once established, Verdi was to dominate as no other the Italian operatic arena for the next 50-odd years, beginning with *Nabucco*, his first enduring success in 1842, and culminating with his comic masterpiece *Falstaff* in 1893.

Having set his course, Verdi quickly found Italian opera still largely governed by the constraints and conventions of the eighteenth century, a world that catered to the dictates of the singer, the schemings of money-hungry impresarios, and an unpredictable public. And nowhere within this system was a greater toll extracted than that on the drama of a work: vocal display was the order of the day. A singer, unhappy with an existing aria in an opera, felt no compunction in inserting another, as Bellini was to discover in 1828. For the *prima donna* Adelaide Tosi he wrote a specifically tailored aria for his opera *Bianca e Fernando*; yet, he says, "as she sang it like a pig and it went for nothing she wanted another. . . . If I didn't change it she would sing one of her *pezzi di baule* ['suitcase pieces' designed to fit stock operatic situations] instead." Verdi throughout his career would be instrumental in altering these conditions, but only with lifelong perseverance. The currents would eventually change but not soon enough to suit him. As late as 1869 he could still write: "While everyone cries out about *Reform* and *Progress*, the audience sits on its hands and the singers can only manage arias, romances, [and] canzonettas effectively. . . . The order is reversed. The frame has become the picture." Later the same year, he would be even more emphatic: "I want *art* in whatever form it is manifest, not *entertainment, artifice,* and *the system.*"

The Verdi of 1843 was not yet the composer so confident as to embrace these novel ideas; "the system," for the time, held firm. *Ernani*, his fifth opera and the first to receive its première at the Teatro la Fenice, still adheres to the majority of formal procedures found in operas from the earlier nineteenth century. Yet curiously, if only in terms of musical innovation, the "Aria con cori per l'Ernani" was to be a tentative break with the prevailing musical conventions. Verdi composed the scene for the tenor Nicola Ivanoff at the request of Rossini. In a letter to Verdi on 28 November 1844 Rossini enclosed Piave's text for the music, not-

ing that it was "poetry that you . . . will know how to adorn with beautiful music and thus make my good Ivanoff happy." The Russian-born Ivanoff, described by the English critic Henry Chorley as possessing "the sweetest voice . . . that ever sang in Italian or Muscovite throat," had become a protégé of Rossini's and it was Rossini who paid Verdi for the music (1500 Austrian lire—about $712). On 28 January 1845 Rossini wrote again to Verdi: "thank you exceedingly for what you have done for . . . Ivanoff, who feels himself blessed to have possession of one of your delicious compositions."

Verdi's work on the music must have proceeded quickly. He received Piave's text from Rossini on 28 November (Piave was the librettist for the complete opera, which is drawn from Victor Hugo's *Hernani*); by 9 December we learn from Verdi's pupil, Emanuele Muzio, that it was then "a beautifully constructed piece" and that Ivanoff was on his way to Milan to learn it from the composer himself. Ivanoff first performed the work at the Teatro Ducale on 26 December where, according to the *Gazzetta di Parma*, it met with "great fortune." The scene was never incorporated into the full score, nor, it seems, was it ever meant to be, for on the first page of the autograph Verdi writes that he cedes the *assoluta proprietà* to the tenor. Thus the "Aria con cori per l'Ernani" was intended for use only in Ivanoff's performances of the complete opera, to be inserted in Act II after the oath in which Ernani places both life and services in the hands of Silva; dramatically it contributes little to the momentum of the plot, yet vocally it is a tour de force. The scene opens with a short recitative followed by a well-proportioned romance for Ernani, "Odi il voto, o grande Iddio," continues with a short transition for chorus, and concludes with his rousing vengeance cabaletta "Sprezzo la vita nè più m'alletta"—described recently by Julian Budden as "so unusual in form and material as to be called experimental."

In August of 1846 it was discovered that Gaetano Fraschini, the first to sing the tenor roles in Verdi's *Alzira, Il corsaro, La battaglia di Legnano,* and *Stiffelio,* was performing Ivanoff's music from *Ernani*. The enraged Ivanoff promptly sought legal redress. Muzio reports that "Ivanoff, owner of the aria which the Maestro wrote him for Parma, has sued Fraschini, because the latter is singing it at Senigania and nobody knows where he got it. But *we* know he got it at Parma; they copied it for him right under [Ivanoff's] nose." Fraschini's copy is presumably the one now in the Biblioteca Palatina in Parma; a comparison of the copy and the autograph reveals a number of variants which in all likelihood were made for, or by, Fraschini. The autograph manuscripts of most of Verdi's operas, including that of *Ernani*, are in the Ricordi archives, Milan.

VERDI: *Ernani*

1848   SAVERIO MERCADANTE, 1795–1870.

La schiava saracena. Draft for Acts I and II. 131 p. 23.5 × 32 cm.
First performance: Milan, 26 December 1848.
Mary Flagler Cary Music Collection.

Although Mercadante's operas have dropped from the modern repertory, they enjoyed tremendous popularity during his own day, bringing him to the forefront of the Italian musical scene. He had a remarkably active career, composing about 60 operatic works and serving as head of the Naples conservatory for the last 30 years of his life. His best operas, such as *Il giuramento* (1837) and *La vestale* (1840), often departed from the traditional Italian conventions and exerted a considerable influence on the younger Verdi, assuring Mercadante at least a position of historical importance today.

La schiava saracena, originally entitled *Il campo de' crociati*, was to be performed in Milan at La Scala in March of 1848, but the political turmoil of that year forced a postponement until December. This was the time of the famous *Cinque Giornate*, the five-day revolt that drove the occupying Austrian army from Milan and gave the city a brief taste of independence before the Austrians recaptured it a few months later. After the Milanese performance the opera traveled to the Teatro San Carlo in Naples.

Francesco Piave, the librettist for many of Verdi's best operas, created the text of *La schiava saracena*, his only work for Merca-

dante. The opera is set against the capture of Jerusalem by the Christians in 1099 during the First Crusade. Its plot revolves around the love between the French crusader Guido and Lea, a young Saracen slave. Lea ultimately decides to take up Christianity and is betrothed to Guido, but their plans come to a tragic end when Guido's Arab rival Ismaele stabs Lea, leaving her to die in her lover's arms.

The draft for the opera in the Cary Collection, bearing the earlier title *Il campo de' crociati*, contains only the first two acts of the four-act work. Act I consists of a "Coro d'introduzione," *cavatine* for both Guido (called "Carlo" in this version) and Lea, and a large ensemble finale. The second act also opens with a chorus, a duet for Guido and Lea follows, and the act concludes with a trio for Lea, Carlo, and Ismaele. The emphasis in the draft is on the vocal parts, which are worked out in detail with usually no more than the bass line of the instrumental accompaniment notated.

The autographs of several of Mercadante's operas, including that of *La schiava saracena*, are in the Ricordi archives, Milan. A large number of copyist's manuscripts survive, many in the Naples Conservatory.

MERCADANTE: *La schiava saracena*

Lalla-Roukh. Piano-vocal score drafts of three passages. 4 p. 35 × 27 cm.
First performance: Paris, 12 May 1862.
Mary Flagler Cary Music Collection.

David is a composer little remembered today, although as recently as 1944 the critic René Dumesnil ranked him second only to Berlioz among the French composers of his day. His fame rested primarily on two works: *Le désert*, an *ode-symphonie* (1844), and *Lalla-Roukh*, the fifth of his seven operas. Both compositions reflect a penchant for orientalism and exoticism, which have attracted composers from Gluck to Messiaen. Orientalism also flourished in David's time in literature and art: one thinks of Goethe's *Westöstlicher Divan*, Hugo's *Les orientales*, Lamartine's *Souvenirs d'un voyage*, and paintings of Delacroix and Ingres.

Thomas Moore's oriental romance *Lalla Rookh* was published in 1817; it was an immediate, dazzling success that has inspired a number of musical compositions, including Spontini's opera *Nurmahal* (1822), Schumann's *Das Paradies und die Peri* (1843), Anton Rubinstein's opera *Feramorz* (1863), and Charles Villiers Stanford's opera *The Veiled Prophet of Khorassan* (1881). *Lalla Rookh* consists of four long poems interspersed with brief narrative passages, which relate the royal progress of the eponymous heroine, an Indian princess, from Delhi to Kashmir, where she is to marry the king of Bucharia. Along the way Feramorz, a poet, joins the caravan and, to relieve the tedium of Lalla Rookh's journey, recites the poems. Princess and poet fall in love; on reaching Kashmir, Feramorz reveals himself to be none other than the king, Lalla Rookh's betrothed.

David's opera is loosely based on this narrative, making virtually no use of the much longer poems. Moore's poet becomes the minstrel Noureddin, whose sweet, melodious singing lightens Lalla-Roukh's boredom. Moore's pedantic Fedladeen, who can find only fault with Feramorz's poetry, has no exact counterpart in the opera, although he sounds, incidentally, very much like Wagner's Beckmesser: "As to the versification," Moore writes, "it was, to say no worse of it, execrable. . . . What critic that can count . . . , and has his full complement of fingers to count withal, would tolerate such syllabic superfluities?"

David's exoticism was not without its detractors. *Le désert*, while it brought him fame throughout Europe and in America, and the admiration of Meyerbeer, Mendelssohn, Berlioz, and Saint-Saëns, elicited from Auber the wish that David "would get off his camel."

The Morgan Library also has portions of the original, second, and third autograph drafts or manuscripts of Moore's poem, the proof sheets with his autograph corrections and additions, and the first-edition piano-vocal score of the opera, inscribed by the composer to Achille-Félix Montaubry, the tenor who sang the role of Noureddin at the première.

DAVID: *Lalla-Roukh*

Mireille. Autograph manuscript of the full score. ca. 1000 p. 35.5 × 26 cm.
First performance: Paris, 19 March 1864.
Mary Flagler Cary Music Collection.

Gounod's *Faust*, first performed on 19 March 1859, has proved to be one of the enduring successes in the history of opera. *Mireille*, whose première fell five years to the day later, has had an oddly checkered career; while it has never secured for itself a permanent place in the repertory, its admirers have done much to save it from obscurity.

The libretto of *Mireille* is based on Frédéric Mistral's *Mirèio*, and tells the familiar story of a wealthy girl (Mirèio) and her humble suitor (Vincent) kept apart by her parents; in desperation, she makes an arduous trip across the Val d'Enfer to the church of the Trois-Maries, where she dies of sunstroke and a broken heart. Mistral was a founder of the *Félibrige*, a movement devoted to restoring Provençal as a living language and to a renaissance of Provençal literature. His poem *Mirèio*, published in 1859, is considered the masterpiece produced by the *félibres*.

Revisions to the opera began soon after its première: by 15 December 1864 it had been reduced from five acts to three, and the ending changed to allow Mireille to live. In 1874, when it first appeared at the Opéra-Comique, it played again in five acts, and Mireille died. In 1889 the three-act, "happy ending" version was again given in a production that, Gounod said, was neither to his taste nor his idea but one to which, for the sake of preserving the work, he was resigned. Finally, in 1898, at Saint-Saëns' suggestion, Gounod's widow asked the French composer and conductor Henri Büsser to restore *Mireille* to its original state as Gounod had conceived it. Working from the orchestral score shown here, Büsser reconstructed the opera; the resulting version was performed at the Salle Favart in 1901. But Mme Gounod did not allow certain of Büsser's discoveries—for example, Gounod's original sung recitatives—to be included, and it was not until 1939 that Büsser's definitive recension was finally given, at the Opéra-Comique. (*Mireille* was first performed at the Metropolitan Opera in the 1918–19 season—paired, oddly, with Stravinsky's *Petrushka*.)

Among the first changes made following the 1864 première were those demanded by Caroline Carvalho, who sang the first Mireille. She asked for a first-act display piece, and Gounod obliged by inserting the *valse-ariette* "O légère hirondelle"—an aria strongly reminiscent of Marguerite's Jewel Song from *Faust*, and one totally inappropriate to place and character. Reynaldo Hahn, who helped prepare the 1939 production, wrote of Mme Carvalho: "This great singer combined a talent which has certainly not been praised too highly, a talent no doubt miraculous, with infallible bad taste, an immense, dissembling, implacable arrogance which her husband [the impresario Léon Carvalho] buttressed with his powerful directorial support."

When the overture to *Mireille* was played at a Gounod memorial concert in London in 1893, George Bernard Shaw, who called Gounod "our nineteenth-century Fra Angelico," wrote that "in the sixties the Parisian critics found [*Mireille*] Wagnerian: nowadays the abyss of erroneousness—not to say downright ignorance—revealed by such an opinion makes one giddy."

GOUNOD: *Mireille*

*Die Meistersinger von Nürnberg. Autograph manuscript of the 1862 libretto. 84 p. 29 × 23 cm.
First performance: Munich, 21 June 1868.
Gift of Mr. Arthur A. Houghton, Jr.*

In 1845, on doctor's orders, Wagner took a rest cure at the Bohemian town of Marienbad. He was there to recuperate from his recent exhausting work on *Tannhäuser*, but he was not idle for long: in July he wrote the first prose draft of what would become *Die Meistersinger von Nürnberg*, and from August to November he outlined and completed the libretto for *Lohengrin*. In "A Communication to My Friends" (1851), Wagner explained the original motivation behind his interest in the *Meistersinger* story: "Just as a comic satyr play followed the tragedy in the Athenian theatre, so I suddenly had the idea of a comedy that could follow my 'Singers' Contest at Wartburg' [that is, *Tannhäuser*] as a truly relevant satyr play. It was the 'Mastersingers of Nuremberg' with Hans Sachs at their head." The 1845 *Meistersinger* draft differs considerably from the form the text would take when Wagner resumed work on it some sixteen years later. The figure of Sachs, for example, is aggressive and irritable, unhappy almost to the point of bitterness at the conservative, rule-bound pedantry of the mastersingers' guild; the guild, in turn, mistrusts Sachs and questions his artistic probity. But in the final version, as Ernest Newman writes, "Sachs bemoans not his personal exasperation and lack of recognition as a poet, but the folly of humanity in general." Wagner both broadened and deepened Sachs's character and refined its dramatic focus; instead of the cynical, truculent figure of 1845, we find a more resigned man, one who accepts the course of his life benignly. This later Sachs is still concerned with tradition and the nobility of his art, but he approaches challenge and disappointment with the wisdom and tolerance of age.

In the 1851 "Communication" Wagner wrote that his friends suggested he write an opera "in an altogether lighter genre; they believed that this would open the doors of the German theatres to me, and so bring a beneficial change to my circumstances." It was in part with this same intent that he returned to *Meistersinger* in 1861. It had been eleven years since a new work of his had been performed (*Lohengrin*, in 1850); there was little hope that *Tristan und Isolde*, completed in 1859, would soon be staged; and the vast tetralogy of *Der Ring des Nibelungen*, on which he had been working since 1848, could not be completed in the foreseeable future. So, in October 1861 he proposed to Schott, his publisher, the scheme for a popular comic opera of modest scale that, unlike *Tristan und Isolde*, "will not call for an outstanding tenor—and this, as things are just now, is almost everything—nor for a great tragic soprano, which is a good deal." What happened, in fact, was that *Die Meistersinger von Nürnberg* was not finished until 1867, called for a tenor and soprano of the first order, included a bass-baritone role that is among the most taxing in the repertory, was the longest opera

ever written, and, when published, the largest score yet printed.

Wagner wrote a second and third prose scenario in mid-November 1861; shortly before, on a train trip from Venice to Vienna, he had conceived "with greatest clarity" the prelude to the opera. The poem itself, completed on 25 January 1862, was written in 30 days in the Hôtel Voltaire in Paris. On 25 September, Wagner sent a fair copy of the libretto to Schott, who published it in facsimile around Christmas; the facsimile was reprinted in 1893, and a third printing is scheduled for 1983, the hundredth anniversary of Wagner's death. It is this state of the libretto which is shown in the Morgan manuscript. The opera was completed on 24 October 1867; in the 22 years since the Marienbad draft, Wagner had composed *Lohengrin*, *Das Rheingold*, *Die Walküre*, two-thirds of *Siegfried*, and all of *Tristan und Isolde*, and had prepared the Paris version of *Tannhäuser*.

Among the many points of difference found in comparing this 1862 libretto with the text as it appears in the completed opera, one might be singled out. In the 1862 version, the Prize Song that Walther von Stoltzing sings at the end of Act III is virtually an exact repetition of the one he sang in Sachs's shop earlier in the act—the so-called Morning Dream Song. On 12 March 1862—that is, *before* he had begun even preliminary composition drafts for Act I—Wagner wrote to his close friend Mathilde Wesendonk quoting the opening text and music of the song. (The text begins: "Fern meiner Jugend goldnen Thoren"; the melody leaves one grateful that Wagner did not always rely on first inspirations.) Over four years later he wrote to King Ludwig II of Bavaria: "I am well into the [music of the] third act, and one of these days I shall have to write the words of Walther's Prize Song." The preliminary composition draft for Act III was begun on 2 October 1866, but once again, as in 1862, Wagner had already sketched the new Prize Song (the sketch is dated 28 September; it does, in fact, have the new words, but they were added later). This new Prize Song tune did not come easily; there are a number of drafts, showing heavy reworking, that suggest how much trouble the new melody gave. Having arrived at the new form of the melody, though, Wagner still had new words to write for it. (One sketch survives with the now-familiar Prize Song music, but with a text beginning "Minnig und mächtig in Lieb' und Leid"; the final song, as we know it today, begins "Morgenlich leuchtend in rosigem Schein.") Once having established the definitive tune, Wagner was apparently unwilling to adjust it to the new words. As a result, there are small problems of declamation in the final Prize Song.

Another problem remained: Wagner's keen dramatic sense made it clear to him that Walther's Prize Song could not be an

Thürme und Bogen,
Häuser, Strassen breiten sich:
durch die Thore zog ich ein;
Dünkte mich
ob er kenn' sie wieder:
auch der alte Flieder
lud mich ein sein Gast zu sein;
auf die müden Lieder
labendlich
goss er Schlaf mir aus,
gleich wie im Vaterhaus.
Ob ich die Nacht
dort wohl geträumt hab', ob gewacht?"

Das Volk
(Leise unter sich.)
Das ist was andres! Wer hätt's gedacht?
Was doch recht Wort und Vortrag macht!

Die Meistersinger
(Leise [unter sich.])
Ja wohl! Ich merk'! 's ist ein ander Ding,
ob falsch man, oder richtig sing'.

Sachs.
Zeuge am Ort!
Fahret fort!

Walther.
"Traum
meiner thäng gold'nen Jugend,
wandest du mich
durch der Mutter zarte Tugend?
Winkt sie mir nach,
folg' ich und fliege
über Stadt und Länder heim zur Wiege,
wo mein' die Traute harrt. –
Kaum
dass ich nah' zu sehn ihr glaube,
blendend und weiss
schwebt sie auf als zarte Taube,
pflückt dort ein Reis,
ob meinem Haupte
hält sie's kreisend, dass ich's raube,
in holder Gegenwart. –
Morgenlicht
dämmerte da wieder:
scherzend und spielend
Täubchen immer ferner wich;
fliegend und zielend
zu den Thürmen lockt es mich;
flattert über Häuser hin
setzte sich
auf dem Haus, dem Flieder
gegenüber, nieder,
dass ich dort das Reis gewönn',
und den Preis der Lieder.
Morgenlicht
hab' ich das geträumt:
nun sagt mir ungesäumt,
was wohl am Tag
der holde Traum bedeuten mag?"

WAGNER: *Die Meistersinger von Nürnberg*

exact repetition of the Morning Dream Song. As Cosima Wagner wrote to King Ludwig early in 1867: "Wagner lately came to the conclusion that it was absolutely impossible to have the same poem sung twice in the same act. It must be the same but different." Wagner's solution was to have the Prize Song be an interpretation of the Morning Dream Song: the beautiful, incorporeal woman of the dream is, in fact, Eva (in Paradise) and the actual Eva of the opera, his "prize." At line six of the Prize Song, Kothner, a mastersinger who has been holding the text for Walther to sing from, lets it drop, allowing Walther to continue on his own inspiration, recasting his song in a way that is both familiar and new.

The Morgan manuscript was once owned by Kaiser Wilhelm II who, according to a long-standing story, showed it to Pierpont Morgan and George Clifford Thomas, a Philadelphia banker and philanthropist. Both men admired the document and Wilhelm (so the story goes) offered it as a gift to one of them—to be decided by the toss of a coin. Mr. Thomas won. The libretto was acquired by Dr. A. S. W. Rosenbach, the noted Philadelphia bibliophile and dealer, from the Thomas estate sometime after 1909, and was purchased from the firm by Mr. Arthur A. Houghton, Jr., in 1951. He gave it to the Morgan Library in 1974 in honor of the Fiftieth Anniversary of the Library as a public institution. Unlike Walther von Stoltzing, Mr. Morgan lost the contest but, through Mr. Houghton's most generous gift, his Library eventually gained the prize.

Wagner gave the full-score autograph manuscript of *Die Meistersinger* to King Ludwig for Christmas in 1867; it is now housed in the Germanisches Nationalmuseum in Nuremberg. The Bayreuth archives contain extensive sketches and drafts for both text and music. The Morgan Library also owns the full-score proof sheets of the opera, extensively corrected for (but not by) Wagner.

La Gioconda. Sketches, drafts, and full-score material for all but Act IV. ca. 800 p. various sizes.
First performance: Milan, 8 April 1876.
Mary Flagler Cary Music Collection.

Ponchielli did not achieve a major success on the operatic stage until the age of 38, when a revised version of his early work *I promessi sposi* was performed at the Teatro dal Verme in Milan (1872). Shortly afterward Ricordi purchased the score, putting the composer's music into print for the first time, and commissioned *I Lituani*. This and each of Ponchielli's following operas were well received and his career became secure, but of his nine completed operatic works only *La Gioconda* holds the modern stage to any extent.

Although *La Gioconda* scored an immediate success upon its première at La Scala in 1876, Ponchielli soon began altering it for a Venetian production later the same year. Revision continued for succeeding performances and by the time the opera returned to La Scala in 1880 it had undergone numerous major changes. The Cary manuscript contains many pages of full score representing material removed from the autograph and replaced by revisions. Among this music are the finales of the first three acts in the form in which they must have been first performed, and much of a second version of the Act I finale, all strikingly different from the corresponding final versions. Act I originally concluded with a festive "Coro della cuccagna" after a scene in which Gioconda laments her lost love. Apparently for the Venetian performance, Ponchielli added a choral *preghiera* to Gioconda's lament and composed a new closing chorus in the form of a *furlana* (a type of dance). Ultimately the composer removed the voice parts from the *furlana* and placed the *preghiera* after rather than before it, achieving a more poignant ending for the act. In the original Act II finale, Alvise boards the ship and, in a rather static trio, confronts Laura, before she escapes, and Gioconda. The final version eliminates this scene and introduces the dramatic duet between Gioconda and Enzo that now constitutes the bulk of the number. The ensemble finale of Act III originally consisted of a scena, in which Alvise reveals Laura's body, followed by a traditional *adagio* and *stretta*. Ponchielli rewrote this entire finale, abandoning the *stretta* and saving the unveiling of the deathbed for a powerful conclusion to the number.

Alvise's aria in Act II caused the composer considerable trouble. When first presented at La Scala, this act began with the aria "Colla stola e colla croce," in which Alvise ironically describes his plans for both Laura's funeral and the upcoming party. For the Venetian production Ponchielli replaced this number with a romance for Laura and added another aria for Alvise immediately before the finale. Even prior to setting Alvise's new text, however, the composer expressed dissatisfaction with its bitter, cynical nature, preferring that the would-be murderer "should be affected somewhat by remorse, by remembrance of the past" as he gazed on the body of his wife, who he thought was dead. Ponchielli finally reverted to his original scheme, removing Laura's romance and the new bass aria and placing the aria for Alvise we know today at the opening of the act. From the second of Alvise's two discarded arias the librettist, Arrigo Boito, salvaged the lines "Death is nothingness / Heaven is an old wives' tale," reusing them in Iago's "Credo" when he collaborated with Verdi on *Otello*.

Additional material in the Cary manuscript testifies to the less significant revisions made in the "Coro d'introduzione," two of the duets in Act II (Laura-Enzo and Laura-Gioconda), and all the numbers in Act III not mentioned above. The composer's continual reworking of musical ideas can be further observed in the vast quantity of sketches and drafts for the opera. Reproduced here is a sketch page filled with different versions of the opening four-bar phrase of La Cieca's romance "Voce di donna o d'angelo." Although the final form of this melody has not yet emerged, the sketch has clearly established the opening rhythm of the finished version. The laborious working-out of this melody, which recalls Beethoven's sketching procedures, continues onto additional pages in the manuscript.

The Cary Collection also contains about 800 pages of drafts and sketches for Ponchielli's *I Lituani*; the full-score autographs of both *Gioconda* and *Lituani* are in the Ricordi archives, Milan.

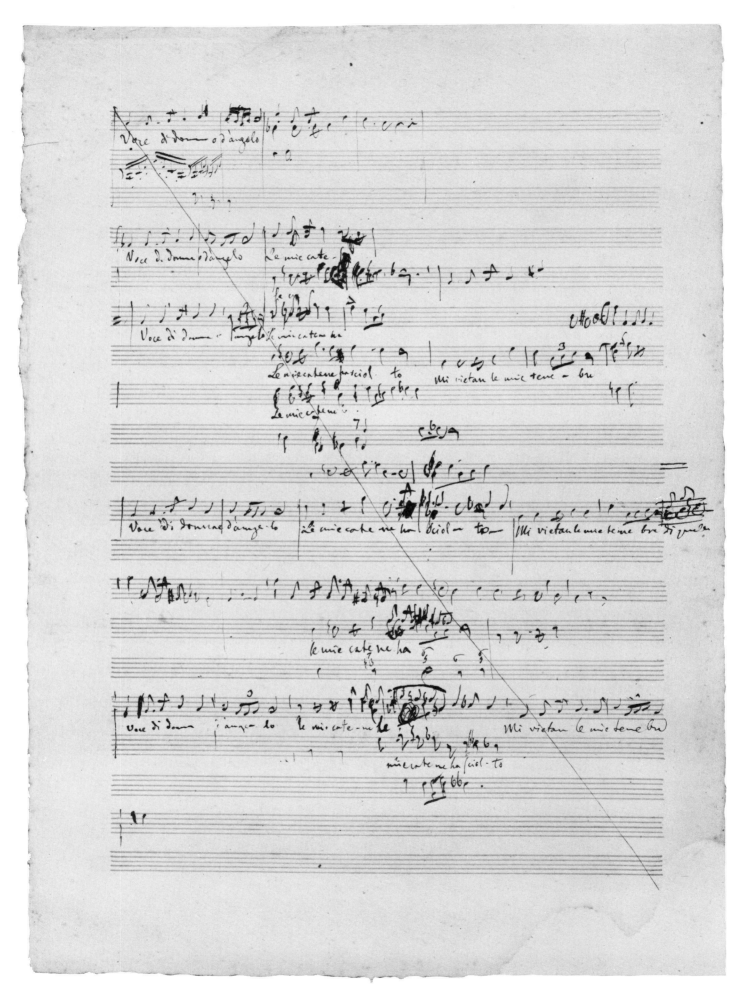

Ponchielli: *La Gioconda*

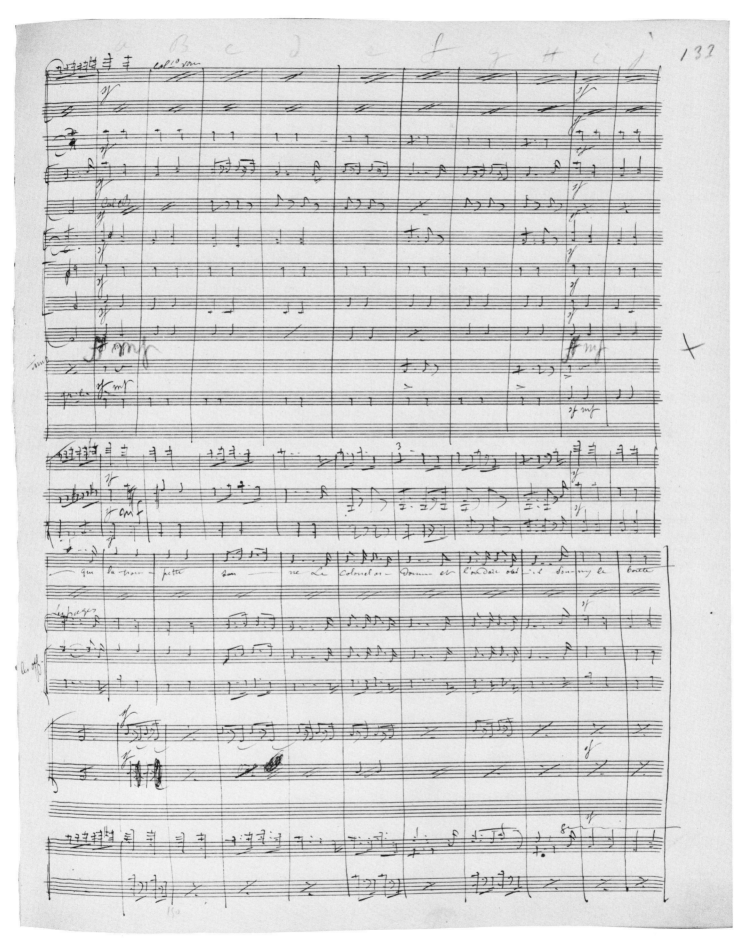

LECOCQ: *Le petit duc*

77

　　　　　　　　　CHARLES LECOCQ, 1832–1918.

Le petit duc. Autograph manuscript of the full score. 446 p. 34 × 26 cm.
First performance: Paris, 25 January 1878.
Mary Flagler Cary Music Collection.

Lecocq, in his day, was among the most successful composers of operettas—or *opéras comiques*, as he preferred to call a number of his works. With Hervé and Offenbach, he enriched the genre of light, graceful theatre pieces that have entertained generations of Parisians and, in Offenbach's case, a more international audience. Among the three, Lecocq possessed the most solid technical resources, although he rarely attained the heights that have assured Offenbach his permanent place in the world repertory.

Lecocq studied harmony with François Bazin; among his classmates was Jules Massenet, whom Bazin dismissed from the class for lack of talent, or simply owing to an antipathy to his musical style. (Ironically, Massenet was to assume Bazin's position on his retirement.) Lecocq reported that his composition teacher, Fromental Halévy, rarely explained his critiques, merely commenting "Not bad, that, but I don't like it!"

The Belgian musicologist Fétis, who did not hold Offenbach's music in high esteem, wrote that while Hervé and Offenbach lowered their musical language to accommodate public taste, the weakness of their early technical schooling allowed them no other resource than flattering the grosser instincts of their audience. Lecocq, he felt, demonstrated the most laudable respect for his art, and tended to refine the taste of his listeners. Fétis, like many writers after him, praised the grace, the elegance, the finesse, and the charm of Lecocq's best work.

Lecocq's most famous piece, and his own personal favorite, was *La fille de Madame Angot* (1872); it was his greatest popular triumph, and ran for 400 consecutive performances at the Folies-Dramatiques. *Le petit duc*, which is still in the French operetta repertory, tells of the young Duke of Parthenay who marries the even younger Blanche de Cambry; on their wedding day Blanche is sent off to an academy for young girls of noble birth, and the duke is put in command of the family regiment, the Parthenay Dragoons. As the first act closes, the duke (now a colonel), his officers, and the ladies of the court sing the lively ensemble shown here: "Que la trompette sonne, le colonel ordonne et l'on doit obéir" ("Let the trumpet sound, the colonel commands and you must obey"). The rest of the work relates the duke's attempts to find and win back his bride. The libretto, written in the freshest comic-opera vein, is by Henri Meilhac and Ludovic Halévy, best known as the librettists of Bizet's *Carmen*, as well as ten of Offenbach's operettas.

Le petit duc arrived in New York in 1879, playing first in English (17 March), and then in French (12 April). It is of interest to note that between 23 April and 12 May one could have seen productions of *Le petit duc* and Sullivan's *Cox and Box* (at the Park Theatre, Brooklyn), and of Offenbach's *Madame Favart* (at Haverly's Theatre, Manhattan); the manuscripts of all three works are owned by the Morgan Library.

The Pirates of Penzance. Autograph manuscript of the full score. 2 vols. 33 × 24 cm.
First performance: New York, 31 December 1879.
Purchased on the Fellows Fund, 1966.

In 1879 what came to be known as "the *Pinafore* craze" swept American theatres. Gilbert and Sullivan's *H.M.S. Pinafore*, first given in London in May 1878, achieved in this country a popularity that had no precedent in our theatrical history. On 19 March 1879 the Philadelphia correspondent for the London *Times* reported: "Such a furore as this opera has created I have never known before in the history of the American stage." More than 150 productions of *Pinafore* were to appear in over 60 American cities; in New York alone eight theatres played it simultaneously. All of these productions had one thing in common: they were wholly unauthorized, either by Gilbert, Sullivan, or Richard D'Oyly Carte, impresario of the newly created D'Oyly Carte Opera Company. There were no international copyright laws in force at that time, and for the D'Oyly Carte triumvirate the American piracies were doubly frustrating: first, no royalties were received from any of the numerous *Pinafore* productions; second, few of these performances bore the faintest resemblance to the authorized version. Gilbert, Sullivan, and D'Oyly Carte were not only deprived of the financial rewards that should have been their due, but their works were being presented in states further and further removed from the carefully planned original. When, in June 1879, D'Oyly Carte saw a performance of *Pinafore* in New York, he reported to his colleagues in London: "The people had all excellent voices—surprisingly good some, but not the remotest idea how to play the piece. The acting, costumes, time of music, etc. were too atrociously bad for words to express."

To counter this deplorable situation, Gilbert, Sullivan, and D'Oyly Carte planned a two-pronged attack: they would come to New York and mount an authorized production of *Pinafore*; then, capitalizing on the *Pinafore* craze, they would introduce a new work. By mid-summer 1879 Gilbert and Sullivan had established the general plan of the new opera; on 5 November they arrived in New York, D'Oyly Carte a week later. The first performance of their version of *Pinafore*, on 1 December, was a revelation to the local critics, one of whom wrote: "We've seen *Pinafore* as a comedy, we've seen it as a tragedy, but the play these Englishmen have brought over is quite a new play to us, and very good it is." (Sullivan conducted—and, as the New York *Herald* of 2 December reported: "It was known to but a few persons in the audience that Mr. W. S. Gilbert was among the chorus, personally superintending the movements on stage.") Sullivan reported to his mother that it was "a success unparalleled in New York. At last I really think I shall get a little money out of America. I ought to, for they have made a good deal out of me." The reviews were uniformly favorable; the *New York Tribune* offered an especially perceptive appreciation: "It is one of the most adroit and delicate of satires upon the absurdities of the conventional Italian opera; not a broad burlesque, but a travesty so witty, and so elegant that it may be called a masterpiece."

The month of December was now devoted to the second stage of D'Oyly Carte's American campaign. Gilbert, drawing on the theme of an earlier collaboration, the operetta *Our Island Home* (music by German Reed), had largely completed his libretto for *The Pirates of Penzance* the previous summer. Sullivan had sketched most of the music, but in early December made a distressing discovery, as he wrote to his mother: "I am working night & day on the 1st Act—the 2nd is done and in rehearsal. . . . I fear I left all my sketches for the 1st Act at home, as I have searched everywhere for them. I would have telegraphed for them, but they would not have arrived in time." Sullivan has provided a fairly detailed description of his composing method, so we know what sort of material those sketches contained, and can appreciate how important they were to him. After he and Gilbert had decided first on a general plot, then a detailed story line, Gilbert worked out the libretto, with lyrics, and sent them to the composer. "The first thing I have to decide upon is the rhythm," wrote Sullivan, "and I arrange the rhythm before I come to the question of melody." Next he sketched the melody "in hieroglyphics which, possibly, would seem undecipherable. . . . When I have finished the sketches the creative part of my work is completed." Following revisions, Sullivan prepared the vocal parts, which were reproduced by copyists, and rehearsals began. After singers' parts had been learned and all stage business set, Sullivan orchestrated the piece, and it was ready for performance.

Gilbert, meanwhile, had had numerous states of the libretto "printed as manuscript"; these, according to Reginald Allen, "more readily won favor with managers, were easier for him to work with making daily changes, and were clearer and more accurate than the copyists' drafts made for use at rehearsals. So, as soon as he completed a manuscript libretto, it was invariably set in type. From then on, author's alterations involved endless resettings."

In New York, Gilbert and Sullivan were now faced with a frantic month of trying to recreate the missing sections of *Pirates*, casting and supervising rehearsals of the new work, and looking after the now-authentic *Pinafore*. Act I of *Pirates* was finished on 29 December; D'Oyly Carte reported in 1902 that Sullivan had been able "to reproduce a considerable part of it—almost note for note, as he subsequently discovered on comparing the new work with the old score." All that remained was the overture, which Sullivan finished at 5:00 A.M. on 31 December, the day of the première. But that New Year's Eve performance was not, in fact, the very first. The day before, at the Royal Bijou theatre in Paignton, on the Devonshire coast, a single performance of *Pirates* had been given, and for one reason only: to secure British copyright. The first-string touring *Pinafore* company was playing in nearby Torquay, and an odd pre-production première it must have been: the only full rehearsal of *Pirates* the company held was on 29 December, on the stage of the Torquay theatre, after a performance of *Pinafore*. A little more than twelve hours later, writes Mr. Allen, "the tired *Pinafore* company were giving a strange rendering of the new opera—scarcely a performance in any accepted sense—dressed in their *Pinafore* costumes augmented by colored handkerchiefs, worn on the head, to indicate who were pirates, and (understandably) carrying their parts on stage with them."

In New York, the true première production of *Pirates* was greeted with great popular acclaim; the press, engaging in the inevitable comparison with *Pinafore*, was by and large favorable, although some reviewers doubted that the new work would ever attain the success of its predecessor. The singular exception to an otherwise well-conceived cast was Hugh Talbot, whose dismal performance as Frederic prompted one critic to recall George Eliot's quip that when Nature made a tenor she spoiled a man. Sullivan called him "an idiot—vain and empty-headed. He very nearly upset the piece on the first night as he didn't know his words, and forgot the music. We shall, I think, have to get rid of him." (There must have been a critical shortage of adequate tenors, for Talbot stayed with the company for over four months.) Immediately following the première, determined to thwart any "piracies of Penzance," Gilbert, Sullivan, and Carte organized three additional companies which, by the end of their respective tours in July, had played over 550 performances in more than 100 cities from Boston to Omaha to San Francisco.

The Morgan Library houses the most comprehensive collection anywhere of source material for the study of Gilbert and Sullivan. In addition to *Pirates*, the Library owns Gilbert's manuscript of the libretto for Act I of the opera and the autograph manuscripts of *Cox and Box* and *Trial by Jury*, and has on deposit the manuscript of *H.M.S. Pinafore*.

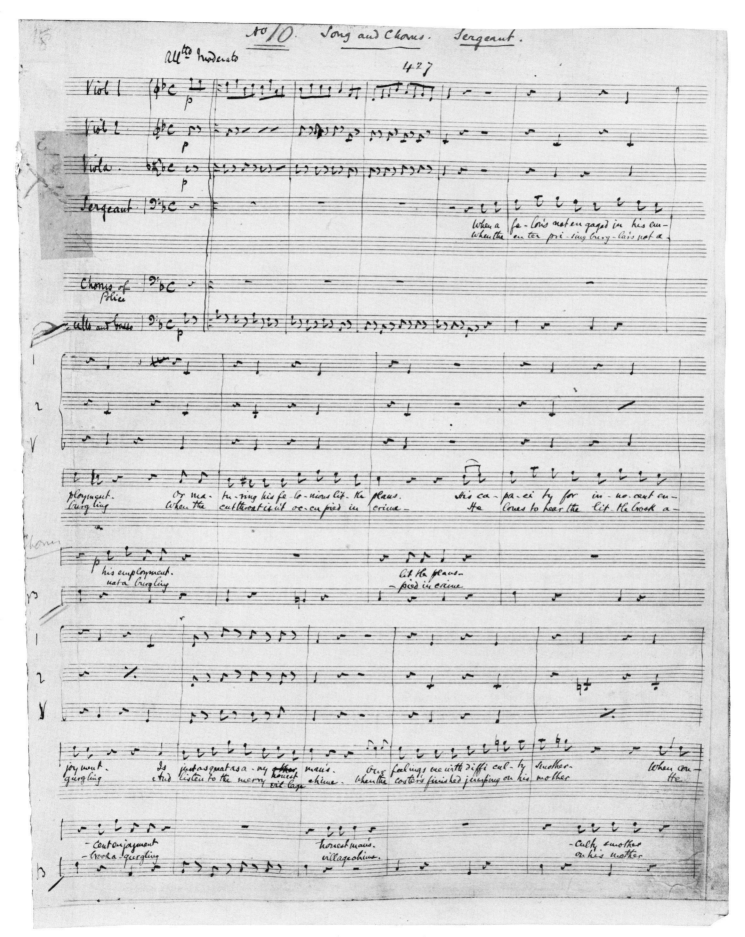

SULLIVAN: *The Pirates of Penzance*

Les contes d'Hoffmann. Sketchbook. 134 p. (of which 48 contain sketches for the opera). 26 × 34 cm.
First performance: Paris, 10 February 1881.
Mary Flagler Cary Music Collection.

When Offenbach died on 5 October 1880 he left *Les contes d'Hoffmann* incomplete in more ways than one: he had not finished writing all of the numbers for the opera, and many of those he had composed were not yet in their final form. Death prevented him from realizing either goal; his working habits had contributed to his not fulfilling them. Offenbach was, above all, a man of the theatre. By the time he started *Hoffmann* he had written over 100 operettas and *opéras comiques*, and had long since mastered the craft of creating effective musical theatre. For Offenbach, the true measure of a work could only be taken by testing it on stage. After sketching and drafting one or two acts, he prepared a skeletal orchestral score with voice parts on their proper staves and piano reduction at the bottom of the page (the instrumentation came later); he then usually insisted on rehearsals—first reading, then singing—so he could *hear* the piece. After he and his librettist(s) had cast their critical eye over it, the work was cut, augmented, rearranged, and otherwise shaped to meet their musical and dramatic standards.

Modifications were also suggested—or demanded—by the impresario; since, in the case of *Hoffmann*, Offenbach died soon after stage rehearsals had begun, and since the impresario of the Opéra-Comique was the autocratic Léon Carvalho, it is not surprising that the *Hoffmann* première presented the work in a state far removed from that which it would have been in had Offenbach lived. The first edition of the piano-vocal score, which appeared, in accord with French practice, at the time of the première, is of little use in establishing an *Urtext*, since it transmits not so much the composer's intentions as a performing version of the opera put together by Carvalho (and others) following Offenbach's death.

All editors and opera directors have had to confront the one unarguable fact about *Les contes d'Hoffmann*: there never was, and never can be, a stage performance of the work as Offenbach conceived it. One can either print only those parts that Offenbach unquestionably wrote, the result being an opera that is too fragmentary to be staged; or one can complete the work, in which case it cannot truly be said to be by Offenbach. Of the many attempts over the past century to prepare a performing edition of *Hoffmann*, the newest is by far the most comprehensive and fully documented, and, there can be little doubt, will be the most controversial. The edition was made by Fritz Oeser and published in 1977; his extensive critical report on it appeared in 1981. There is no question that all who now write about *Les contes d'Hoffmann* are very much in Oeser's debt, regardless of their opinion of his editorial methods and conclusions. The following notes on the *Hoffmann* sketchbook draw heavily on Oeser's fundamental research.

Oeser's single most valuable achievement is to have brought together all sources that document Offenbach's own work on the opera, including a number of manuscripts that, until recently, have been either unknown or ignored. Among these are the orchestral scores of Acts III and V (in the Bibliothèque de l'Opéra, Paris), the Cary sketchbook, and over 1600 pages of sketches, drafts, autograph and copyist's scores (both piano-vocal and orchestral), soloist's and chorus parts, the orchestral score of Act IV, and parts of the text in the hand of Jules Barbier, the librettist. This material belongs to François Cusset, a great-grandson of Offenbach's living in Saint-Mandé, France; it was discovered by the French conductor Antonio de Almeida, another Offenbach specialist to whom all who write about the composer are deeply indebted. The orchestral scores of Acts I and II have not surfaced, and for now must be assumed to be lost. The numbering of the acts will here follow Offenbach's original plan: Act I, Act II (Olympia), Act III (Antonia), Act IV (Giulietta—the Venice Act, omitted at the first performance), Act V.

The Cary sketchbook contains material related to *Hoffmann* on 48 pages: Act I (19 p.), Act II (14 p.), Act III (12 p.), Act IV (3 p.). It is a kind of rough workbook in which Offenbach jotted down ideas he wished to retain, without regard for their continuity, their eventual location in the score, or whether they would ever find their way into any given work. These hastily written aide-mémoire are not always easy to decipher or identify: clefs and key and meter signatures are often absent, the placement of note heads is occasionally equivocal, accidentals must frequently be supplied, and texts are rarely found. Offenbach probably began the sketchbook around the end of 1876 and used it until the fall of 1878, about the time he began Act IV. More precise dating may be possible when other sketches in the book are identified.

Act I opens with a Chorus of Invisible Spirits ("Glou glou glou" etc.) that is found drafted on page 23 of the sketchbook. Most of the Act I finale is based on sketchbook material; it is, in fact, the only autograph source to verify that the whole finale originated with Offenbach. There is, however, no manuscript evidence for the closing measures of the act.

The first of Hoffmann's tales concerns his love for the puppet Olympia; her aria, in Act II, is among the more familiar pieces in the coloratura soprano's repertory. The aria survives in two versions, the second of which is sung today. The first version is found in two copyist's manuscripts, and is also drafted in the sketchbook, in G major, with the note "Chanson d'Olympia en F"—that is, Offenbach intended to transpose it down a tone. The four principal female roles in *Hoffmann*—Olympia, An-

OFFENBACH: *Les contes d'Hoffmann*

tonia, Giulietta, and Stella—were originally to be sung by Marie Heilbron, a young lyric soprano. Offenbach had written most of the parts when, in mid-1879, Heilbron was replaced by Adèle Isaac, a coloratura soprano. (Isaac had recently won acclaim in Gounod's *Roméo et Juliette* at the Théâtre-Lyrique. The tenor Jean-Alexandre Talazac, who sang Roméo to Isaac's Juliette, was the opening-night Hoffmann in 1881.) Offenbach had apparently planned to set Heilbron's aria a tone lower; he was now compelled to transpose the part up and add passages to display Isaac's vocal gifts. Olympia's aria in its final version contains an abundance of virtuosic embellishments that has ever since made it extremely difficult to cast the four roles for a single singer. Oeser prints the aria in G major, but we should not assume that the Ab version in the first edition would not have had Offenbach's approval. In July or August 1880 Isaac visited Offenbach in St.-Germain and asked that Giulietta's F-major song in Act IV be moved up to Ab. It appears that Offenbach's draft of this transposed version was among the last things that he wrote.

Undoubtedly the best-known melody from *Les contes d'Hoffmann* is that of the Barcarolle, which opens Act IV, and it comes as a surprise to many to learn that this gently rocking tune is taken from Offenbach's opera *Die Rheinnixen* (1864), where it suggests not the sway of a gondola on the Grand Canal but the flow of the Rhine, and where, instead of the familiar "Belle nuit, ô nuit d'amour, / Souris à nos ivresses!" of the Nicklausse-Giulietta duet, it is sung by a chorus of elves to the words "Komm zu uns und sing und tanze, / Komm in uns're[n] Rhein." The sketchbook contains a 44-measure piano score of the Barcarolle (without text)—the longest continuous draft found in it. While the idea of adapting the elves' chorus as the Barcarolle no doubt came from Offenbach himself, apart from the sketchbook there is no evidence to support that assumption; moreover, its presence there shows how early in the opera's conception he thought of using in *Hoffmann* music from previous works. As noted above, Act IV (Giulietta) was omitted at the first performance, and is not found in the early editions of the opera. In order to include the Barcarolle in the première, it was transferred to the Antonia act, which in turn was moved from Munich to Venice—a minor adjustment, since the city in which Antonia suffers is irrelevant—although the Barcarolle, when it does appear, serves no discernible dramatic function. The Giulietta act, with the Barcarolle, finally surfaced in the third edition of the piano-vocal score—but was wrongly placed, being printed before, not after, the Antonia act. As a result, the Giulietta act now required an ending, since it no longer flowed into Act V; that explains why the publisher commissioned from Ernest Guiraud the famous (and of course spurious) Septet.

Offenbach had already resorted to this practice of parody, or setting new words to old music, in Numbers 15 and 16 in Act III, where he borrowed, respectively, from his ballet *Le papillon* (1860) and the operetta *Fantasio* (1872); *Rheinnixen* was also used in Hoffmann's "Couplets bachiques," and for part of the "Quatuor avec chœur" in Act IV. It was, in fact, Offenbach's own use of parody that provided Oeser with his solution to completing the opera. In those sections of Acts IV and V for which no firm documentary source material is extant, Oeser used music from *Rheinnixen*, set mostly to text taken from Barbier's newly discovered libretto manuscript, to fill musical and dramaturgical gaps. His guiding principle was that no music should appear in his version of *Hoffmann* that was not by Offenbach, based either on the composer's own manuscripts (or copyist's manuscripts made from them) or, as a last resort, on material from *Rheinnixen*. (Oeser, to be sure, does keep the recitatives, some of which are by Guiraud, but also prints an alternative dialogue text, leaving the choice of sung recitative or spoken dialogue up to the opera director. There is little question that Offenbach would have preferred recitatives.) The Cary sketchbook played a small but by no means insignificant part in Oeser's reconstruction.

The Morgan Library owns a number of Offenbach operetta manuscripts, including all (or parts) of *Les bergers, Madame Favart, La permission de dix heures, Robinson Crusoé, Le roman comique,* and *Scapin et Mezzetin.*

JULES MASSENET, 1842–1912.

Manon, opéra comique en quatre actes et six tableaux. Poème de M.M. Henri Meilhac et Philippe Gille. Autograph manuscript of the piano-vocal score. 288 leaves. 35 × 27 cm.
First performance: Paris, 19 January 1884.
Mary Flagler Cary Music Collection.

In his *Recollections*, Massenet tells how he came to choose the story of Manon Lescaut for his new opera. Léon Carvalho, director of the Opéra-Comique, had shown Henri Meilhac's libretto of *Phoebé* to Massenet, but it did not appeal to him. Visiting Meilhac soon afterwards, the composer spotted a book on the librettist's shelves and cried out *"Manon!" "Manon Lescaut, do you mean Manon Lescaut?"* "No, Manon, just Manon, it is *Manon!*" The very next day Meilhac delivered a draft of the first two acts, and the other three followed in a few days; the final libretto was written in collaboration with Philippe Gille. Preliminary composition was begun in the summer of 1881; the score shown here was completed between May and October 1882, and the orchestration between March and July 1883. The first-night reviews were mixed, but *Manon* was a triumph with the public, and has remained one of the most widely performed of French operas. Massenet himself lived to hear of the 740th performance of his most successful work.

The Abbé Prévost's *Histoire du Chevalier des Grieux et de Manon Lescaut* appeared in 1731 as volume seven of his *Mémoires et aventures d'un homme de qualité.* Manon's story was deemed immoral by French authorities, the book was ordered seized, and its popularity was thus assured. It was set by Halévy as a ballet (1830), and as operas by Balfe (*The Maid of Artois* [1836]), Auber (1856), Richard Kleinmichel (*Schloss de l'Orme* [1883]), Puccini (1893), and Hans Werner Henze, whose *Boulevard Solitude* (1952) is loosely based on Prévost's story and quotes from both the Massenet and Puccini scores. Massenet himself wrote a sequel in *Le portrait de Manon* (1894), portraying Des Grieux at the age of 40 (Prévost's Des Grieux is seventeen); Massenet called it "a poetical souvenir of Manon long since dead." The major change made by the librettists of the 1884 *Manon* was to set the final scene, that of the heroine's death, on the road to Le Havre, rather than in Louisiana. (Puccini retained the American ending. The scene in the convent of St.-Sulpice was retained in Massenet's opera, but not in Puccini's, nor in Scribe's libretto for Auber.) As the title of the Morgan manuscript indicates, Massenet at this stage planned a four-act opera in six scenes: Act I (Scenes 1 and 2), Act II (Scene 3), Act III (Scenes 4 and 5), and Act IV (Scene 6). The final five-act disposition is Act I (Scene 1), Act II (Scene 2), Act III (Scenes 3 and 4), Act IV (Scene 5), and Act V (Scene 6).

We can follow the chronology of *Manon* almost on a daily basis, for Massenet's manuscript contains dozens of indications of date, place, time of day (he apparently favored working in the night and early morning), and occasionally, of the weather and his health and mood. On 16 May 1882—the earliest date in the manuscript—Massenet notes that four of his students are "en loge"—that is, in competition for the prestigious Prix de Rome; on 20 May they were accepted in the following order: Gabriel Pierné, Georges-Eugène Marty, Xavier Leroux, and Paul Vidal. On 4 July he announces that Marty and Pierné have been awarded the First and Second Grand Prix, respectively, and that Leroux has received mention. (Marty is no longer remembered; Pierné was a gifted composer and later had a distinguished career as a conductor.) On 9 July his students were again "en loge," now for the fugue competition (we are not told the results). On 30 July he notes that "I am to leave Paris this evening for Bayreuth: fourth performance of *Parsifal.*" Then: "Being unwell, I remain here." He spent August in Holland and Belgium, and we learn from the *Recollections* that while in The Hague he stayed in the very rooms once occupied by Prévost himself. "His bed, a great cradle shaped like a gondola, was still there." Back in Paris, the usual calm of his nocturnal working habits was broken: "16 October, 3:30 A.M. I finish my work dead tired. I have the pleasure of having next door on the right a violinist, to the left a pianist: it's hell!" Three days later, on 19 October, he finished the opera at 9:00 A.M.

The second act contains two of the best-known passages in the opera: Manon's "Adieu, notre petite table," in which she bids farewell to the table where she and Des Grieux enjoyed so many happy meals, and Des Grieux's "En fermant les yeux"—the first page of which is reproduced here—which tells of his dream of a white cottage deep in a forest; tranquil shade, birds singing. Paradise: but no, all is sad because Manon is not there. It's only a dream, Manon says; no, Des Grieux replies, it will be our life if you want it. It is a brief passage—only 23 measures—of the utmost melodic and harmonic simplicity, but it epitomizes Massenet's unquestioned gift for capturing a memory, a reverie, a fleeting emotion, with music that at once fixes the sensation in its dramatic moment, and lingers long after the event.

The full-score autograph of *Manon* is in the Bibliothèque-Musée de l'Opéra, Paris.

MASSENET: *Manon*

Puccini: *Le villi*

Le villi. Sketches for all but the Preludio and last two numbers; full-score material for the Parte sinfonica and last number. 158 p. various sizes.
First performance: Milan, 31 May 1884.
Mary Flagler Cary Music Collection.

Shortly after his graduation from the Milan Conservatory in July of 1883 Puccini began work on his first opera, a one-act composition originally entitled *Le willis*. The libretto had been derived by Ferdinando Fontana from a legend apparently of Slavonic origin. Composed for an opera competition sponsored by the publisher Sonzogno, the piece was written under tremendous pressure, for the deadline of 31 December 1883 allowed Puccini only four months in which to complete the music. The haste with which the score was written out seems to have been responsible for the failure of *Le willis* to receive even an honorable mention from the judges, who apparently found the manuscript illegible.

In April of the following year Puccini sang selections from the new opera, accompanying himself on the piano, at an elite private gathering held by a wealthy Milanese music lover. Among those present were some prominent members of Italian musical society, including Arrigo Boito, who were impressed enough by what they heard to arrange for a performance of the work at the Teatro dal Verme in Milan (which now has a Via Giacomo Puccini running along one side of it). The première aroused great enthusiasm from public and critics alike and prompted the publisher Giulio Ricordi to purchase the rights for *Le willis* and commission a new work from Puccini and Fontana. Ricordi then asked Puccini to rework the opera into two acts, with a view to performance in larger theatres. The successful première of this revised version took place on 26 December 1884 at the Teatro Regio in Turin, with the title Italianized to *Le villi*. The success was not repeated, however, with subsequent performances at La Scala in Milan and the Teatro San Carlo in Naples.

Although the opera retains the traditional division into self-contained numbers, it shows the influence of Wagner and his followers in the prominence of its orchestra. This prompted Verdi to make the following observation in a letter written about a week after the première of *Le willis*:

> I have heard good things of the musician Puccini. . . . It seems, however, that the symphonic element dominates in his work. All right, but it is necessary to be cautious. Opera is opera and symphony is symphony.

The "symphonic element" was integral to Puccini's musical style, however, and became increasingly pronounced in the composer's later work.

Not only do orchestral sections occur frequently in the opera, but the orchestra often dominates the voices. Some music was originally conceived as purely instrumental, with the voice parts grafted onto it only during revision. Such is the case with the pages reproduced here from the first movement of the *Parte sinfonica* (originally *Intermezzo sinfonico*). Neither this sketch, dated October 1883, nor the full-score fragment of this section includes the choral parts that were added in the revised version.

The full-score fragment of the concluding *Gran scena e duetto finale* also apparently represents the one-act version. It contains orchestral music to which Puccini added the voices of *spiriti interni* (offstage spirits) and *villi* (witch dancers) during the course of revision. He also expanded this number by introducing instrumental music from the second movement of the *Parte sinfonica* with choral lines added to it. In parts of both Anna's *Scena e romanza* and the lovers' *Duetto* Puccini seems to have worked out the music for the orchestra before that of the vocalists. The sketches for these two numbers include sections in which only the instrumental "accompaniment" appears, with the vocal parts not yet added.

The autograph manuscript of the first (one-act) version of *Le villi*, which is unpublished, is in the Ricordi archives, Milan.

Otello. Sketch for part of Act III, Scene 5. 2 p. 35 × 26 cm.
First performance: Milan, 5 February 1887.
Mary Flagler Cary Music Collection.

After the completion of *La traviata* in 1853 Verdi composed operas at an ever slower rate until he reached a stage of semi-retirement in the 1870's. He showed little interest in following *Aïda* (1871) with a new operatic work until his publisher Giulio Ricordi encouraged a collaboration with the librettist Arrigo Boito on a setting of *Othello*. Even after committing himself to the Shakespearean project Verdi was in no hurry to complete it and work progressed slowly and intermittently, interrupted by the revision of both *Simon Boccanegra* and *Don Carlos*. Once *Otello* was finished, however, over seven years after its inception, it emerged as one of the supreme achievements of Italian opera.

Verdi's tremendous admiration for Shakespeare had first borne fruit in his *Macbeth* (1847, revised 1865), which is among the earliest operas closely modeled on, rather than freely adapted from, a work by the great playwright. With *Otello* Verdi achieved a much more faithful and successful rendering of Shakespeare, owing both to the exceptional skill of his librettist and to his own greater maturity as an artist. The correspondence between the composer and Boito as they worked closely together reveals the far-reaching concern that both men had with preserving Shakespeare's intentions. Verdi allowed himself more freedom in shaping the music to the needs of the drama, for in his later years he felt less and less obliged to follow the traditional structural conventions of Italian opera. An unusually meticulous attention to dramatic detail is also evident in the *disposizione scenica* (staging manual) for *Otello*, which is more extensive and detailed than those that survive for other Verdi operas.

Verdi's drafts for all his operas from *Luisa Miller* (1849) through *Falstaff* (1893) are said to belong to his heirs in Sant'Agata, but, so far as we know, scholars have not been granted access to them since the 1940's. The sketch reproduced here, probably a fragment of the draft of *Otello*, involves part of the exchange in Act III between Iago and Cassio, with Otello adding asides as he listens unobserved. This early version of the passage differs from its final form primarily in the voice parts, and Verdi's revisions reveal his concern with the musical delineation of dramatic nuances.

Several of the alterations serve to strengthen the rhythmic pattern of alternating eighth notes and quarter notes in the parts of Iago and Cassio, unifying them and setting them off from Otello's. This rhythmic lilt also helps establish the mood of the conversation; the staging manual specifies that it should be carried on "with animation, with casualness, but always with great elegance." Another change occurs in Otello's music as he exclaims, "now he is telling him the manner, the place, and the hour," believing Cassio to be describing acts of adultery with Desdemona. The original eighth notes become agitated sixteenth-note figures more suitable to the "voice breathless, but full of indignation" called for by the staging manual, and the shorter note-values further separate Otello vocally from the other two characters.

The autograph manuscripts of most of Verdi's operas, including that of *Otello*, are in the Ricordi archives, Milan.

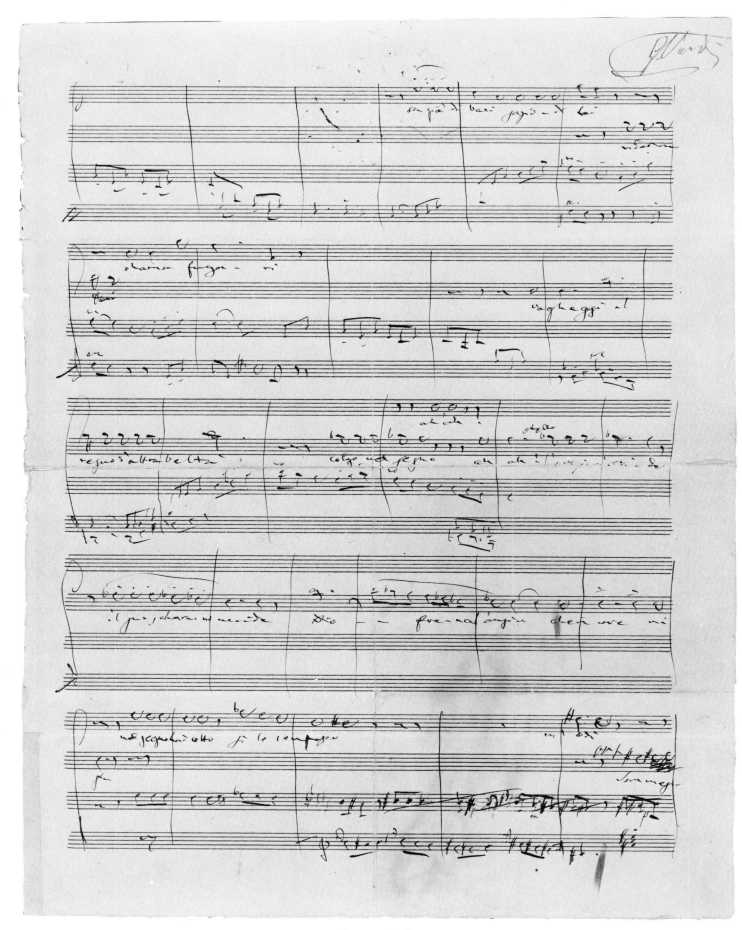

VERDI: *Otello*

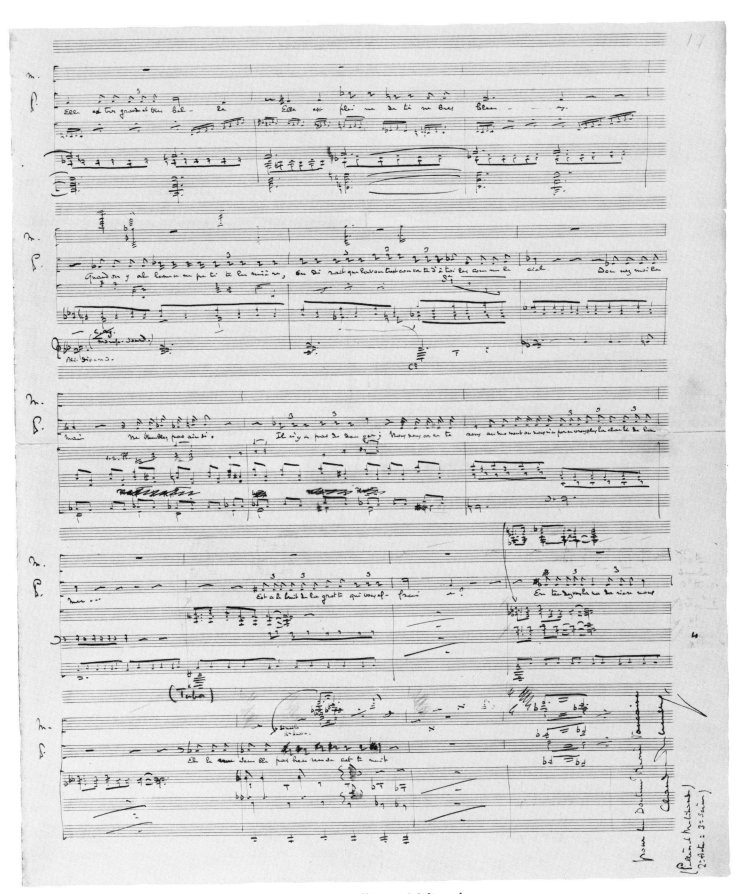

DEBUSSY: *Pelléas et Mélisande*

CLAUDE DEBUSSY, 1862–1918.

Pelléas et Mélisande. Autograph manuscript of the short score, dated September 1893–September 1901. 128 leaves, with music also on 11 facing versos. 39.5 × 30 cm.
First performance: Paris, 30 April 1902.
Frederick R. Koch Foundation Collection, on deposit in the Morgan Library.

Pelléas et Mélisande is profoundly unlike any other opera discussed in this catalogue. Its characters are not drawn from mythology, history, fantasy, or everyday life. They have little discernible past, undergo no apotheosis, and no future is suggested for them. The plot progresses not by discursive, narrative, or other conventional dramatic means, but by discrete and static tableaux, connected only by symbols, allusions, and a few recurring themes. The protagonists are not motivated by greed, lust, revenge, patriotism, or any other traditionally operatic force. The opera has no overture, no arias, no duets, all but no choruses. Musically, nothing in Maeterlinck's play calls for the passionate lyricism of the Italians (such as Verdi), the narrative rhetoric of the Germans (which in the 1880's meant only Wagner), or the tasteful melodiousness of the French (such as Massenet). The play was, in short—and seen with the advantage of hindsight—a libretto in search of a composer named Claude Debussy.

Roger Shattuck, in tracing the origins of the avant-garde in France from 1885 through the First World War, isolated four traits that characterize the arts of that era. Three of them are embodied to some degree in *Pelléas et Mélisande*: the cult of childhood established by the Romantics; the eruption of dream into waking experience; and a "cast of ambiguity or equivocal interpretation which can shape the surface and structure of a work." (The fourth trait, a pervading note of humor often taken to the absurd, is absent—unless, by extension, one sees the futile struggle of Maeterlinck's characters against fate and destiny, if not exactly humorous, at least touched by the absurd.) According to Shattuck, language for the Symbolists, such as Maeterlinck, "was endowed with a mystery of meaning that increased the number of different directions in which each word can point. . . . All this embracing of ambiguity makes the arts difficult of access and occasionally irresponsible. It often renders the extraction of a single meaning infeasible." While we could not hope to draw from *Pelléas et Mélisande* any single meaning—there most likely is not one—or to begin to suggest the levels of symbolism and ambiguity found in the play and opera, it might be of interest to look briefly at a few scenes and isolate one or two of the more exoteric symbolic elements from the many, ranging from the obvious to the impenetrable, that weave through the work.

The first scene of the play, which Debussy omitted, takes place at the castle gate and shows the servants washing the threshold and steps—a symbolic purification of the stage familiar from Greek theatre, and an action that finds a starkly contrasting counterpart in the last act. The porter tells the servants to wait for daylight; one servant replies, "I can see sun through the cracks," and, a few lines later, "the sun's up over the sea!" By the end of this brief scene, many of the symbols that will recur in *Pelléas et Mélisande* have been introduced: the gate, light (especially the sun), water, and the sea. Of these, perhaps light echoes with more, and more varied, reverberations, for it suggests among other things sight (and its opposite, blindness), knowledge, truth, enlightenment, life, security, clarity, openness, and hope.

In Scene 1 of the opera Golaud finds Mélisande by a spring in the forest; she has run away from her home—we are never told where that was—and is lost. Golaud, hunting a boar, has lost his way too. He persuades her to come with him to the castle: " . . . you cannot stay here alone in the wood all night. . . . The night will be very dark and cold." The dark forest, with nightfall approaching, represents Mélisande's flight from some unspecified but terrible past, her alienation from the world from which she has escaped, and a danger to them both from which Golaud offers refuge. (This scene contains at least one exchange that is silly or obscure depending on one's skill at reading between the lines: Golaud: "Do you ever close your eyes?" Mélisande: "Yes, yes, I close them at night.")

In Scene 2 Golaud, who has now been married to Mélisande for six months, is absent on an unnamed mission, and has sent a letter to his half-brother, Pelléas; their mother, Geneviève, reads it to Arkel, King of Allemonde and Golaud's grandfather. Golaud fears that he has lost favor with Arkel because he has married Mélisande instead of the princess Ursule. "But if he consents to welcome her as if she were his own daughter," Golaud's letter reads, "on the third evening after you receive this letter, light a lantern at the top of the tower that looks over the sea." Arkel consents to Golaud's return, and Geneviève tells Pelléas to see that the lantern is lit. Light, here represented by the lantern, is a symbol of welcome and reconciliation, telling Golaud that he may return. In lines omitted from the opera, Arkel, who is nearly blind, says to Geneviève: "One is always mistaken unless one closes one's eyes to forgive or to look more closely at one's own being." Here, blindness or closed eyes signify insight, another kind of knowledge. Light, like all symbols, carries different levels of meanings; it can enable one to see, literally, but can also, figuratively, illumine the inner world of the blind and the wise. Richard Langham Smith has written perceptively on some of the thematic links between Debussy and the Pre-Raphaelites. He notes how the illustrations Dante Gabriel Rossetti and William Holman Hunt made for several Tennyson poems find resonances in *Pelléas*: Mélisande's tresses ("plus longs que moi"), an outward stillness that often conceals profound inner drama, the juxtaposition of beauty and implicit violence, eyes as "lamps of the soul," a ship from an unnamed land with a lighted lantern, and so on.

Act II, Scene 1, "A Well in the Park," is for Pelléas and Mélisande alone. Light as vision is immediately introduced. Pelléas: "They say this was a well with miraculous powers. It would open the eyes of the blind. It is called Blind Man's Well." Mélisande begins to throw Golaud's ring into the air; the sunlight blinds her momentarily and the ring falls into the well. The loss symbolizes both her estrangement from Golaud and the growing intimacy between her and Pelléas. The web of symbols and allusions is especially dense here. When Golaud discovered Mélisande in the first scene of the opera, her crown had fallen into the spring; he offered to retrieve it but she begged him not to. Similarly, Pelléas now thinks he sees Mélisande's ring in Blind Man's Well, but she says, "No, no, that's not it, that's not my ring. My ring is gone. . . . I've lost it." And, as we learn when the next scene opens, while Pelléas and Mélisande were at the well, Golaud was out hunting; at the very moment Mélisande lost her ring Golaud's horse bolted and "ran like a blind idiot into a tree. I fell down and the horse must have fallen on top of me. . . . My heart felt as though it had broken in two."

Act IV, Scene 4, "A Well in the Park," is also for Pelléas and Mélisande alone. Mélisande enters and Pelléas tells her to "come here. Don't stay there, it's too bright in the moonlight. . . . We have so much to say to each other. . . . Come here, in the shadow of the trees." Mélisande wants to stay in the light, but Pelléas warns her that they could be seen from the windows of the tower. They are, of course, hiding; they are children, playing in the dark, afraid of being caught, and also illicit lovers who are using the cover of night to conceal their tryst. Pelléas again asks Mélisande to come where it's lighter; but she resists, saying: "We are much closer in the darkness." Among the many concepts that darkness denotes in Christian theology are sin, spiritual blindness, error, and wickedness: blindness, if willful, becomes sin. Suddenly, the castle gates close. The isolation is complete; they can no longer go back to a safe refuge. They are alone in the darkness with their growing passion—one adulterous in spirit if not in deed. They have confessed their love and are now driven by forces no longer within their power to control. Golaud has seen them; they embrace, oblivious to their fate. Pelléas: "The stars of heaven are falling." Mélisande: "On me as well!" Pelléas: "Again, yes, again, be mine!" Mélisande: "I'm all yours! all yours!" Golaud strikes down Pelléas with his sword; Mélisande flees in terror.

Maeterlinck's first scene of Act V, which Debussy omitted, takes place in a basement room in the castle; the servants are discussing the tragedy that has befallen Allemonde. Golaud and Mélisande had been discovered outside the gate—Golaud, his sword in his side, Mélisande wounded and near death. Their blood on the gateway complements the lustration that opened the play; the clear, purifying light in Scene 1 has been banished by the violence of that sanguinary night in which Golaud killed Pelléas, wounded Mélisande, and attempted suicide. Pelléas's body had been found at the bottom of Blind Man's Well, "but no one, no one has been able to see him." The light that had enabled Golaud to see Mélisande's crown, and Pelléas to see her ring, has failed. The blindness of both fate and of spirit have been visited on husband, wife, and lover; destiny, over which no man has control, has prevailed.

Four years before Debussy encountered Maeterlinck's play, he was asked what sort of poet could provide him with a suitable text for an opera. He replied, with remarkable prescience:

> One who, only hinting at things, will allow me to graft my dream upon his; who will not despotically impose on me the "scene to be set" and will leave me free, here and there, to show more artistry than he and to complete his work. . . . I shall not imitate the follies of the lyric theatre where music insolently predominates and where poetry is relegated to second place. In the opera houses they sing *too much*. One should *sing* only when it is worthwhile and hold moving lyrical expression in reserve. . . . I dream of poetic texts which will not condemn me to long, heavy acts, but will provide me with changing scenes, varied in place and mood where the characters do not argue but submit to life and destiny.

Debussy's music never threatens to overpower Maeterlinck's fragile, fragmented drama. Just as the playwright's symbolism and allusions point in various directions, so Debussy's shifting, unresolved chords do not always follow the lines of traditional harmonic progressions; each chord may imply several functions at once. His harmonic language is as ambiguous as Maeterlinck's verbal one; his music only suggests, Joseph Kerman writes, and in so doing supports the play. Ordinarily, characters as passive as Maeterlinck's would be totally unsuited to operatic treatment. But it is precisely because Debussy denied them the traditional operatic means of expressing themselves that Maeterlinck's shadowy, ambiguous, allusive drama is preserved.

For those who believe in astrological divination, it can be noted that Debussy and Maeterlinck were born within a week of each other; those who find the confluence of their arts sufficiently remarkable in itself may simply agree with Mr. Kerman: "Of all the ingenious, fortunate, magic convergences in the history of opera, *Pelléas* is surely the most extraordinary."

Leaf 17 of Act II of the present manuscript, which Debussy removed and gave to a Docteur René Vaucaire, was acquired by the Koch Foundation shortly after the rest of the autograph; that leaf, which now completes the manuscript, is reproduced here. Other important manuscripts of *Pelléas et Mélisande* include: preliminary drafts and sketches of Act I (fragmentary), Act II, Scenes 1, 2, and 3, Act IV, Scene 4, and Act V (54 leaves, in the André Meyer collection, Paris); a second draft of Act IV, Scene 4 (12 leaves, known as the Legouix manuscript, now on deposit in the Morgan Library); and a rejected draft of the same scene (20 leaves, known as the Bréval manuscript, now in the Bibliothèque Nationale, which also owns the full-score autograph of the opera). The Morgan Library also has on deposit the printed proof copy of the full score, corrected by Debussy, and owns a manuscript of Maeterlinck's *Pelléas et Mélisande*.

1906 — FREDERICK SHEPHERD CONVERSE, 1871–1940.

The Pipe of Desire. Autograph manuscript of the full score, dated 12 August 1905. 227 p. 33.5 × 26.5 and 39.5 × 28 cm.
First performance: Boston, 31 January 1906.
Gift of Mr. Converse.

The Pipe of Desire, described by Converse as a romantic grand opera, was composed between October 1904 and April 1905 at Harvard College, where he had been teaching since the fall of 1903. The one-act opera was first performed in Jordan Hall at the New England Conservatory of Music; the opening-night reviews gave lukewarm praise to the music, found the orchestration commendable, and came down heavily on the libretto. Not only was the story itself judged unoriginal, undramatic, and lacking in human interest: the controversy over opera in English was then, as now, much debated, and many critics simply deemed it a language unsuited to opera. Not so Converse, whose position was unequivocal: "Every nation in which the opera is a national art demands that the singing use the native tongue." The prejudice against opera in English, Converse argued, resulted from "the miserable translations in which operas, if sung in English, are usually presented."

Given Converse's lifelong advocacy of opera in the vernacular, it is regrettable that the text provided by George Edward Barton—he was an architect by profession—should have been so poorly suited as an opera libretto. Iolan, a shepherd, encounters fanciful creatures—elves, dwarfs, gnomes, water nymphs, sylphs—celebrating the first day of spring. The Old One, a symbol of ancient traditions and unchanging laws, possesses the pipe given to Adam by Lilith, "but its charm was rent by woman"; when played by mortal man, its tones arouse the yearning for earthly happiness and Edenic grace. Mocking the Old One's warnings, Iolan plays the pipe, and a vision of all his future desires appears. But when the Old One pipes, reality is revealed: Noaia, Iolan's betrothed, is ill; she makes an arduous journey to him, and dies. Iolan curses God, then denies Him, but eventually acknowledges that he has transgressed eternal laws and must pay the penalty. He sees a vision of Noaia and, calling to her, he dies.

That is, admittedly, not the stuff of which great tragedy is made. The protagonists' punishment is hardly commensurate with their misdeeds: the death of Noaia, who has done nothing wrong, is gratuitous. And inasmuch as Iolan's only wrongdoing seems to be that by an access of concupiscence he is supposed to have committed a mortal sin, it is difficult, at least by today's standards, to feel that his fate was warranted. One is, finally, left unmoved by the drama, and more than a little annoyed by Barton's murky moralizing.

The Pipe of Desire has left its mark on operatic history, however: on 18 March 1910 it became the first opera by an American composer to be performed at the Metropolitan Opera House. The decision to produce the work was made by Gustav Mahler, who conducted at the Metropolitan between 1908 and 1910. Except for the English soprano Leonora Speakes, the principal singers in the première were all American; it was conducted by Alfred Hertz. Converse gave this manuscript of the opera to J. P. Morgan on 15 June 1918, the third wedding anniversary of Emma Louise, Converse's eldest daughter, and Junius Spencer, Morgan's elder son.

Converse: *The Pipe of Desire*

UMBERTO GIORDANO, 1867–1948.

Marcella. Short-score draft. 210 leaves. 31.5 × 27.5 cm.
First performance: Milan, 9 November 1907.
Mary Flagler Cary Music Collection.

Giordano's operatic compositions span almost exactly the same period as Puccini's: his first opera, *Marina* (1888), appeared four years after Puccini's (*Le villi*), and his last, *Il re* (1929), was first performed three years after Puccini's *Turandot*, left incomplete at his death in 1924. The first operas of both composers were entered in the Sonzogno competition, inaugurated by the Italian publisher in 1883: *Le villi* lost to two otherwise forgotten operas; *Marina* lost to *Cavalleria rusticana* by the then little-known Pietro Mascagni. (For a discussion of *Le villi*, see p. 88.) Puccini, of course, would become the most successful composer of Italian operas in this century; Giordano's fame, however, rests on a single work, *Andrea Chénier.*

Marcella, called by Giordano an "idillio moderno" in three episodes, is characterized by a refined, delicate musical style that we do not immediately associate with turn-of-the-century Italian opera. Absent are the violent outbursts of primal emotions and the grandiose orchestral effects characteristic of many *verismo* operas—a genre, in fact, that contains far fewer operas than is commonly assumed. A first-night review said that "the opera is chiseled like a gem. . . . If inspiration is not always ruler and creator here, some details show an excellence of invention and workmanship." Giordano, writing to Luigi Illica a few days after the première, described the opera's reception: "You ask me about *Marcella*. Nothing different from all the first nights of our other successes which are being given in Milan: warmth, indifference; applause, opposition; *bis*, hisses; charming libretto, absentminded music; delightful music, worst libretto; first-rate performance, artists out of breath; vital opera, moribund opera; success, fiasco. [The critics] Macchi, Colantuoni, Pacchierotti howl as though I had stepped on their corns."

Most favorably received, it seems, was the second-act duet between Marcella and Giorgio. "Giorgio's song," wrote a critic, "sent a shudder of commotion through the hall. Impetuous, deafening applause broke out. They want a '*bis*,' they interrupt the performance; the song is repeated." The manuscript of Giorgio's brief aria, "O mia Marcella, abbandonarti?," is reproduced here.

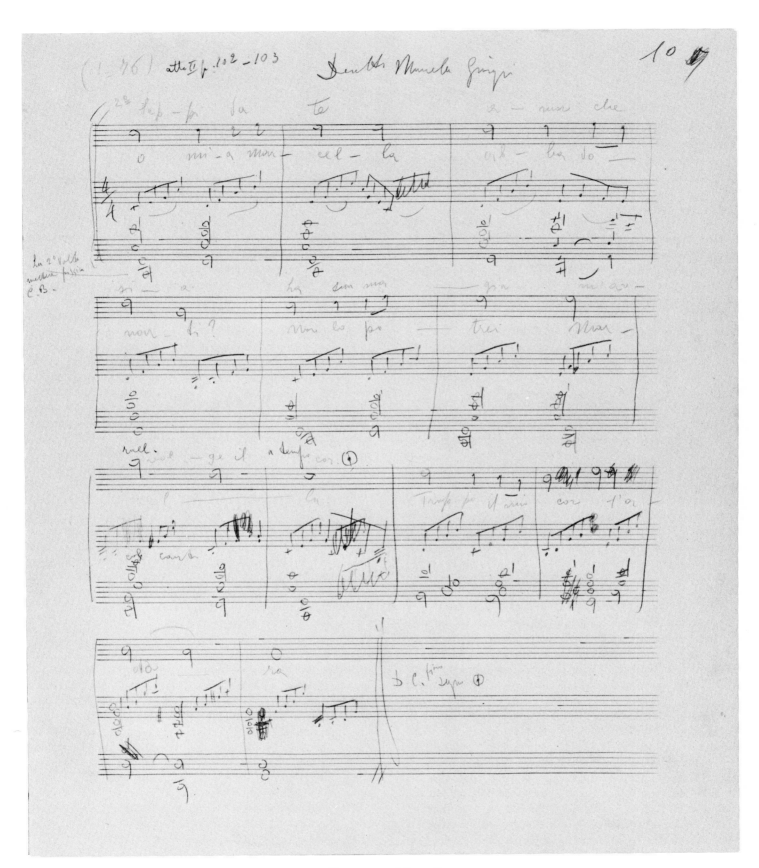

GIORDANO: *Marcella*

La fanciulla del West. Short-score draft of Acts I and II; sketch fragments for Act I. 347 p. various sizes.
First performance: New York, 10 December 1910.
Robert Owen Lehman Collection, on deposit in the Morgan Library.

Puccini saw David Belasco's play *The Girl of the Golden West* during a visit to New York early in 1907. Although at first not strongly attracted to this drama of the California gold-rush days, he eventually developed an enthusiasm for it and abandoned several other prospective operatic subjects in its favor. The resulting "American" opera had its première, appropriately, at the Metropolitan Opera House; it was one of the most spectacular and successful events in the theatre's history.

Puccini played a crucial role in shaping the libretto of *Fanciulla*. Carlo Zangarini, the first of the two librettists who worked on the opera, is reputed to have said that "the real librettist of *The Girl of the Golden West* was not himself—but Puccini." It was the composer's idea to set Act III in the California forest, rather than in the saloon dance-hall, and to incorporate a dramatic manhunt for the bandit, Johnson, into this act. At an early stage in the work Zangarini was obliged to undertake revisions because Puccini felt he "had taken too many liberties with the original." These were finished in late January 1908, and the composer was pleased enough with the result to begin composing the music shortly afterward, even though he felt some further textual alterations were necessary. (The Lehman manuscript contains a folio of preliminary sketches, including several important recurring themes used near the beginning of Act I, dated 1 March 1908, about a month after Puccini received the libretto. The first page of the draft of Act I bears the date 24 May 1908.) Puccini had apparently underestimated either the extent of the modifications that remained to be made or Zangarini's reluctance to carry them out, and in mid-April had Ricordi engage Guelfo Civinini to assist in rewriting the libretto, despite Zangarini's strong protestations. Puccini closely supervised this second librettist as he shortened and reworked the text.

Textual revision continued even after the music had been drafted. Johnson's arioso "Quello che tacete" from Act I, and Minnie's short response to it, were composed to words different from those found in the final version. This original text, in which the lovers describe their emerging feelings of mutual affection, is preserved in the draft of the opera; Puccini replaced it with a text that more vividly evokes these sentiments by depicting the emotions and physical sensations experienced by the lovers. A similar revision seems to have been made to the main portion of the love duet in Act II (beginning at "non ti lascio più"), for an early text of this section has been completely erased in the draft. The new words, a passionate declaration of the love between Johnson and Minnie, have been written over the erasures. Numerous minor textual alterations, which Puccini probably made without the aid of his librettists, are found throughout the draft.

Composing the music of *Fanciulla* was not an easy task for Puccini and occupied him for nearly two and a half years. Progress was seriously hampered by a long depression caused by his wife's accusations of infidelity and the resulting suicide of the girl on whom suspicion was falsely cast. The nature of the music itself also contributed to the slow pace. In his letters Puccini frequently refers to the difficulty he was having with the work, and at one point attributes it to "the distinctive and characteristic features" with which he hoped to endow the opera. He did indeed break new ground with *Fanciulla*, employing a more advanced harmonic idiom and a larger orchestra than in any of his earlier works.

The particular care devoted to the orchestration of this opera is reflected in the detailed indications of instrumentation that are found throughout the draft. Although Puccini apparently added some of these after he had worked out the music, most seem to have been written during the initial stage of drafting, indicating that the conception of the music was often intimately linked with specific orchestral sonorities.

The orchestra was of prime importance to Puccini and often dominates the voices in a *parlante* style; an example can be seen in the page from Act I reproduced here. The main melodic interest is in the orchestral music, which develops the important recurring waltz theme as Johnson and Minnie, alone in the saloon, converse with one another. This same theme receives a similar *parlante* treatment several pages earlier, against the voices of Nick, Rance, and the chorus. In both of these sections the orchestral music was composed first and the vocal music added later. (See *Le villi*, page 88, for similar examples of this.) The instrumental part and barlines are written in ink and the vocal music and text are notated in pencil, with many corrections made in pencil to the orchestral part.

The autograph manuscripts of nearly all of Puccini's operas, including that of *La fanciulla del West*, are in the Ricordi archives, Milan.

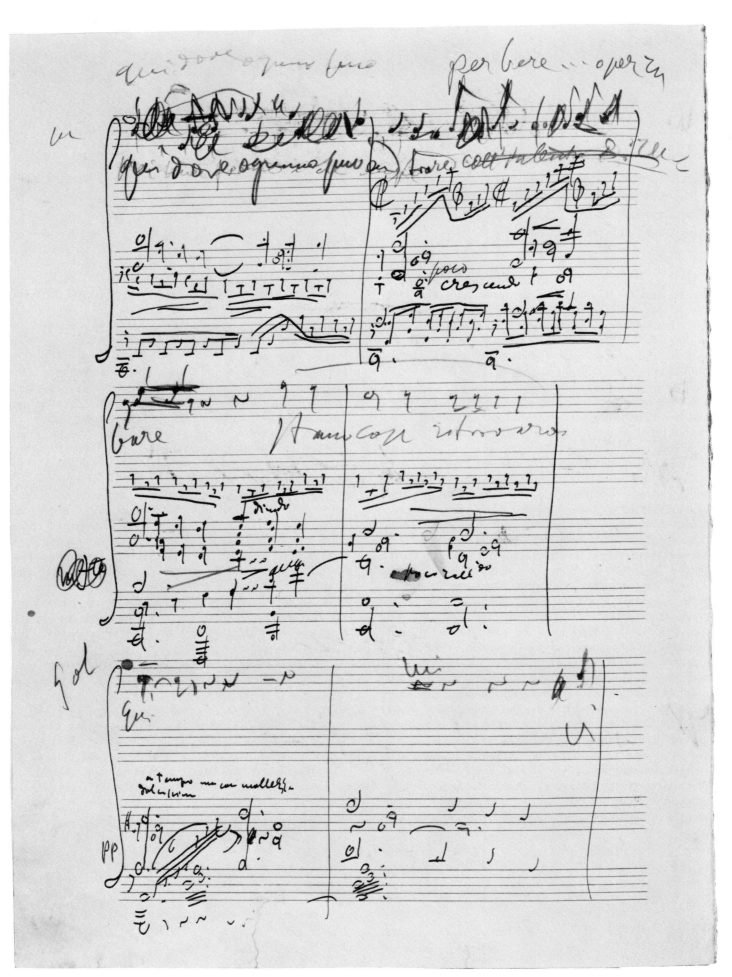

PUCCINI: *La fanciulla del West*

Il piccolo Marat. Autograph manuscript of the piano-vocal score of most of Acts I and II, signed and dated Rome and Ardenza, 1 May 1919–10 March 1920. 137 p. 33 × 24 cm.
First performance: Rome, 2 May 1921.
Mary Flagler Cary Music Collection.

With the première of *Cavalleria rusticana* on 17 May 1890, Mascagni won an immediate, and soon worldwide, renown enjoyed by few composers. (It was his fourth opera, but the first to be performed. The Morgan Library also has the manuscript of Mascagni's student cantata *In Filanda*, which he transformed, around 1880, into *Pinotta*, his first opera; it was not performed until 1932.) *Cavalleria*, now inextricably paired with Leoncavallo's *Pagliacci*, confirmed the public's taste for the veristic works that were to dominate Italian opera for a decade or so. Mascagni never again achieved the meteoric success that *Cavalleria rusticana* brought him; of his dozen or so later operas, only *L'amico Fritz* and *Il piccolo Marat* were to be received with much lasting enthusiasm. "Just when the cliché of Mascagni as a one-opera composer had come to seem irrefutable," writes William Ashbrook of *Marat*, "he unleashed a powerful score that has stirred audiences whenever it is given with a tenor capable of meeting its unremitting demands."

Mascagni had long cherished the idea of an opera on the subject of the French Revolution. (In 1890 and in 1901–03 he had considered, respectively, Charlotte Corday and Marie Antoinette for operatic treatment.) It is not surprising that in the politically and socially turbulent aftermath of World War I he should again have been drawn to a story of heightened collective emotions and of opposing individual passions, a scenario of contemporary relevance drawn from a momentous historical period. Mascagni insisted that the events in the opera be related as a fable: no mention was to be made of actual places, nor were figures of the period to appear; he thought it ridiculous to portray these figures on stage, and could not imagine Robespierre or Napoleon, Julius Caesar or Garibaldi, as operatic characters.

As formal work began on the libretto, Mascagni immediately encountered difficulties. When Giovacchino Forzano, the librettist, agreed to accept Mascagni's changes in the scenario but not those in the text, the composer turned to Giovanni Targioni-Tozzetti (the librettist of *Cavalleria rusticana*), who added new

verses and revised those of Forzano's that Mascagni had found unacceptable. Forzano resumed his work, but was then summoned to Turin by Giacomo Puccini to help in a production of Puccini's *Trittico* (for which Forzano had written the librettos of *Suor Angelica* and *Gianni Schicchi*); Mascagni again called on Targioni-Tozzetti, this time (among other modifications) to finish the love duet that concludes Act II and that was to elicit the greatest acclaim at the première. A review of the opening night describes the tumultuous reception: "The success culminated, and assumed absolutely hyperbolic proportions, after the second act. Two thousand people sprang to their feet in the overflowing boxes, the crowded stalls, the sold-out seats, the mezzanine, the loge."

Our manuscript apparently shows the first stage in composition; it agrees in major outline with the published piano-vocal score but varies in many minor (and a few larger) details. Missing from it are sections corresponding to pages 4–60 and 162–88 of the printed score. The love duet is longer by about 60 measures than its published version. Mascagni signed and dated each section as it was completed; the manuscript contains 50 such datings, allowing us to follow his progress, often day by day. He began on 1 May 1919 with Act II, then worked on both Acts I and II in May and June; Act I was completed on 12 June, Act II on 10 March 1920.

On 2 November 1919 he wrote to the critic Giovanni Orsini: "*Il piccolo Marat* is strong, it has muscles of steel. Its power is in its voice: it does not speak, it does not sing, it howls, howls, howls. I have written the opera with clenched fists, like my spirit. Do not look for melody, do not look for culture; in *Marat* there is only blood! It is the hymn of my conscience."

The full-score manuscript of *Cavalleria rusticana* and the piano-vocal score manuscript of *L'amico Fritz* are in the Memorial Library of Music, Stanford University. The Morgan Library has on deposit the full-score autograph of *Nerone*, Mascagni's last opera.

MASCAGNI: *Il piccolo Marat*

L'enfant et les sortilèges. Autograph manuscript of the piano-vocal score, dated "Divers lieux 1920–25." 75 p. 35 × 27 cm. First performance: Monte Carlo, 21 March 1925.
Robert Owen Lehman Collection, on deposit in the Morgan Library.

Ravel completed two operas: *L'heure espagnole* (1911), a work that captures the spirit of the Italian *opera buffa*; and *L'enfant et les sortilèges*, which has distant roots in the *opéra-ballet* of the late seventeenth and early eighteenth centuries but which is, in the history of operatic genres, *sui generis*. Ravel was faced, as were all composers of the post-Wagnerian generation, with discovering new forms for the lyric theatre. In his opinion, operatic forms had not progressed since Meyerbeer and Wagnerian theatre was absurd, and he lamented the inability of his younger contemporaries to move beyond the stale frameworks of Gounod *et compagnies*. *L'enfant* had no predecessors, and has had few descendants worthy of comparison.

Ravel's first orchestral work, *Shéhérazade* (1898), is all that remains of a projected *opéra féerique* based on an episode from the *Thousand and One Nights*. (Ironically, the last notes he was to write, nearly 40 years later, were sketches for *Morgiane*, a ballet on the Ali Baba story from the same source.) Other subjects he considered—or at least ones for which texts were preserved in his library—included William of Orange, a work laid out in the grand tradition of French historical opera, and *L'or*, *opéra fantastique*, a kind of musical comedy relating a gold-hunter's adventures in the United States, Japan, and Paris that ends on the rather conventional moral that money does not bring happiness. The only project on which Ravel made considerable progress was *La cloche engloutie*, an adaptation of Gerhart Hauptmann's *Die versunkene Glocke*, parts of which were later used in *L'enfant*.

During the main years of work on *L'enfant et les sortilèges*, three additional opera subjects were proposed to Ravel. *Le jongleur et ses moutons*, an anonymous farce set in an oriental port, seems not to have held much interest for the composer. Franz Toussaint's adaptation of the Song of Songs, on the other hand, a blend of orientalism, mysticism, and sensuality, he must have found quite tempting. (He may have been dissuaded from pursuing the project, at least in part, by the fact that Emmanuel Chabrier, a composer he venerated, had already written a major work on the Song of Songs, *La Sulamite*; the Morgan Library owns a manuscript of Chabrier's *scène lyrique*.) Finally, he was offered a one-act *opéra-bouffe* called, simply, *Opéra*, that is set backstage during a rehearsal of Rossini's *Otello*. But it was to be Colette's *fantaisie lyrique* that captured his imagination, and for that we are all in his debt: in *L'enfant et les sortilèges* Ravel produced one of the most enchanting and magical works in the operatic repertory.

To call the association with Colette a collaboration perhaps overstates the case; the few changes that Ravel suggested over the five years he worked on the opera were not substantive, but reflected rather his acute and meticulous ear for vocal and instrumental nuance. In the duet for two cats, Colette reports, Ravel asked "very gravely whether I would mind if he changed 'Mouâo' to 'Mouain'—or maybe it was the other way round." (In the Lehman manuscript, Ravel uses "Mi-in-hou" and "Ou"; in the printed score the onomatopoeia is more precisely notated: "Môr-nâ-ou nâ-ou, Moâ-ou, Mi-in-hou! . . . Mé-in-hou, Mi-in-hon, Moâraïn, Mon-hou, Mô-in-hon.") The teapot and teacup were originally from the Auvergne; Ravel decided against writing a bourrée (a French folkdance that may have originated in that region) and suggested that Colette change their nationality. The result was a black Wedgwood pot and a Chinese cup, for which he wrote a foxtrot. Colette's text here is a combination of American slang (Teapot: "How's your mug?" Teacup: "Rotten!"), a kind of Franglais ("I knock you, stupid chose! Black, black, and thick, and vrai beau gosse"), and some French phrases rendered in pseudo-oriental phonetics: "Puis'-kong-kong-pran-pa, / Ça-oh-râ, / Toujours l'air chinoâ"—that is, "Puisqu'on comprend pas, ça aura toujours l'air chinois" ("Because one doesn't get it, it will always seem Chinese"). Ravel flouts the rules of conventional French declamation governing the *e muet*, or final "e" that is silent in everyday speech but voiced when sung in art music. (The phrase "une petite fille," for example, has four syllables when spoken; when Debussy set these words in *Pelléas et Mélisande*, he used seven notes.) In *L'enfant*, the mother's first words include "sage" and "page"—sung to but one note each. In the final chorus, Ravel "errs" in another direction by setting the *e muet* of "sage" on a *higher* note than that for the first syllable, and then by stretching the word over nearly two measures.

Ravel acknowledged a stylistic source for the rapid, almost cinematic succession of scenes. In an autobiographical sketch, he wrote that "the melody, a dominant preoccupation, has a theme which I have chosen to treat in the manner of an American musical comedy." And in an interview at the time of the première, he said: "Scenically, we have tried for constant movement on the stage; therefore, according to principles of American operetta, dance is continually and intimately involved in the action." (Colette's original title was *Ballet pour ma fille*; but, Ravel said, "I have no daughter." The choreography for the Monte Carlo première was by George Balanchine.) The music

RAVEL: *L'enfant et les sortilèges*

is a mélange of styles of all periods, he admitted, "from Bach—to Ravel!" He took from each era only that which he needed: from the Classical he borrowed dance forms and clarity of line and texture; from the Romantic, the element of instrumental virtuosity; from his contemporaries, the idiom of the music hall and the popular stage. His was an art of parody and pastiche, not unlike Stravinsky's; each borrowed not because he lacked invention but because he readily acknowledged that the models of both past and present might serve his own artistic needs as well. Ravel brought to this amalgam his consummate mastery of orchestration, cast it in a newly evolved texture that stripped away all extraneous elements, and produced an opera that works its magic spell on us all. Writing of the première, Henry Prunières observed that "the child is not alone in being defenseless against the sorceries woven by Ravel and Colette: from the raising of the curtain the audience, too, is submissive to the powerful charms of these two enchanters."

The full-score autograph manuscript of *L'enfant et les sortilèges* is in the archive of Durand and Company in Paris. Mr. Lehman's collection also contains the autograph of the piano-vocal score of *L'heure espagnole*.

ALBAN BERG, 1885–1935.

"Wozzeck. II. Akt, 3. Scene." Autograph manuscript, dated 13 September 1922. 18 p. 33.5 × 27 cm.
First performance: Berlin, 14 December 1925.
Robert Owen Lehman Collection, on deposit in the Morgan Library.

Berg first saw Georg Büchner's play *Woyzeck* at its Vienna première in May 1914 and, as he later wrote to Anton Webern, "at
once decided to set it to music." But he was conscripted into the
Austrian army in 1915—he served until the end of the war in
November 1918—and made little progress on the opera until
1917; the short score of *Wozzeck* was completed in 1921, the
orchestration in 1922. Since its triumphal première, it has remained one of the acknowledged masterworks of twentieth-
century opera.

Büchner died in 1837 at the age of 23; *Woyzeck*, the last of his
three plays, survived only in preliminary drafts and sketches. It
was first published in 1875 in an edition prepared by the Gali-
cian novelist Karl Emil Franzos, and it was he who misread the
name of Büchner's title character. In 1909 the play, still in Franzos' rendering, was published with a revised ordering of the
scenes by Paul Landau; it is this Franzos-Landau recension that
Berg used, with very few changes, as the libretto for his opera.

Büchner's dramas, which strikingly foreshadow the naturalis-
tic and expressionistic works of the 1890's and later, deal with the
ultimate futility of man's attempt to impose order on a universe
he did not create and over which, finally, he has no control.
Büchner had no use for the so-called idealistic poets who "have
produced hardly anything besides marionettes with sky-blue
noses and affected pathos, not men of flesh and blood, with
whose sorrow and happiness I sympathize and whose actions
repel or attract me." Wozzeck—a poor soldier taunted by his
Captain, subjected to worthless experiments by his Doctor, and
deceived by his mistress, Marie (whom he murders)—is that
man "of flesh and blood." The cruel treatment he receives at the
hands of the Captain, the Doctor, the Drum Major (Marie's new
lover) is presented not as an aberration in a normal world, but as
normal behavior in an intractable one.

Scene 3 of Act II is the midpoint of the act and of the opera as
a whole. Wozzeck confronts Marie with his suspicions of her
infidelity with the Drum Major; she denies it but the music, by a
subtle reference to an earlier passage, tells us otherwise.
Wozzeck employs not only *Leitmotive*—that is, recurring musical motifs associated with a specific character, an emotion, an
object, etc.—but also references to works by other composers.
Some, like the thematic allusion to the stage musicians in Act I
of *Don Giovanni*, are quite explicit. Others—an example is the
scene discussed here—are discoverable only by an examination
of the score itself: the instrumentation of the chamber ensemble
is exactly that of Schoenberg's *Kammersymphonie*, op. 9, a work
that influenced the development of Berg's own musical language. This manuscript, in which the full orchestra is notated in
red ink, the chamber orchestra in black, bears an inscription to
Schoenberg dated 13 September 1922—his forty-eighth birthday. (Schoenberg, initially, disapproved of Berg's choice of a
subject, arguing that music should deal "rather with angels than
with orderlies." He even suggested that Wozzeck was "an anti-
musical, unsingable name.")

"When I decided to write an opera," Berg said of *Wozzeck*,
"my only intention, as related to the technique of composition,
was to give the theatre what belongs to the theatre." Those who
have seen this opera, in which both the immediate and tran-
scendent elements of Wozzeck's fate are so powerfully portrayed,
will agree that Berg has indeed succeeded in giving the musical
theatre one of its great works.

The full-score autograph of *Wozzeck* is in the Library of
Congress.

BERG: *Wozzeck*

R. Strauss: *Die ägyptische Helena*

Die ägyptische Helena, op. 75. Two sketchbooks, for Scene 4 and the finale of Act I, and for Act II, beginning with Scene 2. 48 and 64 p. 13 × 17.5 and 8 × 13 cm. Inscribed, respectively, to Max Graf (Garmisch, 1924) and Gustav Brecher (Garmisch, 24 June 1927).
First performance: Dresden, 6 June 1928.
Dannie and Hettie Heineman Collection.

Within the history of opera few collaborations between musician and poet have been more lauded than that of Richard Strauss and Hugo von Hofmannsthal. Composer and librettist of *Elektra, Der Rosenkavalier, Ariadne auf Naxos, Die Frau ohne Schatten, Die ägyptische Helena,* and *Arabella,* their joint achievement was perhaps best summarized by the two men themselves. Strauss wrote to Hofmannsthal early in their association: "Your nature is so complementary to mine! We were born for each other and we are certain to do fine things together." With this Hofmannsthal was in complete accord: "It is more than a possibility, it is certain knowledge on my part, that we are destined together to create some, perhaps a number of works, which will be beautiful and remarkable."

Die ägyptische Helena, the fifth of their six operas, was the inspiration of Hofmannsthal. Broaching the possibility of the work to Strauss, he expressed an interest in "mythological operas," for, as he said, they are the "truest kind that exist." Strauss, returning from a tour of South America and with no other prospect at the moment, received the idea favorably and wrote to Hofmannsthal on 12 July 1923: "I shall be in Garmisch on 15th September, without any work, and should like to find *Helena* . . . waiting for me there! 'Off Kundry—to work!' " And work they did. By mid-October of that year Hofmannsthal's libretto for Act I was in the hands of the composer. On the 23rd of the month Strauss enthusiastically acknowledged receipt of the text, noting that

> the end of Act I is very beautiful and I congratulate the two of us on this piece of poetry which is quite exceptionally suited to music. . . . So far I've sketched out about a third: most of it virtually sets itself to music. . . . I hope to have basically sketched out the first act by the end of November. It's coming on unbelievably fast and is giving me no end of pleasure.

Of his working methods for the composition of an opera, Strauss wrote:

> I often write down a motif or a melody, then put it away for a year. When I return to it I find that quite unconsciously something in me—the imagination—has been at work on it. . . . Before I note down even the slightest sketch for an opera I allow the text to permeate my mind for at least six months and take root within me, so that I am wholly familiar with the situations and characters. Only then do I allow musical ideas to enter my head. The preliminary sketches become more elaborate sketches which are written down, worked on, put into shape as a piano score and worked on again, often up to four times. This is the difficult part of the work. I finally write the score in my study, straight through and without effort.

Additional elucidation of Strauss's compositional habits has been recorded by the conductor Karl Böhm. In 1936, during the early stages of work on *Daphne,* Strauss showed the conductor the libretto of the opera. Böhm noticed that in the margins of the text Strauss had made indications regarding rhythms, tonality, form, and information about several of the characters. As Böhm stated, "he had needed scarcely any more time than it took to read through the text."

With the aid of the Heineman sketches for *Die ägyptische Helena* we are able to see the composer at work on a number of these various stages of composition, for we find both intermediate sketches written in piano score and, in other instances, Strauss's first preliminary outlines. However rudimentary or provisional the sketch may be, one is immediately impressed by a composer working with both self-assurance and a clear vision of what is required for his musical goals. Two examples from the sketchbook for Act I may serve as illustrations. On pages 10 and 11 is found an intermediate version, in piano score, of the concluding music for Scene 4 of the first act. The similarity to the final version is at first glance startling: tonality, melodic contours, and accompaniment appear to be much the same. Upon closer examination, however, we discover many details that are not the same, for the setting of the text and a large part of the melodic figuration for the voices are vastly different.

Strauss's sketch for the finale of the act, reproduced here from the last page of the first sketchbook, is in many ways even more revealing of the composer's working methods. A preliminary sketch, it would seem to be for the closing section of the act. If we may assume that it represents Strauss's first thoughts on the finale, one may posit that all he would need when he turned to the composition of the final version was a broad outline of the harmonic motion and color in order, at a later stage, to complete the finale. If this is so, the music from this sketch is of significance in that it was germinal for the music that precedes it in the finale, and in that it foreshadows to a remarkable degree many of the melodic ideas and harmonic progressions that are ultimately to be found in the entire finale.

Complementing the Heineman sketchbooks for *Die ägyptische Helena* are at least six other volumes of sketches, one in the Gesellschaft der Musikfreunde in Vienna, the others in the Richard-Strauss-Archiv in Garmisch. The full-score autograph of the opera is found in the Österreichische Nationalbibliothek, Vienna.

Dantons Tod. Short-score draft of parts of Scene 6, dated 18 August 1945. 10 p. 34 × 27 cm.
First performance: Salzburg, 6 August 1947.
Mary Flagler Cary Music Collection.

The libretto of *Dantons Tod*, prepared by Einem and the composer Boris Blacher, is based on Georg Büchner's play of the same name. (Büchner's *Woyzeck* was the source for Berg's *Wozzeck*; see p. 105.) *Dantons Tod*, the author's first play, was written in January and February 1835, and was the only one of his literary works to be published in his lifetime. In a letter to his fiancée, Büchner commented on his drama as follows:

> I have been studying the history of the Revolution. I felt annihilated by the terrible fatality of history. I find in human nature a frightful sameness, in human relations an inexorable power, given to all and to none. The individual only froth on the wave, greatness sheer chance, the splendor of genius a puppet show, a ridiculous struggle against an iron law, the recognition of which is the greatest achievement, the mastery of which is impossible.

The opera is set in Paris in 1794. The power of the Revolutionary leader, Robespierre, is absolute. Danton's friend Desmoulins urges him to continue his opposition to Robespierre's Reign of Terror. When Danton does so, both he and Desmoulins are arrested, tried, and sentenced to death—ironically, by the same Revolutionary Tribunal that he himself had initiated a year earlier. The sixth and final scene of the opera takes place in a public square. The mob, anticipating their favorite entertainment, surround the guillotine, celebrating the impending execution by singing and dancing the Carmagnole. To the tune of the "Marseillaise," Danton and his condemned comrades sing, "Our enemy is the stupidity of the masses which can be pierced only by the sword of the spirit."

After the execution, Desmoulins' widow, Lucile, enters and sings the last words of the opera (reproduced here from the penultimate page of the manuscript): "There is a reaper called death, possessing power from God on high; many hundreds of thousands are uncounted—whatever falls under the sickle." Both text and music are taken from what has been called one of the masterpieces of sacred folksong. The text, by an unknown seventeenth-century poet, emphasizes the familiar folk symbolism of the Reaper (death) and the fragile flower (man). One can only imagine the terrible immediacy these words must have had for a Germany just emerging from its own Reign of Terror, as well as for Einem, who had lost both his father and a brother in the War.

For a discussion of John Eaton's *Danton and Robespierre*, see p. 118.

EINEM: *Dantons Tod*

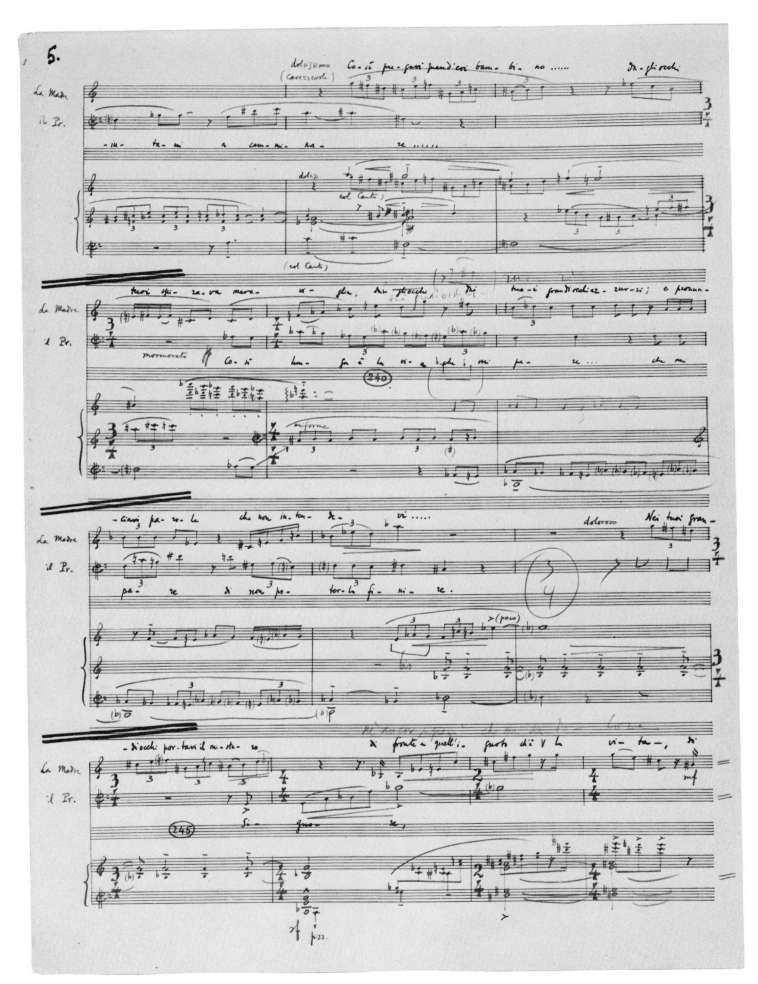

DALLAPICCOLA: *Il prigioniero*

LUIGI DALLAPICCOLA, 1904–1975.

Il prigioniero. Un prologo e un atto da "La torture par l'espérance" del Conte Villiers de l'Isle-Adam e da "La légende d'Ulenspiegel e di Lamme Goedzack" di Charles de Coster. Short-score draft, dated 1945–47. 72 p. various sizes.
First stage performance: Florence, 20 May 1950.
Robert Owen Lehman Collection, on deposit in the Morgan Library.

One day in 1919, in his home town of Pisino d'Istria, a childhood friend of Dallapiccola's related to him an episode from Victor Hugo's *Légende des siècles* called "La rose de l'Infante." The Infanta, a rose in her hand, stands by a pool with her duenna; in the background, Philip II is seen standing in the window of the castle. A breeze blows off the rose petals. When the Infanta asks her governess why, she explains that "Tout sur terre appartient aux princes, hors le vent" ("Everything on earth belongs to the princes, save the wind")—the same words that Philip would speak on learning of the sinking of the Invincible Armada. "I can say that from that day," Dallapiccola wrote later, "the idea of Philip II hovering menacingly over mankind has not left my consciousness," and that if "I mentally identified Philip II with the petty tyrants of the House of Hapsburg, I connected him later with other, more terrible figures."

Twenty years later, in Paris, Dallapiccola read "La torture par l'espérance" ("Torture through Hope") by Count Philippe-Auguste Villiers de l'Isle-Adam, and "reestablished in my spirit the contact with a threatening tyrant, . . . with 'la rose de l'Infante.' " He also reread *La légende et les aventures héroïques, joyeuses et glorieuses d'Ulenspiegel et de Lamme Goedzak au pays de Flandres et ailleurs*, the Flemish epic by Charles de Coster. These two works were to be the main literary sources for the libretto of *Il prigioniero*, drafted between Christmas Eve and

New Year's Eve of 1943. On 10 January 1944, "the first sufficiently clear musical idea came into my consciousness," the twelve-tone row for the aria "Sull'Oceano, sulla Schelda" that constitutes the central portion of the opera. *Il prigioniero* was completed in May 1948, and was first performed on RAI (Radio Audizioni Italiana) on 4 December 1949.

The plot of the opera, which can be epitomized in the phrase "Torture through Hope," is simply told: a jailer speaks of his prisoner as "brother"; the prisoner, finding his cell door open, escapes into the garden—and into the arms of the jailer, who is in fact the Grand Inquisitor. His hope for freedom has become his ultimate torture. The announcement of the first stage performance was greeted with a wave of protests, both musical and political: the twelve-tone system of composition in general was attacked by local music circles; and Communists, Fascists, and Catholics feared that the opera's denunciation of tyranny would be construed as an assault, respectively, on Stalinist Russia, Fascist dictatorship, and (by way of the Spanish Inquisition) the Church. The work today is considered to be one of the most successful operas to employ a strict application of the dodecaphonic technique. Like his *Canti di prigionia* (1941) and *Canti di liberazione* (1955), it grew from an impassioned belief in the evils of repression and in the nobility of man's striving for freedom.

Amahl and the Night Visitors. Partially autograph manuscript of the full score. 227 p. 48.5 × 32 cm. First performance: New York (NBC Television broadcast): 24 December 1951. Mary Flagler Cary Music Collection.

Menotti has described as follows the genesis of *Amahl*:

This is an opera for children because it tries to recapture my own childhood. You see, when I was a child I lived in Italy, and in Italy we have no Santa Claus. I suppose that Santa Claus is much too busy with American children to be able to handle Italian children as well. Our gifts were brought to us by the Three Kings, instead.

I never actually met the Three Kings—it didn't matter how hard my little brother and I tried to keep awake at night to catch a glimpse of the Three Royal Visitors, we would always fall asleep just before they arrived. But I do remember hearing them. I remember the weird cadence of their song in the dark distance; I remember the brittle sound of the camels' hooves crushing the frozen snow; and I remember the mysterious tinkling of their silver bridles.

My favorite king was King Melchior, because he was the oldest and had a long white beard. My brother's favorite was King Kaspar. He insisted that this king was a little crazy and quite deaf. I don't know why he was so positive about his being deaf. I suppose it was because dear King Kaspar never brought him all the gifts he requested. He was also rather puzzled by the fact that King Kaspar carried the myrrh, which appeared to him as a rather eccentric gift, for he never understood what the word meant. . . .

In 1951 I found myself in serious difficulty. I had been commissioned by the National Broadcasting Company to write an opera for television, with Christmas as a deadline, and I simply didn't have one idea in my head. One November afternoon as I was walking rather gloomily through the Metropolitan Museum, I chanced to stop in front of the Adoration of the Magi by Hieronymus Bosch, and as I was looking at it, suddenly I heard again, coming from the distant blue hills, the weird song of the Three Kings. I then realized they had come back to me and had brought me a gift.

Television opera began, at NBC, in 1948, and producers today must look with some envy at the funds the network allocated for those broadcasts. Each cost about $30,000, a budget that included ten days of rehearsals, each of seven working hours. The performing time was just under one hour, so considerable cutting was required; in *Carmen*, for example, the whole subplot with Micaëla was omitted. *Amahl* was the first opera commissioned for television, and was the first of NBC's productions to find a commercial sponsor, the makers of Hallmark Christmas cards. Samuel Chotzinoff, who commissioned *Amahl*, had, in 1939, commissioned Menotti's *The Old Maid and the Thief*, his second opera and the first to be written for radio.

Menotti has long been an advocate of opera that speaks directly to the emotions: "My operas are not cold, intellectual creatures; they are rather nice to look at, impulsive and warmhearted—too warm-hearted at times, so it seems." And there is little question that in Amahl he fashioned a work that has found a large and appreciative audience—especially among children, who are always responsive to a simple tale, simply told. He has his fervent admirers—and, to be sure, his severe critics. Joseph Kerman calls him "a sensationalist in the old style, and in fact a weak one, diluting the faults of Strauss and Puccini with none of their fugitive virtues." Wilfrid Mellers has written that in *Amahl* "the Hollywood gloss is a prostitution of the Christmas mystery. It seems sacrilegious, whether one believes in that mystery or not." But for tens of thousands—or is it millions—*Amahl* has become as cherished a part of Christmas as Santa Claus, or as the Three Kings of Menotti's own youth. Lincoln Kirstein's 1952 prediction that *Amahl* "bids fair to be the American *Hänsel und Gretel*" has proved accurate.

The Morgan Library also owns the autograph full and pianovocal scores of Menotti's *The Medium*; the full score and a large portion of the piano-vocal score of *The Saint of Bleecker Street*; and the piano-vocal score of *Martin's Lie*.

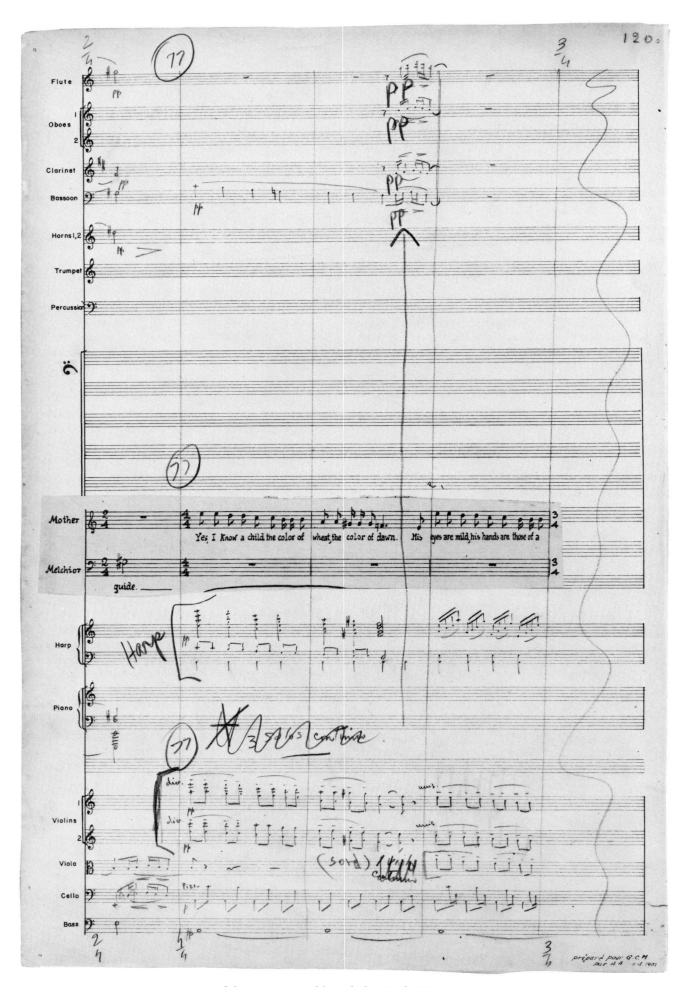

MENOTTI: *Amahl and the Night Visitors*

SCHOENBERG: *Moses und Aron*

Moses und Aron. First draft of Act I, with a few pages of drafts and sketches for Act II, dated (on p. 1) Lugano, 17 July 1930.
78 p. 27 × 35 cm. (and other sizes).
First concert performance: Hamburg, 12 March 1954.
First stage performance: Zurich, 6 June 1957.
Mary Flagler Cary Music Collection.

Schoenberg's deep interest in the Old Testament can be traced in a number of his works. In 1917 he composed the first half of an oratorio, *Die Jakobsleiter* (Jacob's Ladder), in which a number of persons, facing death, come before the archangel Gabriel. Among them is the Chosen One—clearly Schoenberg himself—"whose spiritual understanding," writes O. W. Neighbour, "sets him apart and whose word seems doomed to misunderstanding. . . . He is told to remember all that he has in common with the rest of humanity and to accept his prophetic role." And in the second of his Opus 27 choruses, composed in 1928, "Du sollst nicht, du musst" ("Not 'Thou shalt: Thou must' "), Schoenberg states what was to become the central theme of *Moses und Aron:* "Thou shalt make for thyself no image! For an image restricts, confines, ties down what must stay unlimited and inconceivable."

In 1927 Schoenberg completed *Der biblische Weg* (The Biblical Way), a play concerning the attempts of Max Aruns to establish a new Palestine in an imaginary African country. Aruns fails both because of the imperfect nature of everything human, and because of a tragic flaw in himself: pride. In Act III, David Asseino, whom Aruns had hoped to make High Priest, tells Aruns he failed by trying to be both Moses and Aaron in one, that God did *not* choose to unite the two, and that in trying to be both the eternal Idea (Moses) and its temporal expression (Aaron), Aruns has succeeding in being neither. Aruns replies that he does indeed see the two as aspects of the same person, that in him are found both prophet and preacher: "In him, the purity of the idea is not affected by the work he undertakes in public, and the latter is not weakened by having to take into consideration problems posed by the idea that have not yet been resolved." It is this conflict between the spiritual Idea of God and its verbal, or imaged, representation, that forms the central drama of *Moses und Aron.*

God gives Moses the mission of conveying His message to the Chosen People, the Jews living under Egyptian bondage. When Moses hesitates, saying that he is incapable of expressing the idea of God, the invisible and inconceivable, God tells him that his brother, Aaron, will be his spokesman: "From him will your own voice issue, as from you comes my voice." But when Aaron commands the people to worship a new god and not their old ones, they are confused and rebellious: "Where is He? Point him out!" In short, what they cannot see, they will not worship; Aaron breaks the impasse by making visible the presence of God's power. To heighten dramatic conflict and define character

more sharply, Schoenberg here takes some liberties with scripture. Thus, two of the miracles Aaron performs at this point in the opera (turning Moses' rod into a serpent and making Moses' hand leprous, then curing it) are, in Exodus 3, attributed to Moses alone. But Schoenberg's Aaron is both preacher and politician, and uses many of the tricks of both trades to pacify a restive and querulous people. Moses next promises to lead the Chosen People out of Egypt "to where with the infinite oneness you shall be a model for every nation." But Aaron again intercedes, reducing Moses' spiritual ideal to a sensuous idea, and promises, instead, a land where milk and honey will flow. For the people to believe, they must be given a vision of real, earthly rewards; they will not follow an idea, only an image.

After 40 days in the wilderness, waiting for Moses to descend from Mount Sinai, the people have again become restless, and threaten revolt. They have come with false hopes; they fear that God has destroyed Moses, and demand that they be allowed to worship their old gods. Aaron relents: "O Israel, I return your gods to you, and also give you to them, just as you have demanded. . . . You shall provide the material; I shall give it form: common and visible, imaged in gold forever." Here follows the most famous scene in the opera, "The Golden Calf and the Altar," in which the people indulge in an idolatrous orgy of drunkenness, madness, and wanton sexuality.

Schoenberg was ambivalent about this scene: its dramatic necessity was obvious, but the very effectiveness of its execution panders to artistic tastes of a lower order. "You know I'm not at all keen on the dance," he wrote to Anton Webern in September 1931. "In general its expressiveness is on a level no higher than the crudest program music; and the petrified mechanical quality of its 'beauty' is something I can't stand." As for the staging of the scene, Schoenberg left detailed directions, since "I wanted to leave as little as possible to the new despots of the theatrical art, the directors. . . . The highhandedness of these mere minions, and their total lack of conscience, is excelled only by their barbarity and feebleness." The scene cannot, in fact, be staged as Schoenberg conceived it, calling as it does for the slaughtering and dismembering of animals, people leaping into fire and running burning across the stage, the stabbing of four naked virgins whose blood is then poured on the altar, and so on. Schoenberg suggested one solution in a letter to the conductor Hermann Scherchen in 1950 discussing a possible concert performance of the scene:

I consider a concert performance of the Dance Round the Golden Calf to be nearly impossible, since the music is illustrative throughout. I wish to avoid the mistake of presenting non-symphonic music (however well constructed it may otherwise be) as a symphony, as so many contemporary ballet composers do. You must find a solution that somehow changes an auditor into a spectator, that actually lets one see an approximate representation of the events. Perhaps some film studio is prepared to film the most important moments as a movie.

Moses comes down from Mount Sinai with the Tablets, and berates Aaron for acceding to the people's wishes for pagan worship. Why could they not wait?—"God's eternity opposes idols' transience." Aaron, pointing to the Tablets with God's commandments, tells Moses that "they are images too, just part of the whole Idea." Moses destroys the Tablets and admits defeat: he, too, has fashioned an image (Aaron as his spokesman) and has failed in God's mission. In Act III, for which Schoenberg wrote a libretto but left only a few musical sketches, Moses was to be shown as triumphant. He again accuses the now-captive Aaron of "betraying God to the gods, the Idea to images." Aaron is freed, but falls dead.

"It was not given to Moses to enter the Promised Land," writes Dika Newlin, "nor to Schoenberg fully to complete his magnum opus. But Moses was allowed to behold a vision, and Schoenberg was allowed to formulate in words his lofty idea of the wilderness." As Schoenberg himself wrote about Gustav Mahler: "he was allowed to reveal just so much of the future; when he wanted to say more, he was called away."

Moses und Aron was composed between May 1930 and March 1932. The final autograph manuscript of the opera, along with additional drafts and sketches, are in the Arnold Schoenberg Institute Archive, Los Angeles. The Morgan Library recently purchased the autograph full score of Schoenberg's *Erwartung*, a monodrama composed in 1909.

Danton and Robespierre. Autograph manuscript of the short score. ca. 200 p. 32.5 × 23.5 cm.
First performance: Bloomington, Indiana, 22 April 1978.
Gift of Mr. Eaton.

When we asked John Eaton if he might provide some personal commentary on the background of this opera, he graciously responded as follows:

The idea of *Danton and Robespierre* was hatched by Patrick Creagh, the librettist, and myself some 6 years before the opera was finished, and shortly after Creagh and I had finished the opera *Myshkin*. At first, we were going to have ten characters, named A through J, who would reappear in three different revolutions. We were inspired by Crane Brinton's book *The Anatomy of a Revolution*, and eager to apply the same methods to society that we had to a personality in *Myshkin*. (Awful gutless, abstract stuff!) Then we found everything we needed in the French Revolution, and I was quite inspired by the Büchner play *Dantons Tod*. For a while we thought of using that. However, we wanted a larger curve, historically speaking, than that play uses. At the same time, we found what actually happened and what people actually said to be even more intriguing and exciting than the somewhat falsified events of the play. Any similarity between the play and the final libretto is, in my understanding, purely due to the fact that Patrick Creagh and Büchner used the same recorded speeches and historical material.

It was quite a problem to put the libretto together, with Patrick in Italy and me in Indiana. We sent voluminous letters back and forth with many different trial synopses. Finally, work began in earnest when I was appointed composer in residence at the American Academy in Rome in 1974. During that year we whipped the first act into shape and I composed the first scene. The next academic year my wife, Nelda Nelson, was singing with the Heidelberg Opera, and I was lecturer at The Salzburg Seminar in American Studies. I remember finishing one scene, in the dead of winter, in a three hour layover in the unheated Montevarchi train station, huddled around steaming cups of espresso. At any rate, we managed to have the libretto finished by the summer of 1976 and I was able to then throw myself wholeheartedly into the composition.

Up to this time, I was writing many other pieces while working on the opera. The rate of completion of the opera now accelerated until I was able to write the entire ending from the last third of Robespierre's aria (Act III, Scene 6) in four hours one morning. Would that I had had another two completed libretti to attack then, in that white heat of inspiration!

The central dramatic conflict in the opera arises from the protagonists' opposing means to achieve a common end. Danton would win social freedom for the French people, but never at the expense of any individual's opportunity to pursue his own personal happiness. Robespierre fights for the same freedom, but countenances ruthless means to reach it. Eaton employs specific musical means to express that conflict. Since the early 1960's he had been intrigued with the expansion of pitch—that is, the possibilities of using pitches other than those found in the chromatic scale. In his opera *Myshkin* (1970, based on Dostoevsky's *The Idiot*), he uses sixth tones to suggest Prince Myshkin's irrational states, while quarter tones accompany his more lucid moments. By combining the two microtonal tunings, he was able to present simultaneously two levels of reality. "The thought that fertilized the ground for *Danton and Robespierre*," Eaton has written, "was that Patrick Creagh and I should apply on a social level the techniques explored on a psychological level in *Myshkin*."

Microtones—that is, notes that lie between adjacent keys on the piano—are generated in *Danton and Robespierre* by dividing woodwinds, brasses, and pianos into two groups, one tuned a quarter tone lower than the other, and by using three harps, one tuned normally, the others tuned, respectively, a sixth tone higher and a sixth tone lower. In addition, Eaton calls for an electronic instrument, tuned in what is known as just intonation, that produces wonderfully pure chords in keys harmonically close to C major, but progressively sour and out-of-tune ones as the music moves toward F sharp, the most distantly related key. The first music Eaton wrote for the opera—"a particular and unusual musical continuity"—was the chorale that is used throughout the work to express Robespierre's idealistic vision. In the organ prelude to the opera, the chorale is set to purely tuned harmonies. But when the prelude recurs—in the music accompanying the September Massacres, in Robespierre's hymn that opens Act III, Scene 3, in the scene of terror after Danton has been guillotined—the music moves from "the absolute purity of the basic key to the greatly out of tune final chords." The contrast between the humanist Danton and the tyrannical idealist Robespierre—the dramatic core of the opera—"finds as perfect a musical expression as I could invent in the contrast of tempered, traditional music with just intonation."

It is tempting, and no doubt a bit risky, to try to discover some thread, however tenuous, that connects the earliest entry in this catalogue—Rinuccini's libretto for Peri's *Dafne*—with *Danton and Robespierre*, first performed some 380 years later. But if the nearly four centuries that intervened brought a profound change in degree, the difference in kind is less marked. W. H. Auden, in his essay "The World of Opera," wrote as follows concerning the choice of characters suitable for a libretto: "The most successful heroes and heroines in opera are mythical figures, that is to say, they embody some element of human nature, some aspect of the human condition which is of some permanent concern to human beings irrespective of their time and place."

EATON: *Danton and Robespierre*

Auden's call for characters who transcend their temporal locus, who stand as symbols for ideas and ideals that reach far beyond their momentary incarnation on stage, is surely answered by both operas. And that call is echoed by Eaton himself in an essay addressing the same subject:

> Part of my quest has been to restore heroism and nobility, ingredients so needed in contemporary life, to opera. That banal, ordinary persons should sing as the major characters is absurd and misses part of the major mission of opera: to infuse into a society, through the powerful means of music and poetic vision, high values and purpose. The ultimate models, which though perhaps unrealizable today are nevertheless our goals, are Aeschylus, whose *Oresteia* sought to establish nothing less than trial by jury, and Verdi, whose very name became a call for independence and liberty. Like them, we must find subjects at a sufficient remove from ourselves and resplendent with dignity.

Mr. Eaton has also given the Morgan Library his manuscripts of the short score, and full score of Acts II and III, of his opera *Heracles* (1972). For other operas set in the French Revolution, see Mascagni's *Il piccolo Marat* (p. 100) and Einem's *Dantons Tod* (p. 109).

Opera Manuscripts
IN THE PIERPONT MORGAN LIBRARY:
A SELECTIVE CHECKLIST

This list contains all important manuscripts, both autograph and copyist's, related to opera; a few album leaves quoting a measure or two of music, and other brief excerpts of little historical or musical interest, were omitted. The number of pages (with music on both sides) or leaves (with music on one side only) is, in most cases, the actual number of pages containing music, not the total manuscript count; height precedes width in the centimeter measurements. The names of the collections to which the manuscripts belong are abbreviated as follows:

Cary: Mary Flagler Cary Music Collection
Heineman: Dannie and Hettie Heineman Collection
Koch: The Pierpont Morgan Library, purchased as the gift of Mr. Frederick Koch
Koch Foundation Deposit: Frederick R. Koch Foundation Collection, on deposit in The Pierpont Morgan Library
Lehman: The Pierpont Morgan Library, gift of Mr. Robert Owen Lehman
Lehman Deposit: Robert Owen Lehman Collection, on deposit in The Pierpont Morgan Library

BELLINI, VINCENZO, 1801–1835. [Bianca e Fernando. Overture] 18 p. 24 × 30 cm. On cover: "Sinfonia dell'opera Ernani. Partitura." [Il pirata] 8 p. 24 × 30 cm. Twenty-four measures, in full score, from the Act II "Terzetto." [La sonnambula] 6 p. 28 × 40.5 cm. Sketches for Act I. *Cary*.

BERG, ALBAN, 1885–1935. "Wozzeck. II. Akt, 3. Scene." 18 p. 33.5 × 27 cm. Full score. Dedication to Arnold Schoenberg, dated 13 Sept. 1922. Note at end: "Komponiert Sommer 1920; Instrumentiert Frühjahr 1922." *Lehman Deposit*.

BERLIOZ, HECTOR, 1803–1869. [Gluck, Christoph Willibald, 1714–1787] "Iphigénie en Tauride. Tragédie en quatre actes Par Mᵣ Guillard. Mise en musique et dédiée à la Reine par Mᵣ le Chevalier Gluck." 209 p. 29.5 × 21.5 cm. Manuscript copy of the full score in Berlioz's hand. Dated at end: "Avril 1824." *Lehman*.

BLITZSTEIN, MARC, 1905–1964. "'Theater for the Cabaret.' Opera in one act." 2 vols. 24.5 × 17 cm. Short-score draft. *Cary*.

BRITTEN, BENJAMIN, 1913–1976. [Billy Budd] 3 p. 36.5 × 27 cm. Sketches for parts of Act I, Scenes 1–3, and Act II, Scene 1. *Cary*.

CATEL, CHARLES-SIMON, 1773–1830. "Les artistes par occasion. No. 4. Trio." 50 p. 28 × 21.5 cm. Full score. *Koch*.

CHÉLARD, HIPPOLYTE-ANDRÉ, 1789–1861. "Scène de la Somnambule de l'opéra de Macbeth." Vogt, Album of autographs, p. 100. For English horn and piano. Dated at end: "Paris ce 30 janvier 1848." *Cary*.

CIMAROSA, DOMENICO, 1749–1802. [I tre amanti] 8 p. 21.5 × 29 cm. Full score of an aria for Violante beginning: "Questo soave affetto" (incomplete). *Cary*.

CONVERSE, FREDERICK SHEPHERD, 1871–1940. "The Pipe of Desire. An Opera in One Act Composed by Frederick S. Converse. Text by George Edward Barton." 227 p. 33.5 × 26.5 and 39.5 × 28 cm. Full score. Dated at end: "Lake Sunapee, N.H., Aug. 12, 1905." *Gift of Mr. Converse*.

DALLAPICCOLA, LUIGI, 1904–1975. "Il Prigioniero. Un prologo e un atto da 'La torture par l'espérance' del Conte Villiers de l'Isle-Adam e da 'La légende d'Ulenspiegel e di Lamme Goedzack' di Charles de Coster. Abbozzi." 72 p. various sizes. Short-score draft, dated 1945–47. *Lehman Deposit*.

DAMOREAU, LAURE-CINTHIE, 1801–1863. "Point d'orgue (dans L'ambassadrice)." Vogt, Album of autographs, p. 63. Cadenza (without words) for soprano. Dated at end: "13 mai [18]43." *Cary*.

DAVID, FÉLICIEN, 1810–1876. [Lalla-Roukh] 4 p. 35 × 27 cm. Piano-vocal score drafts of the Entr'acte, the aria "O nuit d'amour," and the song "Ah! funeste ambassade," all from Act II. *Cary*.

DEBUSSY, CLAUDE, 1862–1918. "Pelléas et Mélisande." 128 leaves (with music also on 11 facing versos). 39.5 × 30 cm. Complete short score. Dated September 1893–September 1901. *Koch Foundation Deposit*. [Pelléas et Mélisande. Act IV, Scene 4] "Une fontaine dans le Parc." 12 leaves (with music also on 4 facing versos). 40 × 30 cm. Incomplete short-score draft of the scene. Dated at end: "Septembre-Octobre [18]93." [Pelléas et Mélisande] 409 p. 34.5 × 27.5 cm. Printed proof sheets of the full score with extensive autograph corrections. "Rodrigue et Chimène. CAD. 92." 55 leaves, 40 p., 28 leaves. 34.5 × 26.5 cm. Short score. *Lehman Deposit*.

DONIZETTI, GAETANO, 1797–1848. [Anna Bolena] 4 and 3 p. 23.5 × 32.5 cm. Two drafts for the Act II, Scene 2 duet between Anna and Giovanna beginning: "Va' infelice, e teco reca, il perdono di Bolena." On covers: "Scena dell'opera Anna Bolena per Giuditta Pasta." [Lucrezia Borgia] 18 p. 22 × 28.5 cm. Full score of a recitative and aria written for Nicola Ivanoff. Recitative begins: "Partir deggio lo vuol Lucrezia." [Buondelmonte] 31 p. 26.5 × 38 cm. Eight numbers, in full-score draft, from the additional music composed in altering *Maria Stuarda* to *Buondelmonte*, the form in which the opera was first performed. *Cary. See also* Kreutzer, Conradin, and Vogt, Gustave.

EATON, JOHN, b. 1935. [Danton and Robespierre] Short-score draft. ca. 200 p. 32.5 × 23.5 cm. *With:* Typescript of Patrick Creagh's libretto, annotated by Eaton. 63 p. [Heracles] ca. 500 p. 28 × 21.5 cm. and other sizes. Short-score draft. *With:* the full score of Acts II and III. ca. 280 p. 40 × 30 cm. and other sizes. *Gifts of Mr. Eaton.*

EINEM, GOTTFRIED VON, b. 1918. [Dantons Tod] "VI. Bild. Gottfried v. Einem." 10 p. 34 × 27 cm. Short-score draft of Scene 6. *Cary.*

FLOTOW, FRIEDRICH VON, 1812–1883. [La veuve Grapin] 50 p. 35.5 × 28 and 27 × 17 cm. Piano-vocal score. *Cary.*

GIORDANO, UMBERTO, 1867–1948. "Marcella." 210 leaves. 31.5 × 27.5 cm. Short-score draft. *Cary.*

GLUCK, CHRISTOPH WILLIBALD, 1714–1787. "L'Alceste. Tragedia del Sig: Ranieri de' Calsabigi. Musica del Sig: Cristofano Gluch [sic]." 3 vols. 21 × 28 cm. Copyist's manuscript. [Iphigenie auf Tauris] 8 p. 30.5 × 23 cm. Voice parts, from the middle of Act I, Scene 3 to the end of Act IV, Scene 3. "Orfeo." 470 p. 23.5 × 30 cm. Copyist's manuscript. [Orphée et Euridice] 2 p. 30 × 23 cm. Full score of three passages from the opera. *Cary. See also* Berlioz, Hector.

GOUNOD, CHARLES, 1818–1893. "Cinq-Mars (Trio No. 14)." 4 p. 25 × 31 cm. Short-score drafts for several numbers. *Purchased by the Heineman Foundation.* [Faust. Il était un roi de Thulé] Vogt, Album of autographs, p. 88. For voice and piano; the first four measures. "Mireille." ca. 1000 p. 35.5 × 26 cm. Full score. *Cary.*

GRANADOS, ENRIQUE, 1867–1916. [Follet] 3 leaves. 27 × 35 cm. A fragment of the piano-vocal score. Dated October and November 1901. *Cary.*

HAHN, REYNALDO, 1875–1947. [Mozart] 51 leaves and 8 p., with 26 p. in a copyist's hand, with autograph additions. 34.5 × 27 cm. Piano-vocal score (incomplete). *With:* Typescript of Sacha Guitry's libretto for Act III, with additions in his hand. 23 p. *Koch.*

HALÉVY, FROMENTAL, 1799–1862. [La Reine de Chypre] "17. 3ᵐᵉ Acte. Duo final—Gérard et Lusignan." 61 p. 34.5 × 26 cm. Full score. *Cary.*

HAYDN, FRANZ JOSEPH, 1732–1809. [Ah tu non senti amico / Qual destra omicida, H. XXIVb:10] 2 leaves. 22.5 × 30 cm. Sketches for the recitative and aria for insertion in Tommaso Traetta's *Ifigenia in Tauride. Purchased by Pierpont Morgan about 1907.*

HERBERT, VICTOR, 1859–1924. "'The Nightingale and the Star' (Henry Blossom). Valse brillante (2d Act) Fifi. Henry Blossom. Victor Herbert." 12 p. 34.5 × 27 cm. For voice and piano; from his operetta *Mlle. Modiste. Purchased as the gift of Mrs. Hugh Bullock.*

D'INDY, VINCENT, 1851–1931. "Fervaal." 2 p. 35 × 25 cm. Sketches. *Cary.*

KORNGOLD, ERICH WOLFGANG, 1897–1957. [Die tote Stadt] 152 p. 26.5 × 34.5 cm. and 18 leaves 34 × 27.5 cm. Copyist's manuscripts (in two different hands), with autograph annotations and corrections, of all or parts of seven scenes, and printed proof sheets of part of Act II, Scene 4. *Cary.*

KREUTZER, CONRADIN, 1780–1849. [Donizetti, Gaetano, 1797–1848. Lucia di Lammermoor "Aria di Lucia cantata dalla Sigᵃ Grisi Perrot." 14 p. 26 × 34.5 cm. For voice and orchestra (words lacking); Lucia's scena and aria "Regnava nel silenzio" and "Quando rapita in estasi." The orchestration is almost entirely Kreutzer's own. *Purchased as the gift of Mr. Howard Phipps, Jr.* [Das Nachtlager von Granada] "Romanze mauresque. Romanze aus dem Nachtlager, im maurisch-spanischen Style. Conradin Kreutzer. Paris le 5 Février 1843." Vogt, Album of autographs, p. 68–69. For voice and piano. *Cary.*

LECOCQ, CHARLES, 1832–1918. [Le petit duc] 446 p. 34 × 26 cm. Full score. "Le Petit Duc. Opéra-Comique en 3 Actes de Charles Lecocq." 3 vols. 34 × 26.5 cm. Copyist's manuscript of the full score. *Cary.*

LE SUEUR, JEAN-FRANÇOIS, 1760–1837. [La mort d'Adam] Vogt,

Album of autographs, p. 70–71. Full score. Text begins: "Exauce ô dieu puissant sa timide prière!" *Cary.*

MARCHISIO, BARBARA, 1833–1919. "Cadenze e varianti composte ed eseguite dalle sorelle Marchisio." 53 p. 32.5 × 24 cm. Note on title page dated "27 Giugno 1900—Napoli." A collection of 51 cadenzas for two voices and about 90 for one voice written for *Norma, La sonnambula, Lucia di Lammermoor, Martha, Les Huguenots, Il trovatore,* about 12 Rossini operas, and other works. *Cary.*

MASCAGNI, PIETRO, 1863–1945. "Nerone." 3 vols. 63.5 × 47 cm. Full score. *Koch Foundation Deposit.* "Il piccolo Marat." 137 p. 33 × 24 cm. Piano-vocal score of most of Acts I and II, dated 1 May 1919–10 March 1920. *Cary.*

MASSENET, JULES, 1842–1912. "Manon, opéra comique en quatre actes et six tableaux. Poème de M.M. Henri Meilhac et Philippe Gille. Musique de J. Massenet." 288 leaves. 35 × 27 cm. Piano-vocal score. Dated 15 May–29 October 1882. "Manon. Arrangement pour les traductions." 7 leaves. 35.5 × 27 cm. Thirty measures in full score of cuts and alterations made for later editions. *Cary.*

MÉHUL, ÉTIENNE-NICOLAS, 1763–1817. [Valentine de Milan] "Morceau d'ensemble du 3ᵐᵉ acte." 32 p. 34.5 × 26 cm. Full score. *Cary.*

MENDELSSOHN BARTHOLDY, FELIX, 1809–1847. "Aus der Fremde, ein Liederspiel gedichtet von C. Klingemann, componirt von Felix Mendelssohn Bartholdy zur Feyer des 26 December 1829. Clavierauszug." 56 p. 31.5 × 22.5 cm. Piano-vocal score; the overture and no. 11 are for piano four-hands; no. 5 is in the hand of a copyist. *Heineman.*

MENOTTI, GIAN CARLO, b. 1911. [Amahl and the Night Visitors] 227 p. 48.5 × 32 cm. Partially autograph manuscript of the full score. *Cary.* "Martin's Lie. Opera da chiesa in one act." 81 p. 34 × 26.5 cm. Piano-vocal score. *Gift of Mr. John Davis Skilton, Jr., and Mr. Ernest Hillman.* "The Medium." 225 p. 34.5 × 27 cm. Full score. Dated at end: April 20, 1946. "The Medium. Opera in 2 acts." 79 p. 34.5 × 27 cm. Piano-vocal score. *Cary.* "The Saint of Bleecker Street." 787 leaves. 51 × 33 cm. Full score; the vocal lines and the text (in English and Italian) are in the hand of a copyist. "The Saint of Bleecker Street." 264 p. 34.5 × 27 cm. Piano-vocal score (incomplete; the last 56 measures of Act I and all of Act II are lacking). *Koch.*

MERCADANTE, SAVERIO, 1795–1870. [La schiava saracena, ovvero Il campo di Gerosolima] "Il campo de' Crociati—Mercadante." 131 p. 23.5 × 32 cm. Short-score draft (incomplete). *Cary.*

MESSAGER, ANDRÉ, 1853–1929. [L'amour masqué] "J'ai deux amants." 115 p. 35 × 27 cm. Piano-vocal score. *Koch.* "Véronique." 3 vols. 27 × 35 cm. Copyist's manuscript of the full score. *Cary.*

MEYERBEER, GIACOMO, 1791–1864. [Les Huguenots] "Romance des Huguenots." 2 leaves. 16 × 25 cm. For voice and piano. Text begins: "Parmi les pleurs." Dated at end: "Paris ce 13 May 1836. Giacomo Meyerbeer." *Koch.*

MOZART, WOLFGANG AMADEUS, 1756–1791. [Le nozze di Figaro, K.492. Non so più cosa son] "Atto Iᵐᵒ. Aria di Cherubino. Scena V." 4 p. 22 × 31 cm. Arrangement for voice, violin, and piano. *Heineman.* [Der Schauspieldirektor, K.486] 84 p. 23 × 32 cm. Full score. Dated on the first page of the "Terzett": "Vienna li 18 gennajo 1786." [Die Zauberflöte, K.620] "Atto II. Marcia." 2 p. 14.5 × 31 cm. Twelve bars; the upper three string parts and flute. *Cary.*

MUSORGSKY, MODEST PETROVICH, 1839–1881. *See* Ravel, Maurice.

OFFENBACH, JACQUES, 1819–1880. [L'amour chanteur] 82 p. 27 × 35.5 cm. Full score of the Overture, and nos. 2, 3, 5, and 6. *Koch Foundation Deposit.* [La belle Hélène] 4 p. 27 × 35 cm. Sketches. [Les bergers] 210 p. 27 × 35 cm. Full score. *Lehman.* [Les contes d'Hoffmann] 48 p. 26 × 34 cm. Sketches. *Cary.* [Le fifre enchanté] 13 p. 27 × 35.5 cm. Full score of the Finale. *Koch Foundation Deposit.* [Madame Favart] 117 p. 27 × 35 cm. Full score. *Lehman.* "La Permission de dix heures . . . Jacques Offenbach. 1er Septembre [18]73." 228 p. 27 × 35 cm. Full score. *With:* A different version of the overture. 21 p. 27 × 35 cm. [La princesse de Trébizonde] "La Princesse. No. 1. Introduction." 25 p. 27 × 34 cm. Full score of a scene. *Cary.* [Robinson Crusoé] 687 p. 27 × 34.5 cm. Full score. *Koch.* [Le roman comique] 133 p. 27 × 35 cm. Full-score draft. *Cary.* [Scapin et Mezzetin] 2 vols.(222 p.) 35 × 27 and 23 × 31 cm. Part full score, part draft. *Lehman.* [Scapin et Mezzetin] "Rôle du Capitan. No. 5 Couplets [and No. 6. Duo]." 31 p. 21.5 × 27.5 cm. Copyist's manuscript of the Capitan's voice part, with Mezzetin's vocal cues; two pages have been cancelled and replaced by rewritten versions in Offenbach's hand. *Purchased as the gift of Lauder Greenway.* [Vert-vert] 350 p. 27 × 35 cm. Draft. *Lehman.*

PACINI, GIOVANNI, 1796–1867. [Adelaide e Comingio] "Cavatina di Adelaide. Pacini." 18 p. 22 × 30.5 cm. Full score of the aria "Alme belle che spiegate." At top of title page: "Per l'aimable ed eximia cantata [*sic*] Giuditta Pasta." *Cary.*

PAER, FERDINANDO, 1771–1839. "Gran Scena ed Aria Sedecia con Coro. Atto 2°." 67 p. 22.5 × 29.5 cm. Full score. The opera is otherwise unidentified. *Koch.*

PONCHIELLI, AMILCARE, 1834–1886. [La Gioconda] ca. 800 p. various sizes. Drafts and sketches, in full and piano-vocal score. At end of Act II: "15 Feb. 1876. . . . Genova"; at end of Act III: "7 Marzo 1876. Genova." [La Gioconda] 16 p. 24 × 32 cm. Sketches for Act III. [I Lituani] ca. 600 p. various sizes. Drafts and sketches, in full and short score. [I Lituani] 183 p. various sizes. Early draft in piano-vocal score. *Cary.*

PUCCINI, GIACOMO, 1858–1924. [La bohème] 2 p. 41.5 × 31.5 cm. Sketches for Act IV. Dated "Torre de[l] Lago 12. 12. 90-cinque [i.e. 12 Dec. 1895]." *Heineman.* [Edgar] "Preludio. Atto I° Edgar." 22 p. 35 × 27 cm. Full score. Dated: "Madrid 26 Febbrajo [18]92." *Cary.* [La fanciulla del West] "La Girl. 24 maggio [1]908 milano." 347 p. various sizes. Short-score drafts of Acts I and II. At end of Act I: "28. 4. [19]09." *Lehman Deposit.* "Le Villi. Opera in un atto di G. Puccini." 158 p. various sizes. Part full score, part short-score draft and sketches. *Cary.*

RAVEL, MAURICE, 1875–1937. "L'Enfant et les Sortilèges; fantaisie lyrique de Colette. Musique de Maurice Ravel." 75 p. 35 × 27 cm. Piano-vocal score. At end: "Maurice Ravel Divers lieux 1920–25." [L'heure espagnole] 64 p. 35 × 27 cm. Piano-vocal score. At end: "Maurice Ravel—terminé à la Grangette 10/[19]07." *Lehman Deposit.* [Musorgsky, Modest Petrovich, 1839–1881. Khovanshchina] 40 p. 40 × 30 cm. Portions of Ravel's orchestration of Acts I and II of the Musorgsky opera. *Koch Foundation Deposit.*

RESPIGHI, OTTORINO, 1879–1936. "Maria Vittoria. Partitura. Ottorino Respighi." 3 vols. 43 × 21.5 cm. Full score. *Koch.*

REYER, ERNEST, 1823–1909. "Maître-Wolfram. A Mademoiselle Palmyre Wertheimber, Artiste de l'Opéra." 1 p. 25 × 32 cm. For voice and piano. Dated "28 mars 1864." *Gift of Mr. Ben Meiselman in memory of Herbert Weinstock.*

REZNIČEK, EMIL NIKOLAUS VON, 1860–1945. [Donna Diana] 250 p. 35 × 27 cm. Copyist's manuscript of the piano-vocal score. In Act II, Scene 7 there is an eight-page aria for Floretta in Rezniček's hand, beginning: "Noch niemand hier. . . . Mütterchen, wenn's in Schlaf mich sang." 8 p. 25.5 × 16 cm. *Cary.*

ROSSINI, GIOACHINO, 1792–1868. [La Cenerentola] 3 p. 22.5 × 31.5 cm. Cadenzas for Cenerentola's aria "Nacqui all'affanno e al pianto." On cover: "Cadenze per Giuditta Pasta." [Edipo a Colono] Cori dell'Edipo a Colono posti in musica dal Mro. Rossini." 187 p. 21 × 29 cm. Full score; partly autograph. [Ivanhoé] 32 p. 22 × 29 cm. Full score (not autograph). [Moïse et Pharaon] 3 p. 26 × 34.5 cm. Score, for bass solo and strings, of a recitative beginning

"Vous avez entendu quelle est ma volonté." [Tancredi] 3 p. 27 × 34 cm. Cadenzas for the recitative "Oh patria! dolce, ingrata patria" and the aria "Di tanti palpiti." At end: "Quelques ornements sur L'air de Tancredi pour l'usage de Madme. Gregoire par son ami G. Rossini. Passy ce 15 Août 1858." [Tancredi] 3 p. 22 × 28.5 cm. Cadenzas for "Lasciami, non t'ascolto." On cover: "Cadenze per Giuditta Pasta." *Cary.*

SCARLATTI, ALESSANDRO, 1660–1725. [Tutto il mal non vien per nuocere] "Atto P° Scena Pª." 2 p. 20 × 25 cm. Aria for Olindo beginning: "Luci belle, che siete d'Amore." On p. 2 is a cancelled draft for another aria for Olindo from Act V, Scene 1. *Cary.*

SCHOENBERG, ARNOLD, 1874–1951. "Erwartung (Monodram). Dichtung von Marie Pappenheim. Musik von Arnold Schönberg. Op. 17." 67 p. 34.5 × 26.5 cm. Full score. Dated "Wien 4. Oktober 1909." [Moses und Aron] 78 p. 27 × 35 cm. (and other sizes). First draft of Act I, with a few pages of drafts and sketches for Act II, dated (on p. 1) Lugano, 17 July 1930. *Cary.*

STRAUSS, JOHANN, 1825–1899. [Blindekuh] 401 p. 35 × 27 cm. Full score. *Lehman.*

STRAUSS, RICHARD, 1864–1949. [Die ägyptische Helena] 48 and 64 p. 13 × 17.5 and 8 × 13 cm. Two sketchbooks inscribed, respectively, to Max Graf (Garmisch, 1924) and Gustav Brecher (Garmisch, 24 June 1927). *Heineman.*

SULLIVAN, SIR ARTHUR, 1842–1900. [Cox and Box] ". . . la Triúmvirette musicale 'Coxe et Boxe' et 'Bouncer' composée par Arthur S. Sullivan. Paris, 23 Juillet 1867, Hôtel Meurice." 220 p. 29.5 × 24 and 36 × 26 cm. Full score. *Cary.* [H.M.S. Pinafore] 372 p. 33.5 × 26 cm. Full score. *Arthur A. Houghton, Jr., on deposit.* "The Pirates of Penzance (by A. S. Sullivan)." 2 vols. 33 × 24 cm. *Purchased on the Fellows Fund.* [Thespis] "Little Maid of Arcadee. Words by W. S. Gilbert. Music by Arthur S. Sullivan." 3 p. 24 × 30 cm. Song with piano. Dated "London, June 2nd 1872." "Trial by Jury. Words by W. S. Gilbert. Music by Arthur Sullivan." 165 p. 33.5 × 26 cm. Full score. *Cary.*

THOMAS, AMBROISE, 1811–1896. [Mignon] "Romance." 4 p. 35 × 27 cm. Full-score draft of part of the introduction to "Connais-tu le pays." *Cary.*

VAUGHAN WILLIAMS, RALPH, 1872–1958. [The poisoned kiss] "Evelyn Sharp & R. Vaughan Williams 'The Poison [*sic*] Kiss.' Act III, Vol. I." 31 p. 29.5 × 23 cm. Contains the drafts of nos. 33–36 in the published score, and a six-page ensemble that was later discarded. *Cary.*

VERDI, GIUSEPPE, 1813–1901. [Ernani] "Aria con Cori per l'Ernani. G. Verdi, che cede l'assoluta proprietà di questo spartito all' Egr. artista Nicola Ivanoff." 48 p. 33 × 24 cm. Full score. [Otello] 2 p. 35 × 26 cm. Piano-vocal score draft for part of Act III, Scene 5. *Cary.*

VOGT, GUSTAVE, 1781–1870. [Album of autographs] 198 p. (of which 100 are blank). 30 × 23 cm. Contains entries by 63 composers; operatic entries have been listed separately in this Checklist. [Donizetti, Gaetano, 1797–1848. Maria di Rohan] "Prière de Maria di Rohan." Vogt, Album of autographs, p. 196. For English horn and piano. *Cary.*

WAGNER, RICHARD, 1813–1883. [Lohengrin. Act III, Scene 3] 2 p. 38 × 28.5 cm. Composition draft, beginning with King Heinrich's "Habt Dank, ihr Lieben von Brabant," and ending with the first 22 measures of Lohengrin's "In fernem Land." *Cary.* "Die Meistersinger von Nürnberg, von Richard Wagner." 84 p. 29 × 23 cm. Autograph manuscript of the libretto. *Gift of Mr. Arthur A. Houghton, Jr.* "Die Walküre. Wotan's Abschied und Feuerzauber. Herr Simons. R. W." 5 p. 35 × 27 cm. Short score. *Heineman.*

WEBER, CARL MARIA VON, 1786–1826. "Scena ed Aria dell opera Ines de Castro. Composta per uso della Signora Harlas da Carlo Maria di Weber. Monaco 17–22 Julio 1815." 24 p. 13 × 18.5 cm. Full score. *Cary.*

Printed Operas and Librettos

IN THE PIERPONT MORGAN LIBRARY: A SELECTIVE CHECKLIST

This list contains all important printed opera scores and librettos; reference copies of standard works were omitted. Modern critical editions that were consulted in writing the catalogue entries are listed in the Bibliography. Librettos are listed under the composer's name, in brackets, followed by the librettist's name. RISM refers to: *Répertoire International des Sources Musicales*. Series A/I: *Einzeldrucke vor 1800*. 9 vols. Kassel: Bärenreiter, 1971–81. Sonneck refers to: U.S. Library of Congress. Music Division. *Catalogue of Opera Librettos Printed before 1800*. Prepared by Oscar George Theodore Sonneck. 2 vols. Washington, D.C.: Government Printing Office, 1914. The names of the Library's collections appear here in abbreviated forms; for the full names, see p. 121. Height measurements are given to the nearest half centimeter.

AUBER, DANIEL, 1782–1871. *Fiorella. Opéra comique en trois actes. Paroles de Scribe . . . . Klavierauszug . . . .* Leipzig: Breitkopf & Härtel [n.d.]. [2] [2] 3–71 p. 24 cm. German-French piano-vocal score. Rose morocco gilt and gilt-blocked, onlays of green and brown morocco, cornerpieces *à la cathédrale*; binder's ticket of J. J. Selencka of Brunswick, bound for William, Duke of Brunswick. *Cary*.

BELLINI, VINCENZO, 1801–1835. *Il pirata. Melodramma posto in musica . . . .* Milan: Ricordi [n.d.]. [2] 255 p. 25.5 cm. First edition of the piano-vocal score. *Cary*.

[———.] Romani, Felice. *Norma. Tragedia lirica . . . .* Milan: G. Truffi e comp. [n.d.] [7] 8–32 p. 19.5 cm. First edition of the libretto. With the plot synopses of two ballets: *Merope* (p. [33–36] 37–42) and *I pazzi per progetto* (p. [43–44] 45–48). *Gift of Mr. Ben Meiselman in memory of Herbert Weinstock*.

BERLIOZ, HECTOR, 1803–1869. *Benvenuto Cellini. Opéra Semi Seria en deux Actes . . . .* Paris: Maurice Schlesinger [1839]. [82] p. 33 cm. The first-edition piano-vocal score of nine *morceaux détachés*, with autograph annotations and corrections. *Cary*.

BIZET, GEORGES, 1838–1875. *Carmen. Opéra comique en 4 actes tiré de la nouvelle de Prosper Mérimée. Poème de H. Meilhac et L. Halévy*. Paris: Choudens père et fils [n.d., 1875]. [2] 351 p. 27 cm. First edition of the piano-vocal score. *Cary*.

BOIELDIEU, ADRIEN, 1775–1834. *La dame blanche. Opera comique en trois actes . . . . Clavierauszug*. Bonn & Cologne: N. Simrock [n.d.]. [2] [1] 2–102 p. 25 cm. German-French piano-vocal score. Cream morocco, gilt and gilt-blocked; onlays of pink, green, gray, and maroon morocco; binder's ticket of J. J. Selencka of Brunswick, bound for William, Duke of Brunswick. *Cary*.

[BONONCINI, GIOVANNI, 1670–1747.] Lemer, Gaetano. *Crispo . . . .* Rome: Antonio de Rossi, 1721. [4] 5–60 p. 16 cm. First edition of the libretto. Sonneck p. 336. *Purchased as the gift of Mr. William Kelly Simpson in memory of John D. Barrett*.

[CACCINI, GIULIO, ca. 1545–1618.] Chiabrera, Gabriello. *Il rapimento di Cefalo . . . .* Florence: Giorgio Marescotti, 1600. [3] 4–27 [1] p. 19.5 cm. First edition of the libretto. Sonneck p. 916–17. *Cary*.

[CALDARA, ANTONIO, 1670–1736.] Metastasio, Pietro. *Ciro riconosciuto. Dramma per musica . . . .* Vienna and Rome: Gio. Zempel, 1736. [2] 3–88 p. First edition of the libretto. *Cary*.

CAMPRA, ANDRÉ, 1660–1744. *Tancrede, tragedie, mise en musique . . . .* Paris: Christophe Ballard, 1702. [8] i–l, 291 [1] p. 18.5 cm. First edition. RISM C 745. *Cary*.

CATEL, CHARLES-SIMON, 1773–1830. *Sémiramis. Tragédie lyrique en 3 actes . . . .* Paris: Magasin de Musique [n.d., ca. 1804]. [2] 0–326 p. 32 cm. First edition. *Cary*.

[CAVALLI, FRANCESCO, 1602–1676.] Busenello, Giovanni Francesco. *Gli amori d'Apollo e di Dafne . . . .* Venice: Andrea Giuliani, 1656. engr. plate [4] 64 p. 15.5 cm. First edition of the libretto. Sonneck p. 103. Faustini, Giovanni. *Il Titone. Drama per musica . . . .* Venice: Francesco Valvasense, 1645. [3] 4–66 [6] p. 14 cm. First edition of the libretto. Sonneck p. 1080. Minato, Nicolò. *Scipione affricano. Drama per musica . . . .* Venice: Steffano Curti e Franc. Nicolini, 1664. engr. plate [12] 74 [2] p. 13.5 cm. First edition of the libretto. Sonneck p. 976. *Purchased as the gifts of Mr. James J. Fuld*.

CIMAROSA, DOMENICO, 1749–1801. *Il matrimonio segreto. Dramma giocoso in due atti . . . paroles françaises de Moline*. Paris: Imbault [n.d., ca. 1801]. 2 vols. ([4] 492 p.). 33 cm. First edition of the full score. RISM C 2304. *Gift of Mrs. George A. Carden*.

La clemenza di Tito. Dramma per musica . . . . [Barcelona:] Francesco Generas [1770]. [12] 52 [4] p. 14.5 cm. Silk and silver-wire binding. Libretto; neither composer nor librettist is mentioned. Colophon: Barcelona, y Julio 8 de 1770. Reimprímase. De Hita, Regente. *Purchased as the gift of Miss Julia P. Wightman*.

DAMROSCH, WALTER, 1862–1950. *Cyrano. Opera in four acts . . . . Book by W. J. Henderson after the drama by Edmond Rostand . . . .* New York: G. Schirmer, Inc. [1913] [4] 411 [1] p. 27.5 cm. First edition, signed by the composer. *Cyrano. Opera in four acts . . . . Vocal score arranged by the composer*. [New York: G. Schirmer, Inc., n.d.] [2] [1] 2–190 p. 35.5 cm. First edition of the piano-vocal score, inscribed by the composer to Anne Flagler. *The Man Without a Country. Opera in two acts . . . . Libretto by Arthur Guiterman from a scenario by Walter Damrosch . . . .* New

York: G. Schirmer, Inc. [1937] [6] [1] 2–167 [3] p. 30 cm. First edition, inscribed by the composer to Anne Flagler. *Cary.*

DAVID, FÉLICIEN, 1810–1876. *Lalla-Roukh. Opéra-comique en 2 actes . . . . Paroles de M.M. Michel Carré & Hippolyte Lucas. Partition réduite pour piano et chant . . . .* Paris: E. Girod [n.d.] [6] 221 p. 28 cm. First edition of the piano-vocal score, inscribed by the composer to M. Montaubry. *Cary.*

DEBUSSY, CLAUDE, 1862–1918. *Pelléas et Mélisande. Drame lyrique en 5 actes et 12 tableaux de Maurice Maeterlinck . . . partition pour chant et piano.* Paris: E. Fromont [n.d., 1902]. [8] [1] 2–283 p. 30 cm. First edition of the piano-vocal score, inscribed by the publisher to A. Catherine. *Cary.* Another copy: Paris: A. Durand et fils [n.d., c. 1902 by E. Fromont]. [8] [1] 2–283 p. 32 cm. Inscribed by Jacques Durand to Mrs. William Rodman Fay. *Gift of Mrs. Fay.*

DONIZETTI, GAETANO, 1797–1848. *Torquato Tasso. Melodramma in tre atti di Giacopo Ferretti . . . . Ridotta con accomp^to di pianoforte . . . .* [Milan:] Ricordi and Lucca [n.d., 1833?]. [2] [1] 2–258 p. 25.5 cm. Probable first edition of the piano-vocal score. *Gift of Mr. John Gingrich.*

[GALUPPI, BALDASSARE, 1706–1785.] [Unidentified librettist.] *La partenza, e il ritorno de' marinari. Dramma giocoso per musica . . . .* Barcelona: Giuseppe Altès [1768]. [6] 72 [2] 14.5 cm. Silk and silver-wire binding. Colophon: Barcelona, y Julio 31. de 1768. Reimprímase. De Irabien. *Purchased as the gift of Miss Julia P. Wightman.*

GAY, JOHN, 1685–1732. *The Beggar's Opera . . . . To which is added, the musick engrav'd on copper-plates.* London: printed for John Watts, 1728. [4] [1] 2–58 [2] 16 p. 19.5 cm. First edition, earliest state. Sonneck p. 206. *Cary.*

GERSHWIN, GEORGE, 1898–1937. *Porgy and Bess. An opera in three acts . . . . Libretto by Dubose Heyward, lyrics by Dubose Heyward and Ira Gershwin, production directed by Rouben Mamoulian.* New York: Random House, 1935. [12] 559 [3] p. 31 cm. No. 159 of 250 copies, signed by George and Ira Gershwin, Heyward, and Mamoulian; signed later, for Reginald Allen, by Alexander Smallens, the conductor. *Gift of Mr. Allen.*

GILBERT, SIR WILLIAM SCHWENCK, 1836–1911, and SIR ARTHUR SULLIVAN, 1842–1900. The Gilbert & Sullivan Collection in The Pierpont Morgan Library, assembled and donated to the Library over a period of many years by Mr. Reginald Allen, is by far the largest of its kind, and a complete list of its printed material alone would considerably exceed the length of this Checklist. The Collection includes a virtually complete set of both vocal scores and librettos of the operas, in their many editions, as well as many original programs for each opera, original posters, costume sketches, illustrated sheet music, and several thousand magazine and newspaper articles and reviews.

[GIORDANO, UMBERTO, 1867–1948.] Cain, Henry, Edouard Adenis, and Lorenzo Stecchetti. *Marcella. Idillio moderno . . . .* [Milan:] Edoardo Sonzogno [1907]. [9] 10–47 p. 16.5 cm. Probable first edition of the libretto. *Purchased as the gift of Mr. William Kelly Simpson in memory of John D. Barrett.*

GLINKA, MIKHAIL IVANOVICH, 1804–1857. [*Zhizn' za tsarya . . . .*] St. Petersburg: F. Stellovsky [1881]. [8] [i–iii] iv–xxvii, 3–716 p. 32 cm. First edition of the full score of *A Life for the Tsar. Cary.*

GLUCK, CHRISTOPH WILLIBALD, 1714–1787. *Alceste. Tragedia. Messa in musica . . . .* Vienna: Giovanni Tomaso de Trattnern, 1769. [12] 233 p. 38 cm. First edition of the full score. RISM G 2661. *Cary.*

[———.] Calzabigi, Raniero de'. *Orphée et Euridice. Drameheroique en trois actes . . . .* Paris: Delormel, 1774. [2] 3–38 [2] p. 24.5 cm. First edition of the libretto in French. *Cary.*

GOUNOD, CHARLES, 1818–1893. *Mireille. Opéra en 5 actes, tiré du poëme de Frédéric Mistal [sic] par Michel Carré . . . . Partition chant et piano.* Paris: Choudens [n.d.]. [4] [1] 2–228 p. 26.5 cm. First edition of the piano-vocal score, inscribed by the composer to

Blanchard. *Roméo et Juliette. Opéra en 5 actes de J. Barbier et M. Carré . . . . Partition chant et piano.* Paris: Choudens [n.d., 1867]. [4] 303 p. 27 cm. First edition of the piano-vocal score, inscribed by the composer to his wife. *Cary.*

GRÉTRY, ANDRÉ, 1741–1813. *Colinette a la cour, ou La double epreuve. Comédie lyrique en trois actes . . . .* Paris: Houbaut [n.d.] [2] 244 p. 34 cm. First edition of the full score. RISM G 4061. *Purchased by Pierpont Morgan in 1904.*

HANDEL, GEORGE FRIDERIC, 1685–1759. *Songs in the opera of Rinaldo compos'd by Mr Hendel.* London: for J. Walsh and J. Hare [n.d., 1711]. [4] 65 p. 35 cm. First edition of the full score. RISM H 277. *Cary.*

[HASSE, JOHANN ADOLF, 1699–1783.] Zeno, Apostolo. *Cajo Fabricio. Dramma per musica . . . .* Rome: Antono de' Rossi [1732]. [8] 9–76 p. 15.5 cm. First edition of the libretto. *Cary.*

HUMPERDINCK, ENGELBERT, 1854–1921. *Hänsel und Gretel. Märchenspiel in drei Bildern von Adelheid Wette.* Mainz: B. Schott's Söhne, 1894. [2] 150 p. 27.5 cm. First edition of the piano-vocal score. *Cary.*

KORNGOLD, ERICH WOLFGANG, 1897–1957. *Die tote Stadt. Oper in 3 Bildern frei nach G. Rodenbach: "Bruges la morte" von Paul Schott . . . . Vollständiger Klavier-Auszug . . . .* Mainz: B. Schott's Söhne [c. 1920]. [10] 209 [3] p. 33 cm. First edition of the piano-vocal score, inscribed by the composer to Miss Editha. With the first edition of the libretto. *Cary.*

LULLY, JEAN-BAPTISTE, 1632–1687. *Roland, tragedie mise en musique . . . .* Paris: Christophe Ballard, 1685. [vi] lvi [1] 2–344 p. 36 cm. First edition of the full score. RISM L 3027. *Thesée, tragedie mise en musique . . . .* Paris: Christophe Ballard, 1688. [8] 372 [2] p. 37.5 cm. First edition of the full score. RISM L 3037. *Cary.*

[———.] Quinault, Philippe. *Thesée, tragedie en musique. Ornée d'entrées de ballet, de machines, & de changemens de theatre. Suivant la copie imprimée, a Paris, 1688.* [Amsterdam: Antoine Schelte, 1688.] [3] 4–81 p. 13 cm. Early edition of the libretto. Sonneck p. 1068. *Cary.*

MASCAGNI, PIETRO, 1863–1945. *Il piccolo Marat. Libretto in 3 atti di Giovacchino Forzano. Riduzione per canto e pianoforte . . . .* Milano: Sonzogno, c. 1921. [14] 243 [5] p. 32.5 cm. First edition of the piano-vocal score, inscribed by the composer to Gaspare Fortini, and signed by five members of the first-night cast. *Cary.*

MASSENET, JULES, 1842–1912. *Cendrillon. Conte de fées en 4 actes et 6 tableaux (d'après Perrault) par Henri Cain . . . . Partition chant et piano.* Paris: Heugel et Cie., c. 1899. [10] 366 p. 28.5 cm. *Manon. Opéra comique en 5 actes et 6 tableaux de M.M. Henri Meilhac & Philippe Gille.* Paris: G. Hartmann [n.d.]. [12] 387 p. 28 cm. *Thaïs. Comédie lyrique en 3 actes et 7 tableaux. Poème de Louis Gallet d'après le roman d'Anatole France . . . . Partition chant et piano.* Paris: Heugel et Cie., c. 1894. [6] 275 p. 27 cm. First editions of the piano-vocal scores, each inscribed by the composer to [Jules] Danbé. *Gifts of Mr. Gordon N. Ray.*

MONSIGNY, PIERRE-ALEXANDRE, 1729–1817. *Rose et Colas. Comedie en un acte . . . .* Paris: [on a label pasted over the original imprint] Louis, Marchand de Musique [n.d.]. [2] 154 p. 32.5 cm. First edition. RISM M 3272. *Gift of The Tschaikovsky Foundation in memory of Lois Arvilla Peterson.*

[MONTEVERDI, CLAUDIO, 1567–1643.] Rinuccini, Ottavio. *L'Arianna tragedia . . . .* Florence: Giunti, 1608. [2] [7]–52 p. 20.5 cm. One of four editions of the libretto printed in 1608. See Sonneck, p. 140. *Cary.*

MOZART, WOLFGANG AMADEUS, 1756–1791. [*La clemenza di Tito*, K.621] *Titus. Oper in II Aufzeugen . . . . In vollständigem Clavierauszug mit deutsch und italienischem Texte und zugleich für das Pianoforte allein . . . . Wohlfeile Ausgabe . . . .* Mannheim: K. F. Heckel [n.d.] [2] 3–111 p. 31 cm. German-Italian piano-vocal score. RISM M 5116. *Die Entführung aus dem Serail. Oper in drey Ackten . . . .* Bonn: Simrock [n.d., ca. 1813]. First edition of the full score. K.384. RISM M 4246. [Der Schauspieldirektor, K.486] *L'Impresario. Opéra buffa in un atto composta e ridotta per il cembalo* . . . . Paris: M. Schlesinger [n.d.] [3] 4–41 p. Italian-German piano-vocal score. RISM M 4328. [Der Schauspieldirektor, K.486] *L'Impressario* [sic] *arrangée pour le piano forte* . . . Paris: M. Schlesinger [1822]. [3] 4–9 [1] 10–41 p. 35 cm. Italian-German piano-vocal score. [Der Schauspieldirektor, K.486.] *Ouverture à grand orchestre de l'opera: der Schauspieldirector* . . . . *Edition faite d'après le manuscrit original de l'auteur.* Offenbach: J. André [n.d., 1802]. Orchestral parts. 34.5 cm. RISM M 4329. *Der Schauspiel-Director. Ein komisches Singspiel* . . . . *In vollständigem Clavierauszug mit deutschem Texte u. zugleich für das Pianoforte allein* . . . . *Wohlfeile Ausgabe* . . . . Mannheim: C. F. Heckel [1828]. [2] 3–33 p. 31 cm. Piano-vocal score. *Der Schauspieldirektor, eine komische Oper in einem Aufzuge* . . . . *Klavierauszug.* Leipzig: Breitkopf und Härtel [1808]. [1] 2–31 p. 26 cm. Piano-vocal score. RISM M 4325. *Der Schauspieldirektor. Eine komische Operette in einem Aufzuge* . . . . *Im Klavierauszuge von Siegfried Schmiedt.* Leipzig: in der Breitkopfischen Musikhandlung [ca. 1792]. [2] 37 p. 26 cm. First edition of the piano-vocal score. RISM M 4323. *Cary.*

[———.] Da Ponte, Lorenzo. *Il Don Giovanni, dramma eroicomico . . . messo in musica dall'immortale V. Mozzart* [sic]. New York: Giovanni Gray e Co., 1826. [3] 4–5 [6–7] 8–51 p. 14 cm. *Le nozze di Figaro, dramma eroicomico . . . messo in musica dall'immortale V. Mozart.* New York: Giovanni Gray e Co., 1826. [3] 4–63 p. 14.5 cm. First American editions of the librettos. *Cary.*

OFFENBACH, JACQUES, 1819–1880. *Les brigands. Opera-bouffe en 3 actes; paroles de MM. Henri Meilhac et Ludovic Halévy* . . . . *Partition piano et chant.* Paris: Colombier [n.d.] [2] [1] 2–371 p. Piano-vocal score. *Gift of Mrs. Beulah W. Hagen. Les contes d'Hoffmann. Opéra fantastique en 4 actes de J. Barbier et M. Carré* . . . . *Partition chant et piano* . . . . Paris: Choudens [n.d.] [6] 242 p. 27 cm. First edition of the piano-vocal score. *Cary.*

[PACINI, GIOVANNI, 1796–1867.] Rossi, Gaetano. *Adelaide e Comingio. Melodramma semi-serio in due atti* . . . . Venice: Tipografia Casali [1818]. [2] 3–52 p. 17 cm. Early edition of the libretto. *Purchased as the gift of Sara Greenway O'Dea in memory of Lauder Greenway.*

[PAISIELLO, GIOVANNI, 1740–1816.] Metastasio, Pietro. *Alessandro nell'Indie. Dramma per musica* . . . . Modena: gli Eredi di Bartolomeo Soliani [1773–74]. [2] 3–64 p. 18 cm. First edition of the libretto. *Cary.*

PERGOLESI, GIOVANNI BATTISTA, 1710–1736. *La serva padrona. Intermezzo* . . . . Paris: éditeur, aux adresses ordinaires (imprimé par Auguste de Lorraine). [n.d.] [2] 68 p. 25.5 cm. First edition. RISM P 1393. *Cary.*

[———.] Mariani, Tommaso. *La contadina astuta. Intermezzi tra Livietta, e Tracollo* . . . . [Madrid:] Lorenzo Francesco Majados [1748]. [4] 5–20 p. 19 cm. Contemporary crimson morocco gilt, arms of the dedicatee, Ferdinando VI of Spain, in center of upper and lower covers. *Cary.*

PERI, JACOPO, 1561–1633. *Le musiche di Iacopo Peri . . . sopra L'Euridice del Sig. Ottavio Rinuccini.* Florence: Giorgio Marescotti, 1600. [6] [2] 3–52 p. 32 cm. First edition. RISM P 1431. *Cary.*

[———.] Rinuccini, Ottavio. *La Dafne d'Ottavio Rinuccini* . . . . Florence: Giorgio Marescotti, 1600. [24] p. 21.5 cm. First edition of the libretto. Sonneck p. 339–45. *L'Euridice d'Ottavio Rinuccini* . . . . Florence: Cosimo Giunti, 1600. [4] 16 leaves. 21.5 cm. First edition of the libretto. Sonneck p. 460–61. *Cary.*

PHILIDOR, FRANÇOIS-ANDRÉ DANICAN, 1726–1795. *Le bucheron, ou Les trois souhaits. Comedie en un acte mêlées d'ariettes* . . . . Paris: L'Auteur, Mr. Le Clerc [n.d.] [4] 80 p. 34 cm. First edition. RISM P 1810. *Purchased by Pierpont Morgan about 1905.*

[PICCINNI, NICCOLÒ, 1728–1800.] [Unidentified librettist.] *Il*

barone di Torreforte. Dramma per musica . . . . [Barcelona:] Francesco Generas [1771]. [6] 7–53 p. 15 cm. Silk and silver-wire binding. Colophon: Barcelona, y Deciembre 27. de 1771. Reimprímase. De Lardizabal, Regte. *Purchased as the gift of Miss Julia P. Wightman.*

PONCHIELLI, AMILCARE, 1834–1886. *La Gioconda. Dramma in quattro atti di Tobia Gorrio* [i.e., Arrigo Boito] . . . . *Opera completa per canto e pianoforte* . . . . Milan: Ricordi [n.d.] [2] [5] 6–345 p. 27 cm. Piano-vocal score. *I Lituani. Dramma lirico di A. Ghislanzoni* . . . . *Canto e pianoforte.* Milan: Ricordi [n.d.] [5] 6–23 [1] 1–397 p. 28 cm. Piano-vocal score. *Cary.*

[———.] Ghislanzoni, Antonio. *I Lituani. Dramma lirico* . . . . *Musica di A. Ponchielli.* Milan: Ricordi [1874]. [9] 10–72 p. 20 cm. First edition of the libretto. *Purchased as the gift of Sara Greenway O'Dea in memory of Lauder Greenway.*

PUCCINI, GIACOMO, 1858–1924. *Madama Butterfly (da John L. Long e David Belasco). Tragedia giapponese di L. Illica e G. Giacosa* . . . . *Canto e pianoforte.* Milan: Ricordi & C., 1904. [12] 403 p. 27.5 cm. First edition of the piano-vocal score. *Cary. Madama Butterfly (da John L. Long e David Belasco). Tragedia giapponese di L. Illica e G. Giacosa* . . . . *Canto e pianoforte* . . . . *Nuova edizione.* Milan: Ricordi e Co., 1904. [12] 399 p. 27.5 cm. First edition of the piano-vocal score of the revised version, signed by Puccini, Ricordi, Campanini, Caruso, and Scotti. *Gift of Mr. Reginald Allen.*

[———.] Illica, Luigi, and Giuseppe Giacosa. *Madama Butterfly (da John L. Long e David Belasco). Tragedia giapponese* . . . . *Musica di Giacomo Puccini.* Milan: Ricordi & C., 1904. [5] 6–74 [2] p. 20 cm. First edition of the libretto. *Purchased as the gift of Sara Greenway O'Dea in memory of Lauder Greenway.*

PURCELL, HENRY, 1659–1695. *The vocal and instrumental musick of The prophetess, or The history of Dioclesian.* London: J. Heptinstall for the author, 1691. [6] 173 [3] p. 35.5 cm. First edition. RISM P 5927. *Cary.*

RAMEAU, JEAN-PHILIPPE, 1683–1764. *Les Indes galantes, ballet, réduit à quatre grands concerts: avec une nouvelle entrée complette.* Paris: M. Boivin, M. Leclair, L'Auteur [n.d., ca. 1736]. [4] 226 p. 24 cm. Early edition of selections from the *opéra-ballet.* RISM R 151 (with the corrected title page). *Cary.*

[ROSSINI, GIOACHINO, 1792–1868.] Balocchi, Luigi, and Étienne de Jouy. *Moïse, opéra en trois actes, musique de M. Rossini* . . . . Paris: Aimé André, 1827. [iii] iv–viii, 54 [2] p. 19.5 cm. First edition of the French version of the libretto. *Purchased as the gift of Mr. William Kelly Simpson in memory of John D. Barrett.*

ROUSSEAU, JEAN-JACQUES, 1712–1778. *Le devin du village. Intermède* . . . . Paris: Mdme. Boivin, Mr. le Clerc, Melle. Castagnerie [1753]. [4] 95 p. 33.5 cm. First edition. RISM R 2899. *Purchased by Pierpont Morgan in 1910.*

[SCARLATTI, ALESSANDRO, 1660–1725.] Stampiglia, Silvio. *Turno Aricino. Drama per musica* . . . . Rome: Stamperia del Bernabò, 1720. [2] 3–75 [5] p. 15.5 cm. First edition of the libretto. *Purchased as the gift of Mr. James J. Fuld.*

[SCARLATTI, DOMENICO, 1685–1757.] Capece, Carlo Sigismondo. *La Silvia. Dramma pastorale* . . . . Rome: Per il Rossi, 1710. [4] 5–58 [2] p. 14.5 cm. First edition of the libretto. *Purchased as the gift of Mr. James J. Fuld.*

[———, and NICOLA ANTONIO PORPORA, 1686–1768.] Salvi, Antonio. *Berenice Regina di Egitto, o vero Le gare di amore, e di politica. Dramma per musica* . . . . Rome: Stamperia del Bernabò, 1718. [2] 3–72 [4] p. 15.5 cm. First edition of the libretto. *Purchased as the gift of Mr. William Kelly Simpson in memory of John D. Barrett.*

SCHOENBERG, ARNOLD, 1874–1951. *Moses und Aron. Oper in drei Akten.* Mainz: B. Schott's Söhne, 1957. [5] 6–32 p. 19.5 cm. First edition of the libretto for the first stage performance. *Cary.*

[SCOLARI, GIUSEPPE, ?1720–after 1774.] Metastasio, Pietro. *Ales-*

sandro nell'Indie. Dramma per musica . . . . Barcelona: Giuseppe Altès [1767]. [10] 54 [4] p. 14.5 cm. Silk and silver-wire binding. Colophon: Barcel. y Octubre 23. de 1767. Reimprímase. De Irabien. *Purchased as the gift of Miss Julia P. Wightman.*

STRAUSS, RICHARD, 1864–1949. *Daphne. Bukolische Tragödie in einem Aufzug von Joseph Gregor* . . . . *Klavierauszug* . . . . Berlin: Adolph Fürstner [n.d., 1938]. [5] 6–183 p. 33 cm. *Friedenstag. Oper in einem Aufzug von Joseph Gregor* . . . . *Klavierauszug* . . . . Berlin: Adolph Fürstner [n.d., 1938]. [5] 6–183 p. 33 cm. First editions of the piano-vocal scores. *Cary.*

[——.] Hofmannsthal, Hugo von. *Die ägyptische Helena. Oper in zwei Aufzügen.* Berlin: Adolph Fürstner, 1928. [4] [6] 7–95 p. 18 cm. First edition of the libretto. *Cary.*

STRAVINSKY, IGOR, 1882–1971. *Oedipus rex. Opéra-oratorio en deux actes d'après Sophocle . . . par Igor Stravinsky et Jean Cocteau. Nouvelle révision 1948. Réduction pour chant et piano* . . . . London: Boosey & Hawkes, 1949. [8] 96 p. 32.5 cm. Piano-vocal score, inscribed by the composer to Paul Horgan. *The rake's progress. An opera in three acts by W. H. Auden and Chester Kallman.* London: Boosey & Hawkes, 1951. [6] 414 p. 26.5 cm. First edition of the full score, inscribed by the composer to Paul Horgan. *Gifts of Mr. Horgan.*

SULLIVAN, SIR ARTHUR, 1842–1900. *See* Gilbert, Sir William Schwenck.

[Unidentified composer.] Godi, Giovanni Cesare. *Eraclea. Tragicomedia per musica* . . . . Venice: Nicolini, 1696. engr. plate [2] 3–60 [2] p. 15 cm. Sonneck, p. 445, names Bernardo Sabadini as the composer; *The New Grove Dictionary* (vol. 16, p. 363) states that Sabadini's *La virtù trionfante dell'inganno*, with a libretto by Godi, was originally performed as *Eraclea* (Venice, 1696) with music by an unkown composer. *Cary.*

VERDI, GIUSEPPE, 1813–1901. *Aïda. Opera in quattro atti. Versi di A. Ghislanzoni.* Milan: Ricordi [n.d., 1872]. [4] 293 p. 34.5 cm. First edition of the piano-vocal score. *Cary. Falstaff. Comédie lyrique en trois actes de Arrigo Boïto. Version française de MM. Paul Solanges et Arrigo Boïto.* Paris: Ricordi, 1894. [10] 422 p. 30 cm. French piano-vocal score, no. 17 of 25 copies, with a printed presentation to Jules Danbé, an inscription from Verdi to Danbé, and a special presentation binding with the composer's name and the title in metal work on the upper cover. *Gift of Mr. Gordon N. Ray. Otello. Dramma lirico in quattro atti. Versi di Arrigo Boito* . . . . Milan: Ricordi [n.d., 1887]. [8] 374 p. 27 cm. First edition of the piano-vocal score, inscribed (partly in Boito's hand) to Giovanni Payne. *Cary.*

[——.] Ghislanzoni, Antonio. *Aïda. Opera in quattro atti.* Milan: R. Stabilimento Ricordi [n.d., ca. 1871–72]. [7] 8–58 p. 22 cm. First edition of the libretto, with Verdi's extensive notes, correc-tions, and additions; there are also 16 diagrams indicating the positions and movements of the characters on the stage. *Cary.*

[——.] Piave, Francesco Maria. *Rigoletto. Melodramma . . . musica di Giuseppe Verdi* . . . . Venice: Tipografia Gaspari [1851]. [6] 7–38 [2] p. 17 cm. *La traviata. Musica di Giuseppe Verdi* . . . . Venice: Teresa Gattei [1853]. [5] 6–35 p. 17 cm. First editions of the librettos. *Purchased as the gifts of Sara Greenway O'Dea in memory of Lauder Greenway.*

[VIVALDI, ANTONIO, 1678–1741.] Beregan, Nicolò. *Giustino. Dramma per musica* . . . . Rome: Stamperia del Bernabò, 1724. [2] 3–68 [4] p. 15 cm. First edition of the libretto. Sonneck p. 568. *Purchased as the gift of Mr. William Kelly Simpson in memory of John D. Barrett.*

WAGNER, RICHARD, 1813–1883. [*Die Meistersinger von Nürnberg.* Mainz: B. Schott's Söhne, ca. 1868.] 2 vols. 33.5 cm. Proof copy of the full score (except for the prelude), with extensive manuscript corrections (not in Wagner's hand). *Heineman. Die Meistersinger von Nürnberg. Vollständige Partitur.* Mainz: B. Schott's Söhne [n.d., 1868]. [8] [1] 2–570 p. 33.5 cm. First edition of the full score. *Die Meistersinger von Nürnberg . . . . Vollständiger Klavierauszug von Karl Tausig.* Mainz: B. Schott's Söhne [n.d., 1868]. [4] 402 p. 33.5 cm. First edition of the piano-vocal score. *Drei Operndichtungen nebst einer Mittheilung an seine Freunde als Vorwort.* Leipzig: Breitkopf und Härtel, 1852. [4] [3] 4–352 p. 19 cm. Contains the librettos of *Der fliegende Holländer, Tannhäuser und der Sängerkrieg auf Wartburg,* and *Lohengrin. Parsifal. Ein Bühnenweihfestspiel* . . . . *Vom Orchester für das Klavier übertragen von Joseph Rubinstein.* Mainz: B. Schott's Söhne [n.d., 1882]. [2] [1] 2–261 p. First edition of the piano-vocal score, inscribed by the composer to Franz Liszt. *Cary. Der Ring des Nibelungen. Ein Bühnenfestspiel für drei Tage und einen Vorabend,* [in Wagner's hand] *von Richard Wagner.* [Zurich: Kiesling, 1853.] [4, i.e. 6] 159 [i.e. 285] p. 21 cm. Privately printed in an edition of 50 copies, Wagner's own copy, interleaved, with extensive revisions and corrections in his hand. *Heineman. Der Ring des Nibelungen. Ein Bühnenfestspiel für drei Tage und einen Vorabend.* Leipzig: J. J. Weber, 1863. [6] [v] vi–xxiv [3] 4–443 [7] p. 15 cm. First public edition of the libretto. *Cary. Tannhäuser und der Sängerkrieg auf Wartburg; grosse romantische Oper in 3 Acten* . . . . *Partitur. Als Manuscript von der Handschrift des Componisten auf Stein gedruckt.* Dresden: [Meser] 1845. [4] 450 p. 36 cm. First edition of the full score. *Koch Foundation Deposit.*

[WOLF, HUGO, 1860–1903.] Mayreder, Rosa. *Der Corregidor. Oper in vier Akten von Hugo Wolf. Text nach einer Novelle des Alarcon* . . . . Mannheim: K. Ferd. Heckel, 1896. [3] 4–64 p. 18 cm. First edition of the libretto. *Cary.*

Bibliography

This bibliography serves only to take the place of footnotes—that is, it acknowledges sources that were either quoted, paraphrased, or otherwise found useful in writing the catalogue. In no sense should it be construed as complete for the operas discussed, or even as a list "for further reading." The best bibliographies on opera are those in Grout's *Short History* (see below) and in *The New Grove Dictionary*. For the sake of brevity, the citation in this bibliography of *The New Grove Dictionary* will refer to: *The New Grove Dictionary of Music and Musicians*. Ed. by Stanley Sadie. 20 vols. London: Macmillan Publishers Limited, 1980.

ABBATE, CAROLYN. "*Tristan* in the Composition of *Pelléas*," *19th-Century Music*, 5 (1981), 117–41.

ABRAHAM, GERALD. *On Russian Music*. London: William Reeves, 1939.

ALLEN, REGINALD. *Gilbert & Sullivan in America: The Story of the First D'Oyly Carte Opera Company American Tour*. New York: The Pierpont Morgan Library and The Gallery Association of New York State, 1979.

ALLEN, REGINALD, ed. *The First Night Gilbert and Sullivan*. London: Chappell & Co. Ltd., 1975.

ALMEIDA, ANTONIO DE. [Offenbach Thematic Catalogue; forthcoming]

ALWYN, WILLIAM. "Mascagni's 'Il piccolo Marat,'" *Opera*, 28 (1977), 1128–32.

ANDRÉ, JOHANN ANTON. *Thematisches Verzeichnis derjenigen Originalhandschriften von Mozart, welche Hofrath André in Offenbach besitzt*. Offenbach: André, 1841.

——. *Thematisches Verzeichnis sämtlicher Kompositionen von Mozart, sowie er solches von 9. Februar 1784 an bis zum 15. November 1791 eigenhändig niedergeschrieben hat*. Offenbach: André, 1805.

ANTHONY, JAMES R. "Campra, André," *The New Grove Dictionary*, vol. 3, p. 662–66.

——. *French Baroque Music from Beaujoyeulx to Rameau*. Rev. ed. New York: W. W. Norton, 1978.

——. "The French Opera-Ballet in the Early 18th Century: Problems of Definition and Classification," *Journal of the American Musicological Society*, 18 (1965), 197–206.

——. "Lully, Jean-Baptiste," *The New Grove Dictionary*, vol. 11, p. 314–29.

ARNOLD, DENIS, and ELSIE M. ARNOLD. "Monteverdi, Claudio," *The New Grove Dictionary*, vol. 12, p. 514–34.

ASHBROOK, WILLIAM. *Donizetti and His Operas*. Cambridge: Cambridge University Press, 1982.

——. "Giordano, Umberto," *The New Grove Dictionary*, vol. 7, p. 395–96.

——. "Maria Stuarda: The Opera and Its Music," *The Donizetti Society Journal*, 3 (1977), 73–83.

——. "Mascagni, Pietro," *The New Grove Dictionary*, vol. 11, p. 743–45.

——. *The Operas of Puccini*. New York: Oxford University Press, 1968.

ASHBROOK, WILLIAM, and JULIAN BUDDEN. "Donizetti, Gaetano," *The New Grove Dictionary*, vol. 5, p. 553–70.

BAILY, LESLIE. *The Gilbert and Sullivan Book*. London: Spring Books, 1966.

BARTHA, DÉNES. "Haydn's Italian Opera Repertory at Eszterháza Palace," in *New Looks at Italian Opera: Essays in Honor of Donald J. Grout*, ed. by William W. Austin. Ithaca, N.Y.: Cornell University Press, 1968, p. 172–219.

BARZUN, JACQUES. *Berlioz and the Romantic Century*. 2 vols. Boston: Little, Brown and Company, 1950.

BECKER, HEINZ. "Meyerbeer, Giacomo," *The New Grove Dictionary*, vol. 12, p. 246–56.

BERLIOZ, HECTOR. *Correspondance générale*. Ed. by Pierre Citron. Vols. I and II. Paris: Flammarion, 1972, 1975.

——. *The Memoirs* . . . . Trans. and ed. by David Cairns. London: Victor Gollancz Ltd, 1969.

Berlioz and the Romantic Imagination. London: The Arts Council, 1969 (exhibition catalogue).

BIANCONI, LORENZO. "Sabadini, Bernardo," *The New Grove Dictionary*, vol. 16, p. 362–63.

BLOM, ERIC. "The Literary Ancestry of Figaro," *The Musical Quarterly*, 13 (1927), 528–39.

BOYD, MALCOLM. "Pepusch, Johann Christoph," *The New Grove Dictionary*, vol. 14, p. 357–60.

BROCKWAY, WALLACE, and HERBERT WEINSTOCK. *The World of Opera: The Story of Its Development and the Lore of Its Performance*. New York: The Modern Library, 1966.

BROPHY, BRIGID. *Mozart the Dramatist: A New View of Mozart, His Operas and His Age*. New York: Harcourt, Brace & World, 1964.

BROWN, A. PETER. "Tommaso Traetta and the Genesis of a Haydn Aria (Hob. XXIVb:10)," *Haydn-Studien*, 5 (forthcoming).

BROWN, DAVID. "Glinka, Mikhail Ivanovich," *The New Grove Dictionary*, vol. 7, p. 434–47.

——. *Mikhail Glinka: A Biographical and Critical Study*. London: Oxford University Press, 1974.

BROWN, HOWARD MAYER. "How Opera Began: An Introduction to Jacopo Peri's *Euridice* (1600)," in *The Late Italian Renaissance, 1525–1630*, ed. by Eric Cochrane. New York: Harper & Row, 1970, p. 401–43.

BUDDEN, JULIAN. *The Operas of Verdi*. 3 vols. New York: Oxford University Press, 1978–81.

CAMPRA, ANDRÉ. *Operatic Airs*. Ed. by Graham Sadler. London: Oxford University Press, 1973.

———. *Tancrède. Tragédie lyrique . . . . Reconstituée et réduite pour piano et chant . . . .* Intro. by Arthur Pougin. Paris: T. Michaëlis [188–?].

CARNER, MOSCO. *Puccini: A Critical Biography*. 2d ed. London: Duckworth, 1974.

———. "Puccini, Giacomo," *The New Grove Dictionary*, vol. 15, p. 431–40.

CHARLTON, DAVID. "Méhul, Étienne-Nicolas," *The New Grove Dictionary*, vol. 12, p. 62–67.

CLÉMENT, FÉLIX, and PIERRE LAROUSSE. *Dictionnaire des opéras*. Rev. by Arthur Pougin. 2 vols. New York: Da Capo Press, 1969.

COE, DOUG. "The Original Production Book for *Otello*: An Introduction," *19th-Century Music*, 2 (1978), 148–58.

COMMONS, JEREMY. "Maria Stuarda and the Neapolitan Censorship," *The Donizetti Society Journal*, 3 (1977), 151–67.

COOKE, DERYCK. Liner notes for the London Records recording OSA 1512 of Wagner's *Die Meistersinger von Nürnberg*.

COOPER, MARTIN, and DENNIS LIBBY. "Gounod, Charles," *The New Grove Dictionary*, vol. 7, p. 580–91.

COOPER, MARTIN, and others. "Massenet, Jules," *The New Grove Dictionary*, vol. 11, p. 800–11.

CROLL, GERHARD, and WINTON DEAN. "Gluck, Christoph Willibald," *The New Grove Dictionary*, vol. 7, p. 455-75.

CURZON, HENRI DE. *Musiciens du temps passé*. Paris: Librairie Fischbacher, 1893.

DAHLHAUS, CARL. *Richard Wagner's Music Dramas*. Trans. by Mary Whittall. Cambridge: Cambridge University Press, 1979.

DALLAPICCOLA, LUIGI. "The Genesis of the *Canti di prigionia* and *Il prigioniero*; An Autobiographical Fragment," *The Musical Quarterly*, 39 (1953), 355–72.

"A Dallapiccola Chronology," trans. and ed. by Rudy Shackelford from *Luigi Dallapiccola: saggi, testimonianze, carteggio, biografia e bibliografia*, ed. by Fiamma Nicolodi (Milan, 1975), in *The Musical Quarterly*, 67 (1981), 405–36.

D'AMICO, FEDELE. "Ponchielli, Amilcare," *The New Grove Dictionary*, vol. 15, p. 75–77.

DEAN, WINTON. "Shakespeare in the Opera House," *Shakespeare Survey*, 18 (1965), 75–93.

DE NAPOLI, GIUSEPPE. *Amilcare Ponchielli (1834–1886): la vita, le opere, l'epistolario, le onoranze*. Cremona: Cremona Nuova, 1936.

———. *La triade melodrammatica altamurana: Giacomo Tritto (1733–1824), Vincenzo Lavigna (1776–1836), Saverio Mercadante (1795–1870)*. Milan: Rosio & Fabe, 1931.

DEL MAR, NORMAN. *Richard Strauss: A Critical Commentary on His Life and Works*. 3 vols. Philadelphia: Chilton Book Company, 1962–73.

DEUTSCH, OTTO ERICH. "Mozart und die Schönbrunner Orangerie," *Österreichische Musikzeitschrift*, 9 (1954), 37–42.

———. "Die Orangerie in Schloss Schönbrunn, *Österreichische Musikzeitschrift*, 12 (1957), 384–86.

DEUTSCH, OTTO ERICH, ed. *Mozart: A Documentary Biography*. Stanford: Stanford University Press, 1965.

DEVRIENT, EDUARD. *My Recollections of Felix Mendelssohn-Bartholdy, and His Letters to Me*. Trans. by Natalia Macfarren. London: Richard Bentley, 1869.

DONINGTON, ROBERT. *The Rise of Opera*. New York: Charles Scribner's Sons, 1981.

EATON, JOHN. Letter, dated 19 October 1982, to J. Rigbie Turner, about his *Danton and Robespierre*.

———. Liner notes for the Indiana University Opera Theater recording IUS 421 (distributed by CRI) of his *Danton and Robespierre*.

———. "Stories that Break into Song: Choosing Plots for Opera," *The Kenyon Review*, New Series 4 (1982), 71–77.

FARIS, ALEXANDER. *Jacques Offenbach*. New York: Charles Scribner's Sons, 1981.

FEDERHOFER, HELLMUT. "Mozartiana in Steiermark (Ergänzung)," *Mozart-Jahrbuch*, 1958, p. 109–14.

FÉTIS, FRANÇOIS-JOSEPH. *Biographie universelle des musiciens et bibliographie générale de la musique*. 8 vols. (and 2 vol. suppl.). Paris: Librairie de Firmin-Didot et Cie., 1881–89.

FISKE, ROGER. "Gay, John," *The New Grove Dictionary*, vol. 7, p. 203.

FLOTHUIS, MARIUS. *Mozarts Bearbeitungen eigener und fremder Werke*. Salzburg: Internationale Stiftung Mozarteum, 1969.

GAROFALO, ROBERT JOSEPH. *The Life and Works of Frederick Shepherd Converse (1871–1940)*. Unpublished PhD. dissertation, Catholic University of America, Washington, D.C., 1969.

GATTI, CARLO. *Verdi*. Rev. ed. Verona: Arnoldo Mondadori, 1951.

GAY, JOHN. *The Letters . . . .* Ed. by C. F. Burgess. Oxford: At the Clarendon Press, 1966.

GIANTURCO, CAROLYN. *Claudio Monteverdi: stile e struttura*. Pisa: Editrice Tecnico Scientifica [1978?].

GIRDLESTONE, CUTHBERT. *Jean-Philippe Rameau: His Life and Work*. Rev. ed. London: Cassell and Company, 1969.

GIRDLESTONE, CUTHBERT, and others. "Rameau, Jean-Philippe," *The New Grove Dictionary*, vol. 15, p. 559–73.

GLINKA, MIKHAIL IVANOVICH. *Memoirs*. Trans. by Richard B. Mudge. Norman: University of Oklahoma Press, 1963.

GLOVER, JANE. *Cavalli*. New York: St. Martin's Press, 1978.

GLUCK, CHRISTOPH WILLIBALD. *The Collected Correspondence and Papers . . . .* Ed. by Hedwig and E. H. Mueller von Asow; trans. by Stewart Thomson. New York: St. Martin's Press, 1962.

———. *Iphigenie auf Tauris*. Ed. by Gerhard Croll. (*Sämtliche Werke*, I/11.) Kassel: Bärenreiter, 1965.

———. *Iphigénie en Tauride*. Ed. by Gerhard Croll. (*Sämtliche Werke*, I/9.) Kassel: Bärenreiter, 1973.

———. *Orphée et Euridice*. Ed. by Ludwig Finscher. (*Sämtliche Werke*, I/6.) Kassel: Bärenreiter, 1967.

GOSSETT, PHILIP. *The Operas of Rossini: Problems of Textual Criticism in Nineteenth-Century Opera*. Unpublished PhD. dissertation, Princeton University, 1970.

———. "Rossini, Gioachino," *The New Grove Dictionary*, vol. 16, p. 226–51.

———. "Rossini and Authenticity," *The Musical Times*, 109 (1968), 1006–10.

———. *The Tragic Finale of Rossini's Tancredi*. Pesaro: Fondazione Rossini, 1977.

———. "Vocal Ornamentation in Rossini," typescript of a lecture-demonstration presented at the annual meeting of the American Musicological Society (Denver, 1980).

GRADENWITZ, PETER. "Félicien David (1810–1876) and French Romantic Orientalism," *The Musical Quarterly*, 62 (1976), 471–506.

GREENFELD, HOWARD. *Puccini: A Biography*. New York: G. P. Putnam's Sons, 1980.

GROUT, DONALD J. *Alessandro Scarlatti: An Introduction to His Operas*. Berkeley: University of California Press, 1979.

———. *A Short History of Opera*. 2d ed. New York: Columbia University Press, 1965.

GROUT, DONALD J., and others. "Scarlatti, Alessandro," *The New Grove Dictionary*, vol. 16, p. 549–67.

HAHN, REYNALDO. *Thèmes variés*. Paris: J. B. Janin, 1946.

HALBREICH, HARRY. Liner notes for the Columbia recording M2 33594 of Schoenberg's *Moses und Aron*.

HANNING, BARBARA RUSSANO. "Apologia pro Ottavio Rinuccini," *Journal of the American Musicological Society*, 26 (1973), 240–62.

HARVEY, SIR PAUL, and J. E. HESELTINE, comps. and eds. *The Oxford Companion to French Literature*. Oxford: At the Clarendon Press, 1959.

HAYWOOD, CHARLES. *Folk Songs of the World*. New York: The John Day Company, 1966.

HEARTZ, DANIEL. "Rousseau, Jean-Jacques," *The New Grove Dictionary*, vol. 16, p. 270–73.

HILMAR, ERNST, ed. *Arnold Schönberg, Gedenkausstellung 1974*. Vienna: Universal Edition, 1974.

HOÉRÉE, ARTHUR. "L'œuvre vocale," *Hommage à Maurice Ravel* (Dec. 1938 issue of *La revue musicale*), 103–09.

HOGARTH, GEORGE. *Memoirs of the Opera in Italy, France, Germany, and England*. 2 vols. London: Richard Bentley, 1851.

HOLOMAN, D. KERN. *The Creative Process in the Autograph Musical Documents of Hector Berlioz, c. 1818–1840*. Ann Arbor, Mich.: UMI Research Press, 1980.

HOPKINS, G. W. "Ravel, Maurice," *The New Grove Dictionary*, vol. 15, p. 609–21.

HOPKINSON, CECIL. *A Bibliography of the Works of Giacomo Puccini, 1858–1924*. New York: Broude Brothers, 1968.

ISHERWOOD, ROBERT M. *Music in the Service of the King: France in the Seventeenth Century*. Ithaca, N.Y.: Cornell University Press, 1973.

ISTEL, EDGAR. "Act IV of *Les Huguenots*," *The Musical Quarterly*, 22 (1936), 87–97.

JEFFERSON, ALAN. "Impressions of Manon," *Music and Musicians*, 27 (1968), 28–29.

KENNEDY, MICHAEL, and ROBERT BAILEY. "Strauss, Richard," *The New Grove Dictionary*, vol. 18, p. 218–39.

KERMAN, JOSEPH. *Opera as Drama*. New York: Vintage Books, 1959.

KIDSON, FRANK. *The Beggar's Opera: Its Predecessors and Successors*. Cambridge: At the University Press, 1922.

KINSKY, GEORG. *Manuskripte, Briefe, Dokumente von Scarlatti bis Stravinsky: Katalog der Musikautographen-Sammlung Louis Koch*. Stuttgart: Felix Krais, 1953.

KIRSTEIN, LINCOLN. "Television Opera in U.S.A.," *Opera*, 3 (1952), 198–202.

KOBBÉ, GUSTAV. *Kobbé's Complete Opera Book*. Ed. and rev. by the Earl of Harewood. 9th ed. London: Putnam and Co., 1976.

KÖCHEL, LUDWIG, RITTER VON. *Chronologisch-thematisches Verzeichnis sämtlicher Tonwerke Wolfgang Amadé Mozarts*. 6th ed. Wiesbaden: Breitkopf & Härtel, 1964.

KÖHLER, KARL-HEINZ, and EVELINE BARTLITZ. "Mendelssohn (-Bartholdy), Felix," *The New Grove Dictionary*, vol. 12, p. 134–59.

LAMB, ANDREW. "Lecocq, Charles," *The New Grove Dictionary*, vol. 10, p. 593–94.

——. "Offenbach, Jacques," *The New Grove Dictionary*, vol. 13, p. 509–13.

LARSEN, JENS PETER, and GEORG FEDER. "Haydn, Joseph," *The New Grove Dictionary*, vol. 8, p. 328–407.

LAWTON, DAVID, and DAVID ROSEN. "Verdi's Non-Definitive Revisions: The Early Operas," *Atti del III° congresso internazionale di studi verdiani: Milano, 1972*. Parma: Istituto di Studi Verdiani, 1974, p. 189–237.

[LECOCQ, CHARLES.] "Charles Lecocq Described by Himself," trans. by Edward Biddle, *The New Music Review and Church Music Review*, 12 (June 1913), 294–96.

LIPPMANN, FRIEDRICH. "Bellini, Vincenzo," *The New Grove Dictionary*, vol. 2, p. 446–55.

——. "Belliniana," in *Melodramma italiano dell'ottocento: studi e ricerche per Massimo Mila*. Torino: Einaudi, 1977.

——. *Vincenzo Bellini und die italienische opera seria seiner Zeit: Studien über Libretto, Arienform und Melodik. Analecta musicologica*, 6 (1969), the entire issue.

LOEWENBERG, ALFRED. *Annals of Opera*. 3d ed., rev. and corr. Totowa, N.J.: Rowman and Littlefield, 1978.

LUBBOCK, MARK. *The Complete Book of Light Opera*. New York: Appleton-Century-Crofts, 1962.

MACDONALD, HUGH. "Berlioz, Hector," *The New Grove Dictionary*, vol. 2, p. 579–610.

——. English translation of Maeterlinck's *Pelléas et Mélisande*, published in the Opera Guide series (no. 9) for Debussy's opera. London: John Calder, and New York: Riverrun Press, 1982. Used with permission.

——. Letter, dated 9 May 1982, to J. Rigbie Turner, about Berlioz's *Benvenuto Cellini*.

——. "The Original 'Benvenuto Cellini,'" *The Musical Times*, 108 (1966), 1042–45.

MACDONALD, HUGH, and RALPH P. LOCKE. "David, Félicien," *The New Grove Dictionary*, vol. 5, p. 263–65.

MACDONALD, MALCOLM. *Schoenberg*. London: J. M. Dent & Sons, 1976.

MACNUTT, RICHARD. *Catalogue 106*. Tunbridge Wells, 1975. (Contains a detailed description of Donizetti's *Buondelmonte* manuscript.)

MASSENET, JULES. *My Recollections*. Trans. by Villiers Barnett. Westport, Conn.: Greenwood Press, 1970.

MELLERS, WILFRID. *Music in a New Found Land: Themes and Developments in the History of American Music*. New York: Alfred A. Knopf, 1965.

MENOTTI, GIAN CARLO. Liner notes for the RCA recording VIC-1512 of his *Amahl and the Night Visitors*.

MEYERBEER, GIACOMO. *Briefwechsel und Tagebücher*. Ed. by Heinz Becker. Vol. 2, 1825–1836. Berlin: Walter de Gruyter & Co., 1970.

MONTEVERDI, CLAUDIO. *Letters . . . .* Trans. and ed. by Denis Stevens. London: Faber and Faber, 1980.

MORINI, MARIO, ed. *Pietro Mascagni*. 2 vols. Milan: Casa Musicale Sonzogno di Piero Ostali, 1964.

——. *Umberto Giordano*. Milan: Casa Musicale Sonzogno di Piero Ostali, 1968.

MOZART, WOLFGANG AMADEUS. *The Letters of Mozart and His Family*. Ed. and trans. by Emily Anderson. 2d ed. 2 vols. London: Macmillan, 1966.

——. *Le nozze di Figaro*. Ed. by Ludwig Finscher. (*Neue Mozart-Ausgabe*, II/5/16.) Kassel: Bärenreiter, 1973.

——. *Der Schauspieldirektor*. Ed. by Gerhard Croll. (*Neue Mozart-Ausgabe*, II/5/15.) Kassel: Bärenreiter, 1958.

——. *Der Schauspieldirektor*. Facsimile of the Autograph Manuscript. Intro. by J. Rigbie Turner. New York: The Pierpont Morgan Library, 1976.

MYERS, ROLLO H. *Ravel: Life and Works*. London: Gerald Duckworth, 1960.

NECTOUX, JEAN-MICHEL. "Maurice Ravel et sa bibliothèque musicale," *Fontes artis musicae*, 24 (1977), 199–206.

——. "Notes pour une esthétique de Maurice Ravel," *Revue musicale de Suisse romande*, 29 (1976), 150–57.

NEIGHBOUR, O.W. "Schoenberg, Arnold," *The New Grove Dictionary*, vol. 16, p. 701–24.

NEWLIN, DIKA. "Self-Revelation and the Law: Arnold Schoenberg in His Religious Music," *Yuval* (Studies of the Jewish Music Research Center), 1 (1968), 204–20.

NEWMAN, ERNEST. *The Life of Richard Wagner*. 4 vols. New York: Alfred A. Knopf, 1933–46.

——. *The Wagner Operas*. New York: Alfred A. Knopf, 1963.

NICHOLS, ROGER, and ROBERT ORLEDGE. "Debussy, Claude," *The New Grove Dictionary*, vol. 5, p. 292–314.

NICOLAISEN, JAY. "The First *Mefistofele*," *19th-Century Music*, 1 (1978), 221–32.

——. *Italian Opera in Transition, 1871–1893*. Ann Arbor, Mich.: UMI Research Press, 1980.

ODELL, GEORGE C.D. *Annals of the New York Stage*. 15 vols. New York: Columbia University Press, 1927–49.

OESER, FRITZ. *Jacques Offenbach: Hoffmanns Erzählungen (Les Contes d'Hoffmann). Vorlagenbericht*. Kassel: Alkor-Edition, 1981.

OFFENBACH, JACQUES. *Hoffmanns Erzählungen (Les Contes d'Hoffmann.)* Ed. by Fritz Oeser. Piano-vocal score. Kassel: Alkor-Edition, 1977.

ORENSTEIN, ARBI. *Ravel: Man and Musician.* New York: Columbia University Press, 1975.

ORLEDGE, ROBERT. *Debussy and the Theatre.* London: Cambridge University Press, 1982.

OSTER, OTTO. "Die Meistersinger von Nürnberg: Metamorphosen," *Bayreuther Festspiele. Programm.* Bayreuth, 1964.

PADMORE, ELAINE. "Einem, Gottfried von," *The New Grove Dictionary,* vol. 6, p. 84–85.

PALISCA, CLAUDE V. "The Alterati of Florence, Pioneers in the Theory of Dramatic Music," in *New Looks at Italian Opera: Essays in Honor of Donald J. Grout,* ed. by William W. Austin. Ithaca, N.Y.: Cornell University Press, 1968, p. 9–38.

———. "The First Performance of 'Euridice,'" in *Twenty-Fifth Anniversary Festschrift (1937–1962).* New York: Queens College of the City of New York, 1964, p. 1–23.

———. "Mei, Girolamo," *The New Grove Dictionary,* vol. 12, p. 67–68.

PERI, JACOPO. *Euridice.* Ed. by Howard Mayer Brown. (Recent Researches in the Music of the Baroque Era, vols. 36 and 37). Madison, Wisc.: A-R Editions, 1981.

PERLE, GEORGE. "Berg, Alban," *The New Grove Dictionary,* vol. 2, p. 524–38.

———. *The Operas of Alban Berg.* Vol. 1: *Wozzeck.* Berkeley: University of California Press, 1980.

PIRROTTA, NINO. "Early Opera and Aria," in *New Looks at Italian Opera: Essays in Honor of Donald J. Grout,* ed. by William W. Austin. Ithaca, N.Y.: Cornell University Press, 1968, p. 39–107.

———. "Temperaments and Tendencies in the Florentine Camerata," *The Musical Quarterly,* 40 (1954), 169–89.

POPE, ALEXANDER. *The Dunciad.* Ed. by James Sutherland. London: Methuen & Co. Ltd., 1965.

PORTER, ANDREW. "Favola in musica," *The New Grove Dictionary,* vol. 6, p. 441.

———. *Music of Three Seasons: 1974–1977.* New York: Farrar Straus Giroux, 1978.

———. "Verdi, Giuseppe," *The New Grove Dictionary,* vol. 19, p. 635–65.

PORTER, WILLIAM V. "Peri and Corsi's *Dafne:* Some New Discoveries and Observations," *Journal of the American Musicological Society,* 18 (1965), 170–96.

———. "Peri, Jacopo," *The New Grove Dictionary,* vol. 14, p. 401–05.

POUGIN, ARTHUR. *Méhul: sa vie, son génie, son caractère.* Geneva: Minkoff Reprint, 1973.

PRUNIÈRES, HENRY. "L'enfant et les sortilèges, à l'Opéra de Monte Carlo," in a special issue of *La revue musicale,* 1 April 1925, p. 105–09.

PUCCINI, GIACOMO. *Carteggi pucciniani.* Ed. by Eugenio Gara. Milan: Ricordi, 1958.

———. *Letters . . . .* Ed. by Giuseppe Adami; trans. by Ena Makin. Philadelphia: J. B. Lippincott, 1931.

RAEBURN, CHRISTOPHER. "An Evening at Schönbrunn," *The Music Review,* 16 (1955), 96–110.

———. "Die textlichen Quellen des 'Schauspieldirektors,'" *Österreichische Musikzeitschrift,* 12 (1958), 4–10.

RAEBURN, MICHAEL and CHRISTOPHER. "Mozart Manuscripts in Florence," *Music & Letters,* 40 (1959), 334–40.

RANFT, PETER. *Felix Mendelssohn Bartholdy: Ein Lebenschronik.* Leipzig: VEB Deutscher Verlag für Musik, 1972.

RAVEL, MAURICE. "Esquisse autobiographique," *Hommage à Maurice Ravel* (Dec. 1938 issue of *La revue musicale*), 19–23.

REICH, NANCY B. "The Rudorff Collection," *Notes,* 31 (1974), 247–61.

RENNER, HANS. *Neuer Opern- und Operettenführer, von Monteverdi bis Henze.* Munich: Gotthold Müller, 1963.

RICCI, LUIGI. *34 anni con Pietro Mascagni.* Milan: Edizioni Curci, 1976.

RICORDI, GIULIO, comp. *Disposizione scenica per l'opera "Otello."* Milan: Ricordi, 1887.

RINALDI, MARIO. "Mercadante, Saverio," *Enciclopedia dello spettacolo,* vol. 7, cols. 443–46.

ROBINSON, MICHAEL F. *Opera before Mozart.* London: Hutchinson University Library, 1966.

ROBINSON, PHILIP. "Falcon, (Marie) Cornélie," *The New Grove Dictionary,* vol. 6, p. 367.

ROSE, MICHAEL. "Mercadante, Saverio," *The New Grove Dictionary,* vol. 12, p. 170–76.

ROSENTHAL, ALBI. "A Hitherto Unpublished Letter of Claudio Monteverdi," in *Essays Presented to Egon Wellesz,* ed. by Jack Westrup. Oxford: Clarendon Press, 1966, p. 103–07.

ROSENTHAL, HAROLD, and JOHN WARRACK. *The Concise Oxford Dictionary of Opera.* 2d ed. London: Oxford University Press, 1979.

RUBSAMEN, WALTER H. "The Ballad Burlesques and Extravaganzas," *The Musical Quarterly,* 36 (1950), 551–61.

———. "Ballad Opera," *The New Grove Dictionary,* vol. 2, p. 79–82.

RUFER, JOSEF. *The Works of Arnold Schoenberg: A Catalogue of His Compositions, Writings and Paintings.* Trans. by Dika Newlin. London: Faber and Faber, 1962.

SADIE, STANLEY, and others. "Mozart, Wolfgang Amadeus," *The New Grove Dictionary.* vol. 12, p. 680–755.

———. "Opera," *The New Grove Dictionary,* vol. 13, p. 544–647.

SCHEEL, HANS LUDWIG. "'Le mariage de Figaro' von Beaumarchais und das Libretto der 'Nozze di Figaro' von Lorenzo da Ponte," *Die Musikforschung,* 2 (1975), 156–73.

SCHMID, PATRIC. "'Maria Stuarda' and 'Buondelmonte,'" *Opera,* 24 (1973), 1060–66.

SCHMIDGALL, GARY. *Literature as Opera.* New York: Oxford University Press, 1977.

SCHNEIDER, OTTO, and ANTON ALGATZY, eds. *Mozart-Handbuch.* Vienna: Brüder Hollinek, 1962.

SCHOENBERG, ARNOLD. *Letters.* Selected and ed. by Erwin Stein; trans. by Eithne Wilkins and Ernst Kaiser. New York: St. Martin's Press, 1965.

SELIGMAN, VINCENT. *Puccini among Friends.* New York: Macmillan, 1938.

SHATTUCK, ROGER. *The Banquet Years: The Origins of the Avant-Garde in France, 1885 through World War I.* Rev. ed. New York: Vintage Books, 1968.

SHAW, GEORGE BERNARD. *Music in London 1890–94. Criticisms Contributed Week by Week to the World.* 3 vols. New York: Vienna House, 1973.

SIMON, JOHN. "Les poètes fantastiques," *Opera News,* 45 (28 Feb. 1981), 25–34.

SLONIMSKY, NICOLAS. *Music since 1900.* 4th ed. New York: Charles Scribner's Sons, 1971.

SMITH, PATRICK J. *The Tenth Muse: A Historical Study of the Opera Libretto.* New York: Alfred A. Knopf, 1970.

SMITH, RICHARD LANGHAM. "Debussy and the Pre-Raphaelites," *19th-Century Music,* 5 (1981), 95–109.

SOLERTI, ANGELO. *Le origini del melodramma.* Bologna: Libreria Editrice Forni, 1969.

STERNFELD, FREDERICK W. "The First Printed Opera Libretto," *Music & Letters,* 59 (1978), 121–38.

STIEGER, FRANZ. *Opernlexikon.* 11 vols. Tutzing: Hans Schneider, 1975–83.

STRAUSS, RICHARD, and HUGO VON HOFMANNSTHAL. *A Working Friendship: The Correspondence between Richard Strauss and Hugo von Hofmannsthal.* Trans. by Hanns Hammelmann and Ewald Osers. New York: Random House, 1961.

STROBEL, OTTO, comp. *Richard Wagner: Leben und Schaffen. Ein Zeittafel.* Bayreuth: Verlag der Festspielleitung Bayreuth, 1952.

STRUNK, OLIVER, ed. *Source Readings in Music History from Classical Antiquity through the Middle Ages.* New York: W. W. Norton & Co., 1950.

STUCKENSCHMIDT, H. H. *Schoenberg: His Life, World and Work.* Trans. by Humphrey Searle. New York: Schirmer Books, 1978.

TODD, R. LARRY. Review of a recording of Mendelssohn's *Die Heimkehr aus der Fremde. The Music Review,* 42 (1981), p. 80–81.

TOMLINSON, GARY. "Madrigal, Monody, and Monteverdi's 'via naturale alla immitatione,'" *Journal of the American Musicological Society,* 34 (1981), 60–108.

TRENNER, FRANZ. *Die Skizzenbücher von Richard Strauss aus dem Richard-Strauss-Archiv in Garmisch.* (Veröffentlichungen der Richard-Strauss-Gesellschaft München, vol. I.) Tutzing: Hans Schneider, 1977.

TURNER, J. RIGBIE. *Nineteenth-Century Autograph Music Manuscripts in The Pierpont Morgan Library: A Check List.* New York: The Pierpont Morgan Library, 1982.

TYSON, ALAN. Letter, dated 9 August 1982, to J. Rigbie Turner, concerning Mozart's arrangement of Cherubino's aria from *Le nozze di Figaro.*

——. "*Le nozze di Figaro:* Lessons from the Autograph Score," *The Musical Times,* 122 (1981), 456–61.

U.S. LIBRARY OF CONGRESS. Division of Music. *Catalogue of Opera Librettos Printed before 1800.* Prepared by Oscar George Theodore Sonneck. 2 vols. Washington, D.C.: Government Printing Office, 1914.

"Verzeichnis der verschollenen Mozart-Autographe der ehemaligen Preussischen Staatsbibliothek Berlin," *Mozart-Jahrbuch,* 1962–63, p. 306–09.

VOSS, EGON. "Gedanken über 'Meistersinger'-Dokumente," *Bayerische Staatsoper. Programmheft.* Munich, 1979.

WALKER, THOMAS. "Cavalli, Francesco," *The New Grove Dictionary,* vol. 4, p. 24–34.

——. "Contarini, Marco," *The New Grove Dictionary,* vol. 4, p. 679–80.

WATERHOUSE, JOHN C.G. "Dallapiccola, Luigi," *The New Grove Dictionary,* vol. 5, p. 157–62.

WEINSTOCK, HERBERT. *Donizetti and the World of Opera in Italy, Paris and Vienna in the First Half of the Nineteenth Century.* London: Methuen & Co., 1963.

——. *Rossini: A Biography.* New York: Alfred A. Knopf, 1968.

——. *Vincenzo Bellini: His Life and His Operas.* New York: Alfred A. Knopf, 1971.

WERNER, ERIC. *Mendelssohn: A New Image of the Composer and His Age.* Trans. by Dika Newlin. London: The Free Press of Glencoe, 1963.

WESTERNHAGEN, CURT VON. *Wagner: A Biography.* 2 vols. Trans. by Mary Whittall. Cambridge: Cambridge University Press, 1978.

WESTERNHAGEN, CURT VON, and others. "Wagner, Richard," *The New Grove Dictionary,* vol. 20, p. 103–47.

WESTRUP, JACK ALLEN. "Cherubino and the G Minor Symphony," in *Fanfare for Ernest Newman,* ed. by Herbert van Thal. London: Arthur Barker, 1955.

WHITE, PAMELA C. "The Genesis of *Moses und Aron,*" *Journal of the Arnold Schoenberg Institute,* 6 (1982), 8–55.

WÖRNER, KARL H. *Schoenberg's 'Moses und Aron.'* Trans. by Paul Hamburger. New York: St. Martin's Press, 1963.